The
EVADERS

True Stories of Downed Canadian Airmen and Their Helpers in World War II

Em. Lavender,
Nov. 8, 1993

Emerson Lavender

Norman Sheffe

McGraw-Hill Ryerson
Toronto   Montreal

First published in 1992 by
McGraw-Hill Ryerson Limited
300 Water Street
Whitby, Ontario, Canada
L1N 9B6

1 2 3 4 5 6 7 8 9 0 BG 10 9 8 7 6 5 4 3 2

Canadian Cataloguing in Publication Data

Lavender, Emerson
  The evaders : true stories of downed Canadian airmen and their helpers in World War II

ISBN 0-07-551466-4

1. World War, 1939–1945 – Aerial operations, Canadian. 2. World War, 1939-1945 – Personal narratives, Canadian. 3. Fighter pilots – Canada – Biography. I. Sheffe, Norman, 1924 –   .
II. Title.

D792.C2L38 1992   940.54′4971   C92-094473-6

Typesetting: Jay Tee Graphics Ltd.
Cover and interior design: Dianna Little

Printed and bound in Canada

The basis for this cover is a composite photograph made by the late Denis Budd from articles he left with his Danish helpers in 1943 and which they gave back when he visited them after the war.
  The background is a silk escape map he carried. On it are other items from the kit: fishing line, knife, button compass. In the lower half is his false identity card and a four leaf clover attached to a picture of one of his helpers; in the upper part of the picture is his air gunner's wing and the gold ring he made in his pre-war prospecting days.
  A picture of a small piece of stone from the House of Alphonse and the twenty franc note belong to Ken Woodhouse, momentos of his escape across the English Channel via the Shelburne Line.

For some, it was a time so painful and so tragic that now they wish neither to remember it nor talk about it. For others, it was a time of exuberant adventure. For still others, their experience in that time when they were young was so poignant that nothing that followed would mark them so deeply. Friendships formed in fear and danger back then still live deep in their beings; so deep that they are sometimes divided from those who are closest to them now, but who did not share that poignant time.

With the help of patriots, almost ten thousand airmen evaded capture by the enemy. To these patriots and to the members of the Royal Air Forces Escaping Society, Canadian Branch, this book is dedicated.

TABLE OF CONTENTS

CODA

ACKNOWLEDGEMENTS

We would like to acknowledge the contributions of many people in the preparation of this book. We are grateful for the help of evaders and escapers now living in every region of Canada, and helpers who were active underground workers in Europe during World War II.

The stories in this book are based to a considerable extent on conversations and taped interviews with a great many people. In addition, many of those interviewed made available log books, letters, diaries, illustrations and maps that add considerably to the testimony of their words.

The Directorate of History, Department of National Defence, in Ottawa, provided ready access to Squadron Records, recently declassified Interrogation Reports and other materials, excerpts of which are included in the following pages. We are indebted to the Director and his staff, especially Dr. Steven Harris, for their unfailing co-operation and advice.

Throughout our work we have had the ready co-operation of the Royal Air Forces Escaping Society, Canadian Branch, especially its recent presidents Jim Moffat and Ray DePape.

As always, we appreciate the support we have had from Madeline Lavender and Lois Sheffe.

Emerson Lavender
Norman Sheffe

INTRODUCTION

It was a slow walk from the table to the raised platform at the front of the room. The two walked not with measured tread, but haltingly, hesitantly, almost painfully. As they approached, the applause began and swelled as people rose to their feet. The older of the two men stumbled, turned his head towards the crowd, looking rather bewildered. A pleased smile came over his wrinkled face, and a sparkle appeared in his watery blue eyes. There was a tension to be felt, a tension arising from a yearning to express the depth of feeling in the breasts of the onlookers.

The Canadian, Barry Chaster from New Westminster, B.C., placed a steadying hand under the older man's elbow, supporting him to the raised dais. They stood there for a moment, these seasoned veterans: the Canadian, just about to reach retirement age; the other, a Belgian, now in his early seventies. His light brown suit had been tailored for an earlier time when he had been more robust. But one ignored the fit, focussing on the rows of medals hanging on the left side of his jacket: row after row of shining crosses and gold and silver discs suspended from richly hued ribbons. His face revealed a variety of emotions: pride, pleasure and appreciation. Proud to be among a select group; pleased to renew old acquaintances and appreciative of so significant a recognition, long years after the war.

As the citation was read, the audience showed its pleasure at seeing this Belgian so honoured. To many of the onlookers he was a surrogate for their own heroic friends who had helped them when they were in great danger. As we glanced at the organization's brochure on the table before us, one phrase jumped off the page: "*with the help of patriots*." The phrase haunts us still.

The applause died down and the chairman read the citation:

> Joseph J. Heenen was an officer in the Belgian army captured on May 23, 1940 when the Germans invaded the Low Countries on their drive into France. He escaped and was recaptured, escaped again, recaptured a third time and once again fought to regain his freedom. He began organizing escape lines for Allied troops on the run from the German authorities.
>
> One of the Canadian airmen he assisted was Barry Chaster. Shortly after their encounter, Joseph Heenen was picked up by the Nazis and sent to the notorious concentration camp at Dachau, languishing there until it was overrun by Allied troops in 1945.

We could not help but be stirred by the recitation of selflessness, determination and devotion to the cause of freedom. As the medal of the Royal Air Forces Escaping Society was draped around his neck, the applause swelled to an ovation. The poignancy of the moment was overwhelming; words were inadequate, but the faltering voice and the misty eyes gave an eloquence to the occasion that language could not reach.

Jim Moffat, president of the Royal Air Forces Escaping Society, Canadian Branch in 1989, presents the Society's award to Joseph J. Heenen, an officer in the Belgian army who was captured May 23, 1940. He escaped and began organizing escape lines for Allied troops until he was captured again and sent to Dachau. One of the airmen he helped is Barry Chaster of New Westminster, seen standing behind Mr. Heenen.
COURTESY OF JIM MOFFAT

Six of these helpers were scattered about the banquet room as honoured guests of the Society. Each sat with one of the people who had benefitted from their bravery. At the appropriate moment, the evader escorted his helper to the platform to be honoured by the group assembled. What was going on? Where was this banquet room? Who were these people?

The banquet was being held in downtown Vancouver, British Columbia. It was the Annual General Meeting of the Royal Air Forces Escaping Society (Canadian Branch). Present were about seventy-five members, some with wives and grown-up children. When they were very young, each man had come down in enemy-held territory during World War II, but had evaded capture. They are "the evaders." There were a few present that night who had been captured first, then escaped and evaded until they had returned to safety and they are known as "escapers."

The circumstances of their evasion and escape vary, but all would acknowledge that without people like the evening's special guests, they might not have been able to return to a gathering like this. These special guests, and thousands like them, are gratefully known as "the helpers."

In some cases, the evader, escaper and helper shared only a few hours together. The lives of others were bound together for weeks or months, living cheek by jowl and flitting from shadow to shadow after nightfall, always alert, always aware of the risks, always fearful of the heavy tread, the ominous knock on the door. Capture would have meant a prison camp for the airman in Italy or Germany because both countries recognized the Geneva Convention. No such protection existed for the helper. Capture usually meant death on the spot for the men involved or execution following torture and imprisonment. For the women and children it often meant being sent to prison or a labour camp. So the bond that was forged in war remains strong in ways that the rest of us cannot share. In attempting to explain the singular nature of their experience, one of them said, "You can only touch the rim of our experience."

* * *

Of those aircrew who were shot down and who became prisoners of war, most would have chosen evasion if that choice had been available. But many were injured or captured immediately on coming down, or were traumatized by the knowledge that just minutes before some or all of their crew had been killed. After all, they were young men, most in their late teens or early twenties. They had just survived a close brush with death and they were alone in the darkness of enemy territory.

Such an experience begs the question, "Why evade?"

Fred Reain, a pilot from 428 Squadron, was shot down on January 20, 1944. In spite of the fact that he could not swim, he grabbed a log, paddled across a river somewhere in northern France and holed up in a barn:

> I said to myself, here I am; should I give myself up? For one thing, I didn't feel like submitting to German interrogation.
>
> On the other hand I was still free. In a prison camp I would go through some hardships, too. I didn't know what they would be, but the option was always open to me to give myself up until they caught me.
>
> I chose to be the boss as long as I was on the loose.

Gord Stacey believes that it was partly because of his training that he decided not to give up. By the time he was shot down in April 1944, he knew that the invasion of France was imminent and so he might as well try to make it back. Besides, there was an inherited characteristic that motivated him:

> The prospect of a POW camp for God knows how long didn't appeal to me very much. Besides, my background is Irish and I remember a family story about the Irishman who was the only survivor of a shipwreck. Washed up on some South

Sea island more dead than alive he looked up to see friendly natives offering him some coconut milk. He said: "I don't know where I am, or who you are but, whatever your government is, I'm agin it!"

For the civilian population living in enemy occupied territory, a prudent course would have been to obey orders, observe the curfew and settle down to wait out the war. In view of the fatal risks involved, why did thousands of civilians risk their lives to help save total strangers shot down over their homeland?

Circumstances motivated some: Mlle. Fraipont, a young woman from Fouron St. Pierre, Belgium, for instance, was holidaying at Dunkirk in 1940 as the British army retreated to the coast and was ferried across the Channel in a miraculous rescue. On a stroll near the shore, she and a friend happened upon four or five British soldiers hiding in a cave. The young women arranged for a French fishing vessel to take the soldiers to England. A year later British agents came to Fouron St. Pierre and convinced Mlle. Fraipont to use her house as a safe house for evaders.

Margot Maroldt of Luxembourg City was simply doing her duty when she assisted her husband, Pierre, in his clandestine activities. At first these involved hiding young Luxembourgers who were refusing the German "invitation" to join the German army; by 1943 the Maroldt home was being used as a safe house for evaders.

Anger prompted Mientje Manders of Bakel, Holland, to resist the Germans. She saw a German soldier knock a cigarette from the mouth of an airman captured just a few moments earlier after he had parachuted to earth. Something boiled inside her; every nerve and muscle seemed to grow taut with rage. There and then she decided to act, and by the end of the war, she and her husband Bernard had provided safe haven for over fifty Allied airmen.

Adventure, the sheer frightening excitement of activity, was one of the motivating factors for fifteen-year-old Emmy van Taack, of Rotterdam. In the next five years she and her friends acted as couriers, hid evaders and participated in a number of clandestine actions against the Germans.

Conviction was the most compelling force that drove these women and thousands of other civilians forward in their dangerous activities. No one in this account better exemplifies the strength of personal conviction than Paula Blanchain. Paula Spriewald Blanchain is a German, born in Enneptal, daughter of an anti-Nazi member of the German parliament until the Nazis seized power in 1933. The family fled to Holland and then to Paris. When that city fell the Spriewalds took flight once more, never to be united again. For a time the Vichy French interned Paula with other German nationals in a camp in the south of France. After her release she went to Marseille and became one of the most gallant couriers of the O'Leary Escape Line. She acted as Pat O'Leary's secretary, coded and decoded radio signals between Marseille and London, and acted as a courier for evaders on several occasions.

This book tells the stories of only a few of these helpers and the airmen they sheltered. The opening chapters draw a composite account of the experiences of young Canadians as they joined up, trained, went overseas, and were posted to squadrons. We follow them on operational flying (ops) over enemy territory to the fateful hour when they had to abandon their aircraft far from friendly territory.

Beginning in Chapter 5, the focus narrows to concentrate on the experience of individual airmen and their helpers. Most of these experiences occurred in Northwest Europe, but there were evaders in Italy and North Africa as well. Different in many ways were the experiences of evaders in Burma who had no helpers at all.

The book concludes with another composite picture of that time when the evader and the helper were finally liberated and, now in their early seventies, they can look back, remember and reflect. The half century that has elapsed between the event and the recollection may have somewhat softened the memories of the men and women caught up in the crises of those years. Softened, perhaps, but time cannot blunt the nobility of the risks taken, the deeds performed, or the courage revealed by all the participants, escapers, evaders and helpers.

CHAPTER ONE

I REALLY WANTED TO BE A PILOT

Thousands of young Canadians got their first real job when they joined the air force. The late Denis Budd, from Nelson, British Columbia (Denis died seven months after this interview was recorded), was an exception. Denis had worked at whatever jobs he could find during those bad Depression years of the Thirties, including a stint as a prospector, and he finally joined the army. After more than a year and a half of army life he got some leave and went to Vancouver to try for the air force.

> I went down to the recruiting centre in civilian clothes and, by God, they took me! I said I just had one little problem — I was in the army, and what could they do about it? They all laughed like the dickens and said it was up to me to get out of that.
>
> So was I paraded before the CO of the 10th Corps of Signals, and he looked at me and said: "What the hell are you doing here?" I told him and he said: "Don't be silly; I'll give you three hooks tomorrow and put you in charge of my works department."
>
> But I said, "No sir. I want to go flying." He assigned two guards to me and put me in a truck, and they took me down to the RCAF recruiting office. I was under guard until I was sworn into the air force. By six o'clock that night I was on a train to Edmonton for basic training.

Joe Healey, of Cartierville, Quebec, had a similar experience. He was working in an aircraft factory but really wanted to be a pilot. However, he had only a Grade 11 education.

> That put me down the drain; they wouldn't even look at me in '41. I heard that out west they were taking failures from the pilots' course and training them as gunners. I went out there and tried again and again to get accepted for aircrew. Finally I went down to the recruiting office one time and the guy said, "Oh God, not you again! Okay, c'mon in and I'll give you a test!"
>
> So he gave me a test and I asked, "How did I do?" "Not bad, not bad; you haven't got the requirements for a pilot, but you can train as a wireless air gunner or as an air gunner."
>
> "Which is the quickest course?" I asked. Well, they lied to me. They said that air gunner was the shortest course. That was a lie. I wish I'd had the wireless, because that would have helped me when I was down in Belgium with the Underground."

Clayton Leigh, from Orillia, Ontario, had only a Grade 9 education when he joined the air force. He knew that to become a pilot he would have to find a creative way around the education criteria that existed at that time.

1

So I thought the best way to become a pilot was to get close to Command. To do that I took a crash course in typing and shorthand and in six weeks I qualified as a clerk. That got me into an orderly room, where I saw the CO daily. That was in 1940, when I was 20. I remember one CO — a tall, white-haired older man who drank like a fish. I think he drank a bottle before breakfast, because he couldn't see in the morning. So with the mail, all he could do was to sit with his letter opener and hand the letters to me and I dealt with everything from there on. But he was a wonderful man — a real father-figure — and maybe he was the one to push me through for pilot's training.

When John Millar turned eighteen on June 12, 1940, he went with a chum to enlist in the air force in Winnipeg. He trained as an air frame mechanic and was sent overseas in December 1941.

We went over in a convoy of troopships, one of which was the French liner *Louis Pasteur*.

The food was terrible. Somebody asked for two volunteers to work in the galley, and two of us volunteered. Back home I had delivered meat on a bicycle and I guess that qualified me to work in a galley, because we were signed on as fifth and sixth butchers and got ten shillings a day for it. All we had to do was to bring the meat up to the galley from the ship's hold. We ate better than the captain and had milk to drink every day. We lived like kings for the thirteen days that it took to cross the Atlantic. A few months after I arrived in Britain I was accepted for training as a flight engineer at Topcliffe.

Joe Petsche, now living in Burlington, Ontario, got into the air force a little differently.

I joined up in Montreal. When the war started I desperately wanted to join the Black Watch, but they wouldn't let me unless I got my mother's signature, and there was no way she would sign. So I joined the air force, where they didn't ask for her signature. I wanted to be a pilot, but they said my eyes didn't quite balance and I'd have trouble landing a plane; so I became a gunner and I guess it was just as well.

Brock Christie, of Lethbridge, Alberta, had a very clear reason for joining the air force:

I joined for the spirit of adventure. At that age you think you're never going to die. Being in the air force, open to all that adventure, the flying and the camaraderie — that's the life!

I was at Manning Pool when it was the Royal Texas Air Force. Twenty-five percent of the group I was in were from Texas. I saw my first plane close up when on guard duty at Picton, Ontario. Some fellow yells at me, "Hey kid, you want to go for a ride?" That was the greatest experience of my life up to that time: riding in a Fairey Battle. That was the life for me!

Training in Canada completed, young airmen took troopships to England and were usually sent to a holding centre at the seaside resort of Bournemouth on the south coast. All the hotels, apartment buildings and many large houses had been taken over to accommodate officers and men.

Bob Bodie, from Warner, Alberta, trained as a navigator. He has pleasant memories of his time in Bournemouth:

> It was a real nice place — a real luxury. They had a swimming pool where I was billeted and I liked swimming so I had a great time.

Gordon Stacey's recollections of the town are less pleasant. Now retired from his position as general manager of Guelph Hydro, Gordon joined the air force in his home city of Toronto, trained as a navigator and went overseas in January 1943.

> Like all the rest, we were sent to Bournemouth for a while. I have grim memories of that place. We were there during one of those raids when the Germans came in at zero feet across the Channel and then up and over the cliffs to strafe the parks with gunfire. One Sunday in May they came in. It was a beautiful afternoon, with people lying out in the park and so on, and they swept the whole area — bombed and strafed and were away again before anybody knew what was happening. They left absolute carnage behind.
>
> I had been on leave up in London, but when we got back to Bournemouth we were met at the station with lorries and were told to leave everything where it was and get into the trucks. We had to go and help clean up the mess in the park. A lot of Aussies were killed when the Germans hit a couple of hotels. I remember that the bar in one of them had fallen into the basement when a bomb hit, and everybody in that bar was thrown into a pile of debris in the basement. We pulled out several people who were still alive and some who weren't. That was a grim one.

Joe Healey survived the same raid.

> I noticed a large group of aircraft coming over the sea towards us. I thought at first they were Spitfires — so much for aircraft recognition classes!
>
> Suddenly one opened fire and I recognized the radial engine of a Focke Wulf. I started to run but somebody said to hit the ground, so I did. Machine-gun bullets and small bombs were dropping all around us. It was over in seconds and there were dead airmen all over the place.

Fred Reain was in Bournemouth in 1942. A friend of his lost a hand in one of those raids. Before he joined 428 Squadron, Reain trained on Oxfords at Cirencester, where flying was not without its exciting moments.

> A fellow from Vancouver, whose name was Cook, and I would go flying all the way to the Bristol Channel. For excitement, we would do low flying and chase ducks. One day Cook got too low and the sea was rough enough that he caught his prop and shattered it. In his report, which I confirmed, he said that he had indeed hit a duck, but it was while he was flying at 5,000 feet!

Halifax bomber "R" for Robert. LQ were the letters to identify it as an aircraft from 405 Squadron based at Leeming until it was transferred to the Pathfinders at Gransden Lodge, Bedfordshire. Note the mid-upper gun turret and the rear gun turret just visible between the rudders. A Halifax like this one from 427 Squadron was involved in a mid-air crash on March 30/31, 1944, described on page 138. The collision sheared off the upper turret and instantly killed all but two of the crew; one of them died soon after reaching the ground. Jim Moffat, the tail gunner and sole survivor, had heard his pilot say, "What the hell?", followed by a loud crash. He looked out to the right and saw that the big port rudder was still there. But, when he looked to the left, there was nothing left of the starboard rudder and he knew that the aircraft was doomed. D.N.D.

If the Canadian airman was slated for a bomber crew he was usually sent to one of the Canadian squadrons of 6 Group, most of which were based in Yorkshire. At no time in the war, however, did Canadian squadrons have exclusively Canadian or British crews; as the need arose for particular specialties, airmen were assigned to squadrons regardless of nationality.

No. 6 (RCAF) Group was formed at Linton-on-Ouse, Yorkshire, on October 25, 1942. Its headquarters was at Allerton Park. By the end of the war, 6 Group consisted of fourteen squadrons at eight stations plus supporting units. Canadian bomber squadrons were identified by number, and each had a name and crest: for example, 408, "Goose"; 415, "Swordfish"; 419, "Moose"; 420, "Snowy Owl"; 424, "Tiger"; 425, "Alouette"; 426, "Thunderbird"; 428, "Ghost"; 429, "Bison"; 431, "Iroquois"; 432, "Leaside"; 433, "Porcupine"; 434, "Bluenose". Squadron 419 became known as the "Moose" Squadron, in honour of its first CO, Wing Commander "Moose" Fulton.

Squadron 434, the Bluenose Squadron, was adopted by the Rotary Club of Halifax. Perhaps 427 had the most glamour attached to it, if only because its symbol was the MGM lion, and the names of movie stars were attached to specific planes. The telegram sent to the squadron from the beauteous Hedy Lamarr (as shown on p. 6) illustrates this connection. For some reason the wartime censor seemed to believe it necessary to indicate that he had examined Miss Lamarr's telegram and found it contained no vital secret of value to the enemy.

Crewing Up

Crewing up was an interesting procedure, according to Gord Stacey, who joined 434 Squadron.

> It was like a high school dance — you waited to be picked. We all milled around in a big room — pilots, flight engineers, navigators, bomb aimers, gunners, wireless air gunners — and you got picked. A pilot from Vancouver came over to me; his name was Sands. We liked the look of each other, so we went around the room

On March 30, 1945, 424 (Tiger) Squadron flew its 2000th sortie from Skipton-On-Swale, Yorkshire. None of the ground crew in this picture is identified. D.N.D. PHOTO

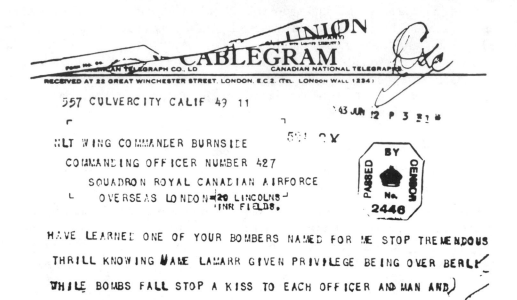

427 Squadron was adopted by MGM movie studios in 1943 and the squadron became known as the Lion Squadron for that reason. Many movie stars such as Spencer Tracy, Judy Garland and Walter Pidgeon sent telegrams to the squadron. This one from the gorgeous Hedy Lamarr must have stirred the blood a bit. But why did Censor Number 2446 find it necessary to indicate that Miss Lamarr's message was safe to pass on?

to see who was still available. It was catch as catch can. First we went after a bomb aimer. We had seen this fellow who was an RAF type; he looked a little older than most. We found out later that he had been on a squadron and done some trips, but had pranged and lost the rest of his crew. The engineer and the wireless operator came along later. Sandy, our skipper, went as second dickey on a raid on Frankfurt and didn't come back, so we had to pick another skipper, and we lost him and the next one as well. We figured we were ill-fated and I think we were considered a Jonah crew.

Bob Bodie got talking to Art Debreyne, a pilot:

Art figured I was his type, for we seemed to get along pretty well. We talked with some of the fellows and most would have been glad to get on with him, because he was a crackerjack and we'd heard about him before. Crewing up is where I met Andy Mynarski for the first time. This was in January '44. We had another fellow who was our mid-upper gunner, but he got in a fight one night and got his jaw broken, I guess, and Mynarski took over. I got to know Andy quite well. He was a nice, quiet sort of fellow, an unassuming type, but very conscientious, no matter what we were doing.

When Fred Richards arrived at 412 Fighter Squadron, then based at Heescht, Holland, he saw at once that his situation was a bit different from that of other airmen there:

I was an old married man, so I didn't go on the drinking toots into the pubs in town. Our squadron had about twenty or twenty-five aircrew. There were changes in personnel all the time — postings and losses — but there were quite a few like myself who hung on and on.

Fighter Command was different from Bomber or Coastal Command. We had one-man crews. Associations built up among crew members in the other Commands. Four of us in the squadron were very close friends, and we made it all the way through and are still close today. We all live in Metro Toronto and go out for dinner every few months. They are just like family.

Gord Stacey went from Bournemouth to air navigation school.

I had no particular problem because I had trained as a navigator in southwestern Ontario, but some of the navigators who had trained out west knew only two forms of navigation — CN and CP. What I mean is that the country out there is so flat and so free of landmarks that all a navigator had to do was pick up one of the two transcontinental railroads and get his bearings by following one of them along until he could identify a town by the name on the grain elevator. When they got to England, however, it was a real problem for some of them.

After navigation school I went to Middleton St. George, just before Christmas 1943. By the time we were shot down, in April '44, we had seen a lot of crews come and go. No crew completed a tour of operations during that time, because they were all shot down.

Some evaders recall advice they got about how to evade capture if they came down in enemy territory. Under the terms of the Geneva Convention, prisoners of war were to be removed from combat zones and treated humanely. They were not to lose their citizenship or their identity and they were not required to give any information other than their name, rank and service number. Prisoners were to be placed in camps that were clean, dry and warm and no less sanitary than the barracks of their guards. Most important, a prisoner knew that he would survive, at least as far as the Geneva Convention was concerned. Helpers could expect no such considerations.

As the war progressed and evasion tactics were improved, aircrew were given training exercises in evasion. Gord Stacey's crew was attached to an RAF regiment in Yorkshire. They were taken out in a blacked-out lorry so they couldn't see where they were going. They were given a map and a rough idea of where they were within thirty miles or so. Dropped off two at a time, they were to find their way back to base within three days without being caught and without using any form of transportation.

Some of the fellows didn't play fair at all. They would make for the nearest pub and hole up waiting to be picked up by the Home Guard, or they would get somebody to drive them back to base. I remember the exercise we were on. Several of these groups of two got together and found that they were just outside an army transport camp. They sneaked into this camp and made off back to camp in all kinds of vehicles — all of which had to be returned the next day! In our case, we headed for a railway line, walked to the nearest station to find out where we were and set course from there.

Chapter Two

ON OPS

After training in Canada and the United Kingdom, the young men were finally ready for operational duty. For some of them, actual flying operations were very short. Ray DePape's first trip (see Chapter 8) was also his last, while John Dix, at nineteen, was a veteran of twenty operations when his plane went down.

Bob Morgan went to a Boston Conversion Unit and then to a Turbilite Squadron, 533, RAF. The turbilite was a device that was created in the early days of nightfighting to help against German intruders.

It was a Douglas A-20 with the nose cut off and a great big light in what was left of the nose. In the bomb bays there was about a ton of batteries, and there were special navigating lights on the wingtips. When you took off there was a Hurricane fighter at either wingtip. By then we had radar to help us locate Jerry nightfighters. All we were supposed to do was to approach a German nightfighter from astern and flash the light. The Hurricanes were then supposed to blast the target we had caught in the light. But the light was only good for about a minute, and the other problem was that when you flashed the light on, the Hurricanes were always too far back and the light would fail before they got close enough. That turbilite idea didn't last too long.

Clayton Leigh became a Typhoon pilot with 182 Squadron, a rocket squadron, and he was proud of it.

The Spitfire boys might object to this, but there were two kinds of fighter pilots. A Spitfire was primarily a defensive weapon to drive away enemy fighters and to protect the bombers in raids, whereas the Typhoon was purely an offensive weapon. If a flight of Spitfires flew over occupied France, nobody bothered to shoot at them because they weren't going to do any damage. But if a Typhoon went over, every gun in France opened up on him, because they knew he was going to attack something on the ground — a tank or a train or infantry or whatever.

The Typhoon was a deadly weapon and the Germans were frightened of them. It was a big, fast, powerful aircraft. A Spitfire was a joy to fly, but flying a Typhoon was a real chore. It had a fourteen-foot prop going round like a windmill and it was a tricky thing to fly. That's why the Typhoon losses were so dreadful. Twenty-six of us went over with 439 Squadron, and only four of us came back.

I didn't get over until just before D-Day, and then got transferred to 182, a rocket squadron. We used to do operations from England, attacking the buzz-bomb bases or the bombs themselves when they were in flight. We attacked tanks and

A Typhoon similar to that flown by Clayton Leigh, armed with rockets and cannon and ready to take off from the steel mesh temporary runway that was laid down in France after D-Day. Its engine developed 2,180 hp and it had a maximum speed of 405 mph at 18,000 feet. Its service ceiling was 34,000 feet. D.N.D. PHOTO

V2 installations in two flights of eight aircraft in daylight. We flew in fingers of four. The most experienced man was the flight commander and the least experienced man would be his number two, who had to watch behind. The next most experienced would be number three, and number four had a little experience, and that was me. The trouble was that when four of us peeled off to go down and attack something, I was the last man down so everybody on the ground would be shooting at me.

We went in at sea level across the Channel, just above the waves. Some guys hit them and came back with bent props. We would come up over the French coast at treetop level and then pull up to 4,000 feet to attack. This gave us enough time to get the aircraft into a dive and properly trimmed before firing and pulling up.

The first time I was hit badly, we were on an armed recce into France and I was hit and the plane went into full fine pitch for take-off; you can't fly like that or you'll tear the engine right out of it. With full fine pitch the engine was screaming, and I had the throttle way back almost at stalling speed. I cruised right over Le Havre at just about stalling speed, but nobody shot at me. There I was, pooping along over the most heavily defended port in Europe and nobody shot at me, so I made it back to base.

On D-Day I was sitting beside my aircraft, waiting to be called. There was nothing for us until they had established a beachhead. We moved to France a few days after that. They had scraped out a level field with a bulldozer and had put down some wire mesh. We continued to live in England but they took gas and ammunition over to this landing strip. We would sleep in England, get up, go over, attack, land at this strip, load up with fuel and ammunition and go again all day until the last sortie, after which we would fly home to England. I did a complete operation one time in something like eighteen minutes. That's getting out of the foxhole, running to the aircraft, jumping in, firing up, flying back towards the coast to get some height and then back to attack, then to the strip to land and jump into the foxhole again — under fire the whole time from machine-gun nests that hadn't been mopped up.

We never had time to form close friendships. When we got to France we lived in tents, four to a tent, and there was nearly always an empty bed in that tent, with one of us gone.

The first operation for Joe Petsche was a mining over the Frisian Islands in the Baltic. At about eight hours, it was one of the longest trips his crew ever made, and they got hit by an Me-110.

He came up underneath us and I was the mid-upper gunner. If I hadn't had a steel seat I wouldn't be here now. Even so, I got some shrapnel in my leg, and I still have it. The attack set the aircraft afire and I helped put it out. We made it back to England, but they wouldn't let us land at our base because the mines were still on board, and we couldn't dump them because the hydraulic system was shot up. We couldn't get rid of them manually either. Finally, we were ordered to land at an American Air Force base. It was the best thing that ever happened to me while I was in England. The pilot set it down so gently that I didn't even feel it when we touched down.

I was in hospital there for three weeks and that was the lap of luxury. Boy! I'm telling you, there were three classes of aircrew — American, Canadian and British. On our base all we ever got after a trip were two eggs, but at this American base there were eggs on the table every morning and there was chicken and everything. When I was in that American hospital my commission came through and I also found out that I had been awarded the DFM.

John Millar and his crew from 431 Squadron did eighteen ops, three of them to Berlin, before they were shot down. In November 1943, they were on a raid to Mannheim when a 2,000-pound bomb got hung up in the bomb rack and wouldn't release. Jack Hill, the pilot, told Al Donnell, the bomb aimer, to get rid of it, but it wouldn't budge. Jack reached over and pulled the override switch, which would jettison the bomb racks and all the bombs, but that didn't work either. Millar picks up the story:

We still had to have the engines revved higher than normal, but we were gradually losing altitude, even though we were at full bore on the engines. The ice we had picked up must have weighed about 2,000 pounds. When we opened the panels on the floor we found that there were three bombs there! We couldn't see the bomb racks because they were all covered with ice, and all we had to chip the ice was a screwdriver. Al Donnell and I took turns doing this for almost two hours, and all that time more ice was building up because we were flying through freezing rain. Finally, the pilot said that we didn't have enough fuel to get to England and that if we didn't get rid of the bombs in the next half hour at the latest we were going to head down towards the south of France and bale out.

Al and I worked at it in turns and finally she went. We got one end free and they all tore loose. The pilot throttled back and took another look at the amount of fuel we had. By this time we were somewhere near Cherbourg. He said he would have a go at getting to a base in southern England. To get there, we had to go through a wall of searchlights, but just as we got there the lights went out for some reason.

We crossed the Channel and got to this base. As we were coming in, the starboard outer engine went out. On touchdown the port inner went. After we taxied to the end of the runway the third engine died. We parked the aircraft and shut down the fourth engine on our own.

CHAPTER THREE

ONE IN A HUNDRED

Sooner or later in their tour of operations, disaster struck each of the airmen in this book. Yet, as the following statistics indicate, because of good luck, personal qualities, the quick action of brave civilians, or whatever fates decide these matters, they were to survive. In his book *The Nuremberg Raid*, Martin Middlebrook gives the following statistics, based on the overall 1939–1945 casualty figures, for any 100 aircrew who joined heavy-bomber crews:

Killed on operations	51
Killed in crashes in the United Kingdom	9
Seriously injured in crashes	3
Prisoners of war	12
Survived unharmed	24
Shot down; evaded capture	1

Typhoon pilot Clayton Leigh remembers that twenty-six of his class went overseas and only four came back. What is remarkable is that even if a crewman did complete a tour, his time was measured in months, not years.

Denis Budd and his crew joined 405, a Pathfinder squadron, at Gransden Lodge, near Cambridge. On August 16, 1944, Denis had heard that his commission had come through, and his buddies were looking forward to a few beers at his expense when he got back from that day's raid on Stettin in the Baltic. They got to the target, marked it and were headed home when it happened. Denis remembers it vividly:

> Being a tail gunner, it was awfully hard to know where you were, because things were gone before you saw them. I heard this *thump, thump, thump*, right down the side of the aircraft, and I knew right away that it was anti-aircraft fire. Then a cannon shell came through the bottom of my turret, hit the base of the outside gun and buggered it up completely. The intercom was out, flames were coming out the port engine, and then I saw a nightfighter come up from underneath.
>
> When I realized that the intercom was out, I decided that things were getting too hot and I should get the hell out of there. I had a seat pack instead of the usual chest-type parachute. This was unusual because there was not much room in the rear turret for a parachute. The chest pack was kept inside the plane, but if I had flown with one of them I wouldn't be alive today.
>
> I wound the turret around on the beam with the hand crank, got the sliding door open and stuck my ass out, took off my helmet and intercom and fell out backwards, almost. I got my left leg out all right, but my right leg was jammed between the turret and the body of the plane just above the ankle.

There I was, hanging upside down outside a burning plane at 18,000 feet. At times like that you get a tremendous rush of energy, so I was able to pull myself up, in spite of hanging backwards in the slipstream. I managed to get to the top of the zipper of the outer flying suit, and I kept wiggling it down inch by inch as far as I could. I kept wriggling my foot out of the boot and finally my foot slipped out and I broke free. I came down with one boot and a leg that was as black as the ace of spades.

On the way down I thought, "Holy doodle, what if the skipper gets that fire out and he flies home to Britain without a tail gunner. What a fool I'm going to look like, because nobody told me to bail out." Then I started to think of the craziest things. I used to take a lot of photographs — I had stacks of them at home — and I wondered what would happen to them. Eventually I made a perfect landing with only one boot. I rolled over and was up in a flash and buried my 'chute in a patch of cabbage.

Joe Healey didn't get the chance to bail out. He was training to be a dispatcher with 138 RAF, an SOE (Special Operations) squadron based at Tempsford.

We were carrying a crew of eight and two spies on the night of October 18, 1943. We were hit by light flak, and it kept on hitting us. Because we were so low we had no chance of getting away. The truth was, we couldn't find the target. We were going back and forth, back and forth, looking for the signal light from the Maquis that would identify the drop zone, and the Germans just nailed us. We were too low to jump, so we got into crash positions and, BOOM, we were down — a good belly landing except that we hit a tree. However, everybody got out. This was near Herantels, just east of Antwerp.

Clayton Leigh, with 182 Squadron RAF, thinks he just might have shot himself down:

I was hit at low level either by ground fire or, because we were so cocky by the summer of '44, by shrapnel from my own rocket. We weren't pulling up to our correct height to get into proper flying position before we fired the rockets, so when a 60-pound rocket burst on pavement and you were 1,000 feet up, the shrapnel from it could do your plane some real damage.

I knew I was hit, and at that point there is a sudden moment of decision after which you cannot change your mind. You either have to shove on full throttle and get high enough to jump, or you pull the throttle off to save your engine so she won't burn until you can do a belly landing. If you decide to throttle back, you assume that the glycol leak is not bad enough to burn before you hit the ground. If you guess wrong, you fry: you are just a ball of fire. A pilot's inclination is always to stay with the aircraft, because you feel more secure there than on the end of a parachute. But the day before, I was flying behind a Rhodesian when he was hit. I saw black smoke start to come from his engine, so I yelled on the radio for him to get out. However, he tried to pull out, went into a dive and hit the ground. That was in my mind now.

I landed the plane, wheels up in a field. When I came to a stop I realized I wasn't hurt and that nobody was showing up to help me. There were German shells landing to my left as they attacked our troops and I realized I was down between the lines. I got out of the plane, ran through a hedge, a hellish thing, and went down into the river at the end of the field.

Bob Morgan was on his second tour when he was shot down. On April 19, 1944, he had just returned to 169 Squadron RAF from a bit of leave. He went down to Flights to see how the fellows were making out before he turned in. The wing commander spotted him and said that one of the crew was sick and could he go?

"No sir. I'm just back from leave, and I didn't bring my flying gear down to Flights with me."

"Borrow some," he said, "and take the nearest aircraft."

Morgan found out, too late, that the nearest aircraft was a Mosquito that had been sitting out in the rain at the base, and the radar was fouled up because of the damp. Cologne was the target.

Our instructions were to go south and east and come at it from the Ruhr. We ran into a fearful storm, but got to the target and waited for our bombers to arrive. We got radar contact with an enemy fighter dead ahead, but I couldn't see it, so we backed off, took another run at it and still couldn't see anything. Then we realized we were overshooting it because the radar was haywire.

The nightfighter came in underneath and his tail gunner got our port engine, with the only generator for electrical power. Ten minutes later we were hit again, this time in the starboard engine, and we were in trouble. I had to get my navigator out first: he was a big man and it was really difficult to get him out of the hatch of a Mosquito. He tried going out head first and got stuck. I managed to get him back in, turned him around, put my foot on his head and shoved him out. The hatch was on the other side of the plane from where I was sitting, and we were not flying very well. We had enough height at 25,000 feet, so the only thing I could do was to bring it right up to a wing stall, get my parachute harness ready, get out on the starboard nacelle, and jump.

It was about two o'clock in the morning, and we were near Wavre, Belgium. I landed in a ploughed field, having suffered excruciating pain all the way down. It was bloody awful. I didn't realize pain could be so devastating. When you jump from an aircraft you have these parachute straps that go between your legs; they are relatively loose until the 'chute opens, and then all the straps tighten up. One of the family jewels was under the bottom strap and there was nothing I could do until I hit the ground and released the harness. That was the start of my European summer vacation.

Joe Petsche of 434 Squadron landed in a tree at about 2:30 A.M. on July 13, 1944, after bombing the railway yards at Arras. He hung in that tree about six feet off the ground for a few minutes and then realized he was in a German truck compound. He dropped quietly to the ground, climbed a fence and took off.

Russ Jones was a navigator. When he was about to bail out, he remembered the strangest thing. In wartime, pencil erasers were very hard to come by, and navigators were always being warned to preserve them carefully. So before he jumped he went back to his navigator's table and retrieved his pencil eraser.

Chances of evading successfully in the spring, summer or fall were better than in the winter. The weather was warmer; often there would be food — vegetables or fruit — that could be foraged, and there was no snow to mark the evader's footsteps. Not many evaders made it to freedom in the winter. Fred Reain, a pilot from 428 Squadron, is one of the exceptions.

Fred was shot down on January 20, 1944. His plane was at 9,000 feet when it was hit. He bailed out, and on the way down experienced a lot of snow, which turned to rain as he approached the ground.

> It was a miserable night, but it wasn't very cold. The first obstacle I had to cross was a river. I never learned to swim so this was a bit of a problem. I grabbed a big log or something, made sure my mae west was secure and paddled across. I still don't know where the hell it was, but I think it was near Metz in France. I holed up right away as soon as I got rid of my chute.
>
> My favourite hiding places were barns, because I was a farmer and I knew what to expect in them. Invariably they had straw or hay and grain. The big thing was to find a way to get into them. I found a barn and stayed in it for almost two days. I crawled on top of a great pile of sheaves of grain and burrowed down as far as I could get, then camouflaged where I had come in. There was lots of air down there and all kinds of mice. I still had my mae west, with its little light, and I kept that as long as the batteries lasted. I'm convinced there was a search made while I was there, because I could hear people talking and I assumed they were Germans, but I sat tight and they didn't find me.

Gord Stacey was shot down on April 27, 1944. He landed very hard in a ploughed field, having misjudged the distance. He found out later that he had cracked his collarbone, but it didn't develop into anything serious.

> I could hear sounds around me, and I could hear the boys going over and the crumps of their bombs as they fell. I could see the flashes as the bombs hit the target — Montzen, about twenty miles away.
>
> My bomb aimer, Johnny Arscott, had shrapnel in his legs when he jumped and somehow or other his chute hadn't buckled properly, so one buckle let go and he came down in a spiral as the 'chute was spilling air. To make matters worse he landed on the back end of a cow! He says all he remembers was that the cow took off across the field, bawling its head off, and he crawled after it, hissing, ''Shush, shush!'' He managed to crawl into a ditch, where members of the Dutch Underground found him and took him to a doctor.
>
> I started walking southwest into Belgium, navigating with my compass and the stars.

Perhaps the best-known incident concerning a Canadian bomber crew during the Second World War occurred on the night of June 13, 1944, near Cambrai, France. Seven days after the Allied armies had landed in Normandy the Germans were trying desperately to bring up reinforcements and drive them back into the sea. Bomber Command's major role during those few days was to disrupt major lines of transportation leading from Germany to Normandy.

QUESTIONNAIRE FOR RETURNED AIRCREW

LOSS OF BOMBER AIRCRAFT

NUMBER   RANK   NAME

Squadron   **419**   Aircraft Letter   **A**   Type of Aircraft **Lanc. X**

Date of Loss **12/13.6.45**   Target **CAMBRAI**

How many Ops. had you done   Duty in Aircraft

Date of Interrogation   Information extracted from **POW Questionnaire**

NARRATIVE OF EVENTS FROM TAKE-OFF TO LANDING:-

PILOT   F/O   DE BREYNE A.
NAV   F/O   BODY A.R.
B/A   SGT   FRIDAY W.J.
W/OP   W/O   KELLY J.W.
M/U   W/O   MYNARSKI A.C.
F/E   SGT   VIGARS R.E.
R/G   F/O   BRODY G.P.   **INTERROGATED**

NARRATIVE

        Approaching target, 8000', dark night, no previous warning of attack.
M/U called something about e/a light below, go stbd, R/G saw nothing.
A/C then on fire - turret and i/c u/s. Turn turret manually. Got
chute and turned it back half way. Hand rotation gear came off in hand.
R/G trapped in turret and saw M/U approaching, chute harness on fire. Waving
and R/G waved to tell him to go away. R/G stayed in a/c to ground. Broke off
port wing, a/c careened madly. This turned turret onto beam, shaking R/G out.
Landed about 60' away. Bombs all on, 2 exploded after ½ hrs., one an hr.
later. No information of remainder of crew. E/a seen after attack JU88, as
it passed below. R/G fired guns manually. Attack almost directly below.

This questionnaire from F/O G.P. Brophy (not Brody) has several points of interest. The report is not dated but it does indicate that the information was extracted from a POW questionnaire; therefore, it was probably made in May of 1945. No doubt there is a typographical error in the Date of Loss. The correct date, of course, was June 12/13, 1944. This record may well be one of the earliest recorded statements of Pat Brophy that led to the posthumous award of the Victoria Cross to Andy Mynarski. Bob Bodie's account of his bailing out appears on page 18.

Bob Bodie, the navigator in Art Debreyne's crew in 419 Squadron, tells what he remembers:

We had smooth trips until June 13. Our target that night was the marshalling yards at Cambrai. This was a night raid, but we didn't get there. We were supposed to go in at 2,000 feet and we were coming down, getting ready for the run-in on the target. All of a sudden this Ju-88 came in from pretty low and astern. Pat Brophy, our tail gunner, said he came in at six o'clock.

The fighter knocked out two motors on one side, and the fuel tanks were burning. Between Brophy's position in the rear turret and Mynarski's in the mid-upper, all the glycol was burning. I heard Art on the intercom say: "Jump! Jump!" because we were only at 2,000 feet. I jumped, pulled the ring and felt the 'chute open, which is a nice feeling.

I found out many months later what happened. Andy Mynarski saw that Pat Brophy was trapped inside the rear turret and tried desperately to free him in spite of being engulfed in flames himself. Finally Brophy waved Mynarski away; Andy stood to attention, saluted and jumped. The aircraft crashed and hit a tree; the rear turret broke open and Brophy landed some yards away, shaken, but alive. I didn't know any of this for some time, nor did I know until later that Andy's burns were fatal and that he had been awarded the Victoria Cross posthumously.

It's a funny thing, you know, but there was another incident in those few seconds as we were bailing out. It was the bomb aimer's job to pull the hatch open. Jack Friday was the bomb aimer, and as he pulled on the hatch it flew back and knocked him unconscious. Roy Vigars, the engineer, saw him lying there, got Friday's parachute, put it on him, loosened it but, keeping it closed with his foot, stepped on the ring and pushed him out. Vigars didn't get any award for that, but I often think that what he did was quite a feat, you know. You see someone lying there, but you want to get out yourself because you are only at 2,000 feet and there isn't any time. He did it anyway and saved Friday's life.

I heard one person say that Andy was still alive when he landed but that he didn't live very long. It was Brophy who recommended him for an award, because he was the only one who saw it. Friday and Vigars became prisoners of war. Art Debreyne, Jim Kelly, Pat Brophy and I evaded and eventually got out together.

Mynarski's gallantry is commemorated in the name of a school in Winnipeg and also in the only airworthy Lancaster bomber in Canada, carefully restored by the Canadian War Plane Heritage Museum at Mount Hope, Ontario.

When they eventually returned to England, Vigars and Friday were asked to complete a POW questionnaire. The documents that appear on pages 17 and 19, describing the loss of the aircraft, were extracted from that questionnaire. Friday's statement is particularly eloquent for its brevity:

Took off the from Middleton St. George. Do not remember briefing or takeoff. First thing I remember is coming to in a hospital in Amiens.

```
QUESTIONNAIRE FOR RETURNED AIRCREW

LOSS OF BOMBER AIRCRAFT

NUMBER  1852652     RANK  SGT       NAME  VIGARS  R.E.

SQUADRON   419    AIRCRAFT LETTER   A     TYPE OF AIRCRAFT  LANC X

Date of Loss      12/13.6.44            Target     CAMBRAI

How amny ops. have you done   13     Duty in Aircraft  F/E

Date of Interrogation 7.5.45      Information extracted from  POW QUESTIONNAIRE

NARRATIVE OF EVENTS FROM TAKE-OFF TO LANDING:-


          Took off approx 10.15 p.m. from Middleton St George, on 12-6-44.
No events until approx 00.10 hrs.  R/G reported fighter below our tail.
Our own stream prevented any evasive action.  Fighter opened fire.  Near
Albert.  A/C hit around photo flush, a/c lost height, pilot regained
control.  Bale out over i/c.  I tryed to reply but mouthpiece u/s.
Moving into B/A compartment found him laying on floor, so loosening
his chute and pulling it, keeping it closed with my foot I managed to get
him out.  He landed safely as I saw him later.  He was unconscious for
approx 4½ days.  Escape hatch was jammed when I tryed to get out but freed
it.  I landed very heavily on left hip but no bones broken.  Weather clear but
no moon.  Bombs were still on a/c when I left.  I do not know what happened
to a/c.
```

This questionnaire describes the action that Roy Vigars took on the night of June 12/13, 1944, when he saved John W. Friday from the same aircraft from which Andy Mynarski valiantly tried to rescue Pat Brophy who was trapped in the rear turret.

The most evocative description of being shot down comes from John Dix, a bomb aimer with 158 RAF Squadron, whose story appears in Chapters 5 and 6. The account that follows is from John's unpublished manuscript and is his recollection of being shot down on his twenty-first trip on August 27, 1943.

Upon reaching our altitude we carried out a gentle weaving from left to right, right to left, and slight alterations in altitude to confuse any unseen enemy fighters that may have been following our course. This continuous weaving, combined with operating at high altitudes for many hours, and breathing pure oxygen from our face masks, tended to make one a little drowsy.

The noise of the four powerful engines, unscreened by any insulation, had become part of our daily lives. Our senses were attuned to their continuous roar. Any slight change in this comforting tune was always instantly noticed by all seven of us on board. Any change in the pulse of the engines could mean that the pilot or the engineer was changing throttle or power settings to conserve fuel, gain or lose altitude, or just to synchronize the four engines to avoid vibration.

The first reaction of all of us to such a change, however, was always the same — it meant trouble, danger and a vague feeling of fear deep inside. This increased the beat of our hearts and caused an involuntary halt in our breathing.

Within seconds we could diagnose which of these contingencies had caused the change in the steady roar of the engines. The voice of the pilot or the engineer would usually be heard on the radio, putting our minds at rest.

Tonight was to be different. Our navigator was in the habit of advising us every fifteen minutes or so of our approximate position. He had just told us we were about to cross the Moselle River between Luxembourg and Saarbrücken and would be flying across the Rhine in about fifteen minutes. The night was very clear, with no clouds in sight, and the stars were shining very brightly. I could see a faint winding ribbon of water 18,000 feet below — the Moselle. There had been no sign of enemy activity since crossing the French coast some two hours before. Just a few sporadic bursts of anti-aircraft shells below us at the coast, and as this was a normal occurrence we had taken little notice of it.

A few minutes after the navigator advised us we were approaching the Moselle I heard several heavy thuds and a change in the roar of the engines, then a small flaming incendiary shell passed between my legs from behind. It left a neat round hole in the perspex nose dome in front of me and continued on in my line of sight for several seconds. There was a steady chatter from our machine guns in the

OVERSEAS

MISSING ON ACTIVE SERVICE AFTER AIR OPERATIONS

Allan, A., F/O, Toronto.
Applin, D. J., Sgt., Westmount.
Armstrong, A. T., F/O, Millbrook.
Bedford, Gordon William, F.O., J20133, Mrs. G. W. Bedford (wife), Makinak.
Body, A. R., F. O., Edmonton.
Brophy, George Patrick, F.O., J35142, Capt. G. P. Brophy (father), 100 High St. S., Port Arthur.
Byers, J. E., Sgt., Calgary.
Bzowy, M. A., WO., Rycroft, Alta.
Carruthers, G. W., Sgt., Malton, Ont.
Christoff, C., Sgt., Oba, Ont.
Couper, M. W., Sgt., Montreal.
Dagenais, J. J. G., F/Sgt., Montreal.
Davies, D. I., Sgt., Walnut Grove, B.C.

Reported wounded in action, LIEUT. JOHN GEORGE KARASIVICH is an officer in the Royal Winnipeg Rifles and went overseas in August, 1942. His wife and two children reside at 717 Jarvis ave.

Murray, D., F/O, Red Deer, Alta.
Murray, R. W., F/O, Vancouver.
Mynarski, Andrew Charles, WO., R134239, Mrs. Stanley Mynarski (mother), 846 Manitoba ave., Winnipeg.
Phillips, R. J., WO., Edmonton.

The 937th Casualty List of the RCAF, published July 18, 1944. This list contains the names of F/O Debreyne's crew in which Bob Bodie was the navigator, the late Pat Brophy the rear gunner, and Andy Mynarski, the mid-upper gunner, who was to receive the Victoria Cross posthumously. Other members of the crew were J.W. Friday, Roy Vigars and Jim Kelly. Vigars' name does not appear on this list because he was with the RAF.

turrets behind me. The voice of the rear gunner came across the radio in the form of a scream with a vague reference to a fighter approaching, then silence from him and his guns. In the same instant, the pilot called to say that both starboard engines were on fire, and that the aircraft was becoming hard to control.

I glanced behind me and saw the flight engineer slumped over his control panel minus his helmet, with blood pouring from a wound in his scalp. I realized then that we were in serious trouble. Our gunner in the middle turret called that the fighter appeared to be firing again from the right side, that the bomb bays underneath him were on fire and the flames from it and the engines were preventing him from sighting the fighter.

Tracer shells were thudding into our aircraft and our middle gunner was firing blindly into the night. Our plane was now obviously out of control. As I was thrown violently against the side of the fuselage, the pilot was shouting over the radio for us to bail out — he had no control over the plane, which was tossing violently from side to side.

The escape hatch in the nose section was a panel measuring two feet by three feet in the floor under the navigator's seat. He had to lift up his seat and pull an emergency handle, which released the hatch into the night. This became quite difficult as we were being tossed about inside the fuselage like peas in a can. We finally released it. The terrific noise from the air rushing by this gaping hole in the floor was very frightening, but our reactions were swift, and I know I was acutely aware of every second of time.

Our navigator took his position facing the rear, sat down on the sill of the open hatch, gave a quick glance at the two of us waiting, then disappeared in a flash. I caught a momentary glimpse of him as he fell free and shouted to my radio man that he was on fire. I sat on the edge of the hatch and hesitated for a moment in fear of catching fire myself as I jumped.

Before I had made up my own mind to jump, a violent manoeuvre of the crippled plane threw me bodily out into the night. I received a terrific jolt as I left the plane, my head wrenched backwards, my helmet and both my flying boots were torn off by the rush of air. My right hand was locked tightly on the release handle of my parachute and I must have pulled it immediately I was thrown from the plane. I received another bone-shaking jolt as my 'chute opened above me. I lost sight of the furiously burning plane as it plunged earthward.

For the next few minutes I believe I lost consciousness, as my next memory was of a terrible loneliness. The lack of noise was the most striking thing; all I could hear was the faint hum of bombers continuing on their way high above me. I was swinging gently from side to side beneath the huge canopy of my parachute. When I looked up to see it there was a sharp pain in my throat. I instinctively put my hand to the pain and it came away covered with blood. I was too scared to explore my body further, as the thought crossed my mind that my neck was broken. I vomited from shock and fear as I slowly floated down in the darkness. . . .

I was still swaying very gently from side to side like a pendulum when I glimpsed what appeared to be a small patch of trees flashing by below me. I realized I was moving quite fast across them. Before I could brace myself for the shock of landing I hit the ground quite hard and rolled into a heap of soft ploughed earth, and my parachute settled softly into a heap beside me.

Northwest Europe

CHAPTER FOUR

ON THE RUN IN NORTHWEST EUROPE

Prior to the First World War, there had been an age-old military tradition that capture meant disgrace. There were escapers and evaders in the First World War, and some of their stories appeared in school library books like A.J. Evans' *The Escaping Club*. These inspired many of the young men who found themselves alone in enemy territory after 1939.

By the Second World War, however, because of the changing military tactics that involved swift encircling movements, and due to the increasing numbers of downed airmen, being captured by the enemy had lost the taint of dishonour. The British had also come to realize that there were many civilians in enemy-occupied countries willing to help an evader. And so, by 1940, they had established M.I. 9 (Military Intelligence section 9). It had a number of objectives: one was to provide evasion training to airmen as to how to evade capture. Another was to organize and finance escape lines run by civilians in occupied countries. Radio communication links were also very important. These contacts were made either through two-way radio with trained operators dropped into Europe or through coded messages delivered through the nightly broadcasts from the BBC. As escapers and evaders successfully made their way back to Britain, they became valuable resources for M.I. 9 and were subjected to sometimes gruelling interrogation.

By 1941 the method of evading capture was fairly well defined. A downed airman was to bury his parachute and immediately get away from the area and stay out of sight, especially during daylight. The airman should make an approach only to a person who was alone. To sustain an evader, an escape kit contained a silk map of the area, some money in local currency, a compass, a hacksaw blade, a water bottle, desalination tablets, concentrated chocolate, some fishing line and hooks, needle and thread, benzedrine, chewing gum and matches. Once an airman made contact with a civilian who was willing to help, an evader could look forward to some kind of lodging, food, false identity papers, civilian clothing and transport — sometimes by bicycle or car and, on long journeys, by train. Local resistance groups provided much of the practical assistance. Sometimes the groups received direct or indirect support from British Intelligence.

Three of the major European escape lines are described in detail in this book. Two were initiated by M.I. 9. The O'Leary Line helped over 600 Allied servicemen evade capture. "Pat O'Leary," who said he was a French Canadian, was known as its leader. His real name was Dr. Albert Guerisse, a Belgian army surgeon.

Late in 1943, M.I. 9 dropped two French Canadian soldiers into occupied France to organize the Shelburne Line. By the summer of 1944, Lucien Dumais and Ray

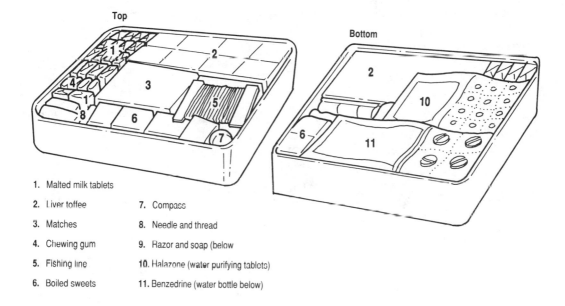

1. Malted milk tablets
2. Liver toffee
3. Matches
4. Chewing gum
5. Fishing line
6. Boiled sweets
7. Compass
8. Needle and thread
9. Razor and soap (below
10. Halazone (water purifying tablets)
11. Benzedrine (water bottle below)

Diagram of an escape kit

LaBrosse had organized this Line which rescued 138 evaders and agents from the coast of Brittany by Royal Navy gun boat.

European civilians organized and staffed the third line mentioned in this book. In the three years of its life the Comet Line saved over 800 Allied airmen. It was the creation of Andrée "Dedee" de Jongh, a young Belgian girl. Dedee lived with her parents at 73 Ave. Emile Verhaevan in Brussels, and had been much inspired by the heroism of nurse Edith Cavell in the First War. Dedee's father, Frederic, was a school master. After Dedee got the Line organized, his school office was used as the Line's headquarters for a time.

In August 1941, Dedee made the first of thirty-three trips across the Pyrenees. She went to the British Consul in Bilbao, Spain, and succeeded in convincing this sceptical official that she could and would organize the safe houses, recruit the helpers, see to the provision of false identity papers, food, clothing and all the necessary items for a successful escape operation. All she required from the British was

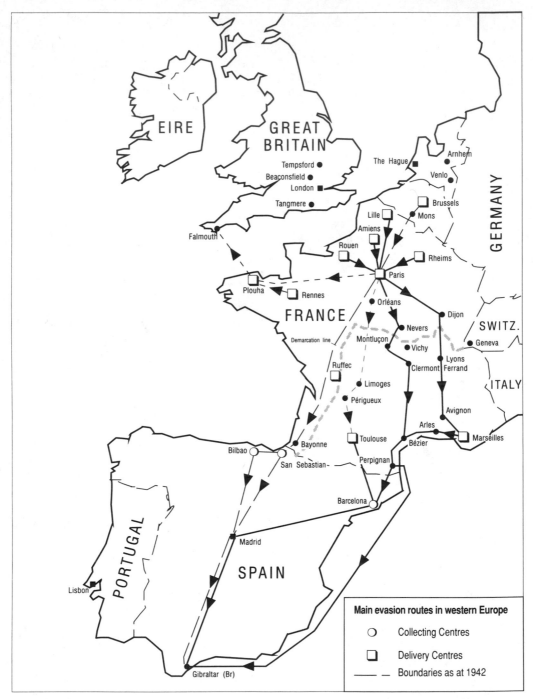

The following text appears on the map:

EIRE

GREAT BRITAIN

GERMANY

Tempsford ●
Beaconsfield ●
London ■
Tangmere ●

The Hague ■   Arnhem ●
Venlo ●
Brussels □
Lille □   Mons
Amiens
Rouen ●   Rheims □

Falmouth

Plouha   Rennes □   Paris ■

FRANCE

Orléans ●   Dijon ●

SWITZ.

Demarcation line   Nevers ●
Montluçon   Vichy ●
Ruffec □   Clermont Ferrand   Lyons
Geneva ●

ITALY

Limoges ●
Périgueux ●   Avignon ●

Arles ●   Marseilles □
Bilbao ○   Bayonne   Toulouse □   Bézier
San Sebastian   Perpignan ●

PORTUGAL   Barcelona ○

Madrid ●

SPAIN

Lisbon ■

Gibraltar (Br)

Main evasion routes in western Europe

○   Collecting Centres

□   Delivery Centres

———   Boundaries as at 1942

———— **O'Leary Line** in which Paula Blanchain and Alex Wattebled worked and through which Mel Dalphond escaped in 1943.

— — **Comet Line** down which John Dix escaped in September, 1943 followed by Ray De Pape about a month later.

- - - - **Shelburne Line** through which Ken Woodhouse made a successful escape in March, 1944.

money to pay the Basque guides for the dangerous trips across the Pyrenees and for the other expenses. At the same time, however, she and her fellow organizers in Comet insisted on running the Line their own way with no interference from the British. It has been estimated that 216 members of the Line were executed or died in captivity. Andrée was arrested in January 1943, and sent to concentration camps Mezum, Essen, Kraizburg, Ravensburg and Mauthausen. She was freed on April 22, 1945. Her father was arrested in June 1943, and was shot at Mount Valerien, Paris, on March 28, 1944.

* * *

By the summer of 1940, Hitler's forces occupied all of Denmark, Holland, Belgium and Luxembourg. France was divided until November 1942; the Germans occupied the coastal areas and that part of France north of the Loire River. A French government with headquarters at Vichy administered the rest of the country in collaboration with the Nazis.

The German successes in Europe in 1940 created a crisis for Britain. Not only had vast amounts of Allied arms and munitions been left behind but, more important, thousands of soldiers were stranded in German-occupied territory. Many became prisoners of war, but thousands of others evaded capture. It has been estimated that from the fall of Dunkirk in June 1940, to the end of the war in 1945, 35,000 British Commonwealth and American soldiers and airmen regained Allied lines. Twenty-three thousand were men who had escaped after being captured; over 9,000, mostly downed airmen, evaded capture and returned to friendly territory.

The reasons for their successful evasion are many and varied, depending upon their own personality, the time of year, a great dose of luck and, without question, the help of thousands of civilians in the occupied countries.

The Helpers

Some civilians had but a single opportunity to help a young airman escape. On the afternoon of June 17, 1944, for instance, Monsieur Galvaire of the French village of Carency, near Vimy Ridge, found a young Canadian pilot from 405 Squadron hiding in the woods on his farm. His Lancaster had been shot down the night before after successfully marking the target of the marshalling yards at Lens. Twenty-year-old Warren Morrill of Schreiber, Ontario, was the mid-upper gunner in that crew. He died a sergeant but, his commission having coming through, was buried as a pilot officer along with the five others who died that night.

While Madame Corneille and others of the village tended to the bodies of the six young airmen who were killed in that crash, giving them a Christian burial in the local cemetery, Monsieur Galvaire hid the young Canadian in his house for three days until arrangements could be made with a member of the local Resistance to start him on the dangerous trip to eventual safety in Britain. Had the Germans captured this young airman he would have become a prisoner of war. Had they captured M. Galvaire, he would have been shot on the spot or sent to a concentration camp. In the event, M. Galvaire was not arrested, and he still lives in Carency, carrying with him the proud memory that he helped save one young man by risking his own life and that of his family.

Unlike Monsieur Galvaire's experience, often one small act led to another and another until many civilians became deeply involved. Mlle. Fraipont is one such person. Incredible as it may seem, she and her friend Fiorella had been holidaying in Dunkirk when the battle and the evacuation raged around them. After the British surrender on June 4, 1940, Mlle. Fraipont and Fiorella went for a walk along the sea front. They heard someone calling to them from the cliffs and discovered four or five British soldiers hiding there. The two girls arranged for a local fisherman to pick them up after nightfall and take them across the Channel.

The two friends didn't think much more about that incident and a few days later they returned to their home near Liège. Fifi, as Mlle. Fraipont was known, had a little house of her own situated not far from the Dutch border in the village of Fouron St Pierre.

Gordon Stacey of 434 Squadron picks up the story.

> Fifi was contacted by British Intelligence in 1941 and asked if she was still willing to help. Apparently some of the soldiers Fifi and Fiorella had helped told the British Secret Service of their assistance. She asked how she could help and they said that her house was a handy spot for getting people across the border and on down the escape line. It would be a matter of finding safe houses for evaders and arranging their onward movement. So she became more and more involved.
>
> She had worked as a seamstress and had also helped at the local chateau in various ways. Fiorella was the daughter of the landowner.

From 1941 on, Fifi became increasingly involved and assisted scores of downed airmen at considerable cost. After many months of providing safe passage and onward movement for evaders it came to the point that Fifi had no more room in her small house. In desperation she went to her family in Liège and asked if, for one night only, they would put up a young airman from Scotland.

> Her parents agreed, although her father was distraught to learn of the extent of Fifi's involvement in the Resistance. By a tragic coincidence, Fifi's younger sister had just broken off a relationship with a fellow and in retribution he went to the local authorities and told them of the Scotsman in the Fraipont home. That night they were raided and the Scot was taken to a POW camp. The rest of the family, except for Fifi, were arrested. The mother went to Buchenwald, the father to Auschwitz and the sister to a factory in East Prussia. While they all survived, the parents came out of the camps in very poor health and didn't live long after my last visit with them in 1947.

It is important to note that Resistance groups did not start out with an overall master plan to help evaders on a country-wide basis, but rather one evolved from the spontaneous links that were forged in thousands of communities, large and small.

As well, the participants were, to a very considerable extent, very young, many of them women still in their teens or early twenties. Thousands of women helped Allied servicemen evade capture and many of them became leaders of escape organizations. Several of these women became well known for their exploits. The women whose stories are mentioned in this book would regard themselves as just ordinary people and tend to discount their extraordinary achievements. The experience of Emmy van Taack, now of Toronto, is a clear example.

Emmy van Taack was fourteen when the Germans bombed Rotterdam on May 14, 1940.

I was going to high school at the time. When the bombing started my mother, father, sister and I were sitting on the stairs, where the walls were closest together. When the bombing stopped we climbed onto our roof and were stunned by what we saw. There in front of us our city was burning to death. The warehouses were full of goods from all over the world — lumber, oil, spices, rice, sugar, rubber — everything was burning.

By 1941 the bombings were so bad that my mother and sister and I moved to our country house about 120 kilometres away from Rotterdam. My father had to stay in the city because he was a teacher. And anyway, the general feeling was that the war would not last long!

I became actively involved in the Resistance when I was fifteen. Our country house was ideally situated as a place to hide people fleeing from the Germans. These people also needed ration cards, false papers and food, so a group of my friends got organized. Joop Migchelsen, aged nineteen, was our leader. We had people working at City Hall who would steal German rubber stamps for authorizing the required papers.

My main job in the beginning was as a courier in a network that brought information from other parts of the country and carried it from village to village. My run was usually to Harderwijk from Hulshorst, about eight kilometres. I would pick up the "mail" and put it on my body or on the bike and away I'd go. Sometimes the trips would be as long as twenty kilometres. I would have a contact in a farmhouse, where I would meet the courier from the next village. I would only know their code name. I didn't know where they lived or their background.

We listened to the English radio for news of the war. I knew how to type, so we mimeographed the news and spread it throughout our small area. Because of my age I was in a very favourable position because there was a lot of innocence there!

In the villages we would know who could be trusted. The biggest threat was that people talked too much — just in a friendly way. It was so interesting to tell your neighbour what you had seen or done. If neighbours were quiet about it that would be fine, but they might tell somebody else, and that was how a lot of information eventually got into German hands.

We got weapons by air drop from Britain — sten guns and handguns. Joop and the boys would go out and get the crates when they were dropped and take them to a little house in the woods where they would be buried for the time when we would need them.

Money was not provided by anybody. We got help from the farmers who would share some of their milk and grain with us even though it was all supposed to go to the Germans. Food in the stores became very scarce in '44 and '45. Thousands of people died from hunger.

In 1944 Jimmy Branford, of the RAF, was shot down over Germany and got to the Dutch border by himself. We kept him for some time in a little house he called "Uncle Tom's Cabin." Since Jimmy was my responsibility, and because collecting food was becoming more and more difficult, I had to quit a job that I had at a bank.

When the organizations were betrayed by collaborators or Nazi spies, they had to be reorganized. As the map on page 26 indicates, evading airmen who were downed in Luxembourg, Holland, Belgium and France were brought to collection points like The Hague, Amsterdam, Brussels and Liège, and then sent to Paris. From Paris they were escorted down one of the major escape lines through Toulouse to Marseilles or St Jean de Luz and across the Pyrenees to neutral Spain.

If an airman came down in Denmark, the route of evasion was often in the other direction — north or east by sea to Sweden. Denis Budd's experience illustrates this route. As related earlier, Denis had bailed out of a 405 Squadron Lancaster on August 16, 1944. He landed in a cabbage patch with a very painful right leg and minus one shoe and one flying boot. After a delightful sleep in a little nest he made for himself in a grove of trees, he took stock of his situation. What struck him was that he was not the least bit frightened. He made up his mind that he was "going to beat those buggers" and so, in late afternoon, he made contact with a farmer.

I asked him for water to drink and a place to sleep. He was ky-eying at me, not being able to speak a word of English. But he pointed to the barn and took me in and showed me some hay where I could lie down. Then he went out and locked the door.

Instead of lying where he told me, I took some hay and put it behind the barn door so that I would be behind it when it opened. Later that evening I heard voices and a big ky-eying back and forth, and the farmer and another man came in. They went to the end of the barn where I was supposed to be and I turned and went out the door! But I couldn't get far because of my leg, and the big guy with the farmer caught me and held me by the scruff of the neck. He couldn't speak English either, and there was a lot more ky-eying.

I complained as best I could about my sore leg and they finally put me in a car. It turned out that the big fellow was Magnus Neilsen, a Danish policeman who worked for the Gestapo, but whose real activity was as one of the top men in the Danish Underground. He brought a doctor to treat my leg and then delivered me to Roskilde

On his silk escape map, which his Danish helpers had saved for him until he returned after the war, the late Denis Budd photographed a number of mementoes of his evasion experience: his gunner's wing, a four-leaf clover and a helper's picture, and equipment from his escape kit including a compass and fishing line. In the upper right-hand corner of the picture is the gold ring he made from the gold he found as a prospector before the war and which he gave to his Danish helpers in 1943.
COURTESY OF THE LATE DENIS BUDD

and the home of Mr. and Mrs. Tholstrup and their two daughters, Lisbeth and Kirsten. The girls could speak a little English and I answered their many questions as best I could.

Mrs. Tholstrup got me a bottle of beer and a tomato sandwich — boy, did I ever appreciate that! In front of their home, quite close to the water, was a little log cabin where they took me to sleep. If the Germans came or if there were any problems, they would push a button in their home which would sound a buzzer in the cabin. I was told to immediately crawl out the window and get away from the house as quickly as possible. There was a small boat on the beach and I was to push out in that and get away.

Next morning they asked me if I would like to have a shower. When I took off my clothes and my watch I arranged them in a very particular way. When I came out of the shower I knew that they had been through every piece of clothing. Obviously they were still not sure of my identity. Later they brought someone who was introduced to me as Joseph. I found out later that he was Joseph Fisher Holst, the chief wireless operator of the Danish Underground in Copenhagen. He questioned me some more and then said: "We are reasonably sure that you are who you say you are and we are going to give you a choice. We can give you food and some money and you can go your own way. You will probably be picked up by the Germans and put in a prisoner-of-war camp, and you will outlast the war and get home safe and sound. The other choice you have is that we get you false identity papers and you get to know some different people in the Resistance movement. You have to do exactly what we tell you — no ifs, ands or buts. If we tell you to jump, you jump! You don't ask why and you do it right away. If you don't follow our instructions, it won't be the Germans who shoot you; it will be us. We will give you a day to think about it and I will be back tomorrow and then you can tell us."

He came back the next day and I said, "Well, you people have been so kind, and if you are willing to risk your neck I am sure as hell willing to risk mine!"

Denis became Albert Dennis Jensen, an architect from Roskilde, and he stayed with the Tholstrups for some time. Roskilde was famous in the area for the unique clock in its cathedral. Every hour on the hour the figures of two knights ride out from the body of the clock and charge each other. Lisbeth, who was seventeen at the time, wanted to show Denis the clock and so they went to the cathedral on bicycles, went in, sat down, and immediately in walked five German soldiers. As soon as Lisbeth saw them she said to Budd: "Don't say a word. When I talk and laugh, you laugh too, but don't speak."

The soldiers sat about ten feet from Denis and Lisbeth. All seven sat and watched the clock strike the hour, two of them much more frightened than the others. Eventually the soldiers left the church and Denis and Lisbeth, heaving a great sigh of relief, returned to the relative safety of the Tholstrups' home.

One day Joseph arrived with the news that it had been decided it would be better if Budd were moved to Copenhagen. He was taken to a small cottage owned by a Jew whom the Resistance had managed to get out to Sweden. At this stage of the war the Gestapo were getting particularly vindictive and vicious. It was soon decided that it was time to get Budd out of Denmark.

They had arranged for me to get out on a coal boat. It was sailing for Germany, but it was going to pass through Swedish waters and I was to give myself up to the captain during the time the ship was in those waters. Joseph took me down to the docks where I met O.B. Bertelson. His code name was O.B., and I didn't know him by any name but that till after the war. O.B. took me past German soldiers and onto this freighter that was supposed to sail at midnight.

Midnight came and the ship did not sail! And I had lost my contact with the Underground. To get this far and now this! I was afraid they might bring dogs on board to search the ship and in the early hours of the morning I heard a noise. A man came down to the hold, and I was relieved to hear that he was whistling *God Save the King*. I gave myself up to him and he took me off to a large house. And who should be there but my pilot, Bruce Walter!

We learned that another ship was sailing the next day, and that night Bruce and I were taken down to the hold of that ship. When we got on board there was Ralph Rafter, our wireless operator! The ship sailed out of the harbour at Copenhagen and into Swedish waters. At that point a Swedish pilot came on board to take the ship through Swedish minefields. Since the Swedish pilot was in charge of the ship in Swedish waters we gave ourselves up to him.

After considerable discussion we were taken to a big compound in Malmo, Sweden. We got ourselves cleaned up there — that was the first place that I had ever slept in paper sheets. We entered Sweden as civilians so were not interned. From Malmo we went by train to Stockholm and stayed in the Astoria Hotel after reporting to the British Legation.

We were able to draw some pay from the Legation so we had a ball for the short time we were there. Then, one foggy night, Ross Wiens, Ralph Shafter and I were flown out to Leuchars airfield in Scotland in a DC-3.

A year earlier Donald Smith, now of St. Catharines, Ontario, took the same route from Denmark to Sweden, but he was no stowaway: he had to work his way across in a very literal sense. Smith joined the air force in 1940, and within a year he was in England working as a mechanic on RAF Hurricanes and Spitfires. In a matter of months he was able to remuster and he became a flight enginer with 75 (New Zealand) Squadron.

On the night of April 20/21, 1943, Smith, his pilot Flight Lieutenant Parish and crew were leading a force of bombers on a raid on Stettin. Their Stirling was attacked by Me-110s; the plane suffered heavy damage — one engine gone and the fuselage on fire. Smith recalls: "Because we had an extra pilot on his first trip, I was told to go out the back way instead of the front if we had to bail out. When the order came, I went out the back hatch and, as I came down, I saw the Stirling blow up. I was the only survivor."

Smith practically walked across the whole of the Danish peninsula. He was eventually taken in by a man who could speak English and he was given a bath, a meal and a bed to sleep in. Smith remembers a telephone conversation his host had while he was there, though he doesn't know who it was with:

"What would you do if a Canadian airman came to your house?"

"I'd get him over to Sweden, of course," seemed to be the reply.

"Well, I have one for you at my house; come and get him!"

Smith was put in touch with the Danish Underground. The plan was that he would cross the strait separating Denmark from Sweden. There was constant traffic in that waterway, mostly freighters, ferry boats and German naval craft. The Nazis kept a close watch on these ships, so Smith's was to be no ordinary journey.

He was to go by kayak! Had he ever had any experience in a kayak? Well no, but he was a strong young Canadian and of course he could do it. It was just as well he was not familiar with the waters of the Baltic and its bays, gulfs and straits, because that knowledge might have given him second thoughts. Tidal waters poured through the narrow channels creating very rough seas, even for a large ship. In a tiny, two-man kayak it would be a bouncy and dangerous trip.

Lars Troan, a young police cadet, had been held by the Gestapo accused of sabotage. Lars had escaped and was to accompany Smith. Unlike Smith, Lars had previous experience in a kayak. He also had a special flashlight and the correct recognition signals for the day. In addition, he had a photograph of Gestapo headquarters which the Resistance wanted the British to bomb. The RAF was to be informed that the top floor was used to hold Gestapo prisoners, so only the bottom two floors were to be bombed. A tricky bit of flying would be needed and indeed, on March 25, 1945, a bombing raid was successfully completed.

Smith remembers the crossing very well:

> The water in the Sound was very cold, with fast currents and heavy swells. This proved to be a blessing to us when a German patrol boat headed in our direction with its searchlight sweeping over the water. We stopped paddling and laid our heads flat on the gunwhale. Just at the right moment the kayak dropped between two waves and the searchlight went over our heads. After paddling for three hours we passed the Swedish island of Ven and were now safely out of Danish waters. Lars decided to go up the coast to a point where the Swedes had left a stretch of beach without barbed wire. We finally landed at three A.M. on May 1, 1943. After beaching the kayak, I took out my dagger and slit it below the water line and shoved it out into the Sound.

Smith turned himself in to the British Legation, who were expecting him, as the Danish Underground had reported he was on his way. By May 13, 1943, Donald Smith was back in Scotland, just over three weeks from the time he had left.

CHAPTER FIVE

WHEN YOU ARE INVOLVED YOU HAVE NO FEAR

At six o'clock on the morning of May 10, 1940, German armour swept across the Luxembourg border and, by the end of that day, the swiftness of that attack had brought not only Luxembourg but also Holland and Belgium to their knees.

Margot Maroldt remembers that day very well. Born in Larochette, Luxembourg, in 1915, she had married Pierre Maroldt in 1938. He operated an agricultural supply store and had many contacts with other businessmen and farmers in the area.

Margot recalls:

> We had no idea the Germans would come that day. We knew they were on the other side of the river very near to us, but we didn't expect them to come that day. We expected that there would be a war, but we didn't think they would come over here. But at six o'clock that morning a very nice German worker we knew came and told my husband that the German army was here.
>
> For the first few months the German army was in charge of the occupation and everything was correct, and apart from food rationing we had little trouble. But In August, German civilians arrived — the Gestapo and so on — and that's when our troubles began.

AVIS

Toute personne du sexe masculin qui aiderait, directement ou indirectement, les équipages d'avions ennemis descendus en parachute, ou ayant fait un atterrissage forcé, favoriserait leur fuite, les cacherait ou leur viendrait en aide de quelque façon que ce soit, sera fusillée sur le champ.

Les femmes qui se rendraient coupables du même délit seront envoyées dans des camps de concentration situés en Allemagne.

Les personnes qui s'empareront d'équipages contraints à atterrir, ou de parachutistes, ou qui auront contribué, par leur attitude, à leur capture, recevront une prime pouvant aller jusqu'à 10.000 francs. Dans certains cas particuliers, cette récompense sera encore augmentée.

Paris, le 22 Septembre 1941.

Le Militärbefehlshaber en France,
Signé : von STÜLPNAGEL
Général d'Infanterie.

A notice posted throughout France by the German General von Stulpnager, September 22, 1941. Since this notice was posted before the formation of the Comet, Shelburne and O'Leary escape lines, it is obvious that successful evasion by downed Allied airmen was already a serious problem for the Nazis.
COURTESY OF KEN WOODHOUSE

WARNING

All males who come to the aid, either directly or indirectly, of the crews of enemy aircraft coming down in parachutes, or having made a forced landing, help their escape, hide them, or come to their aid in any fashion, will be shot on the spot.

Women who render the same help will be sent to concentration camps in Germany.

Persons who will capture or detain landing crews or parachutists or will contribute by their attitude to their capture will receive a reward of up to 10,000 francs. In certain particular cases this compensation will be increased.

Paris the 22, September 1941

Le Militerbefohlohaber en France
Signed: von Stulpnagel
General of the Army

For more than a year Margot did not know of the secret activities that had begun to occupy Pierre's time. He wanted to keep her out of all that — it was too dangerous for her to know anything in case she was picked up for questioning.

> I had a feeling that he was involved in something because there were always people coming to our house. There was Leo Koob, who owned a small coffee shop, and Hubert Glesener, a fitter and metal worker, and several others. I asked myself, "Why do they come?" I knew they didn't come for business. And when they came they all talked together very quietly. I asked Pierre what this was all about, but he wouldn't tell me.
>
> I knew many of these men who came to our house. One in particular I had no confidence in. I told Pierre that I knew he was a very nice young man, but if the Gestapo got their hands on him and tortured him he would tell everything he knew because I thought he didn't have a very strong character.

In view of the tragic events that were to follow, it is important to pause to make a point here. Thousands of civilians who worked in the Resistance were betrayed by Nazi sympathizers. Some of these collaborators were caught, tried and convicted of war crimes after the war. However, the Germans were able to arrest many other patriots betrayed by their friends — not willingly, of course, but because they broke down at some point during interrogation or torture. And it was often not possible for anyone to prove who betrayed whom. To this day there are festering doubts and suspicions among older Europeans about their former friends and allies.

As the war progressed young men from Luxembourg were being conscripted into the German army (the present chaplain to the Luxembourg royal family, Abbé Georges Vuillermoz, was one of them), or being sent to labour camps in Germany. Some of these young men were able to evade their German masters, hiding in a succession of homes in Luxembourg. By September 1943 Margot was brought fully into the Resistance work with Pierre when she took in two civilians hiding from the Gestapo.

One day Pierre came to Margot with the news that another house had to be found for these men because there was an English airman whom they had to hide. This would be more difficult, more dangerous and more urgent.

Pierre had found out about this airman through contacts with the "chain." We didn't know at that time that there was something called the "Comet Line." Pierre only knew to whom these young men should be sent as the next step. A cousin of Pierre's, a young girl, knew that we had hidden men in our house and she contacted Pierre to tell him of this airman who needed help. Pierre told me, and that was a fact I accepted.

The young British airman was John Dix, from 158 Squadron based at Lisset. His twentieth birthday had been celebrated in memorable fashion a few days before in another safe house in Luxembourg. John had defied his father when he was just over seventeen by joining the Royal Air Force. He trained as a navigator and, on August 27, 1943, was acting as the bomb aimer in a Halifax raid on Nuremberg. It was his twenty-first operation. Half a century later John Dix still remembers the night he was taken to the home of Pierre and Margot. He had come down several nights before, making contact with friendly people who hid and clothed him. One of his strongest supporters was Nicole (not her real name).

Nicole said a truck would be along in a few minutes and I was to remain hidden until she called me. The truck would stop at an intersection and then back up about fifty yards; this would be the signal to Nicole that it was the right truck. Sure enough, a few minutes later, I heard one approaching, its lights very dim. The driver flashed them a couple of times as he approached. He went by us, stopped and backed up. Nicole left the bushes and I could hear her talking to the driver. I was told to get into the back, and lay down under a tarpaulin and a pile of empty grain sacks. Nicole covered me completely and warned me under no circumstances to move until she told me to. It was possible that the truck would be stopped at a checkpoint. Since our plane had been shot down, additional checkpoints had been set up and the driver did not know where they all were.

She sat up front with the driver and was now his girlfriend whom he had taken along for the ride on his delivery of grain to a warehouse in the frontier area. He had a special permit to be out after dark. Off we went, every bone in my body shaken with each bump in the road. I held my arm over my head to hold up the tarpaulin and give some breathing space; it was very uncomfortable. After about half an hour the truck stopped suddenly. There were loud guttural voices, followed by footsteps at the side of the truck, and the driver got out. More talking in German and I could hear Nicole's voice. I put my hand over my mouth to stifle a sneeze; I was terrified and soaking with perspiration. A few seconds later the truck door closed, the engine revved up and we were on our way.

A short while later we started to make many stops and turns. I could hear other vehicles and could sense that we were in a big town. Finally the truck stopped and the engine was turned off. I could hear sounds of trains nearby and knew we were near a railway station. The driver called for me to come out, but I did not move at first, remembering Nicole's final instructions. Then I scrambled out from under the grain sacks and tarpaulin into wonderful fresh air. I jumped down from the truck and was led through the back door of a house. The yard was filled with stacks of lumber and two warehouses. Nicole led me into the house and introduced me to Pierre and Margot, the owners of the truck and the house where I would now be hiding. From my window I could look over the yard to the main Luxembourg railway station.

A few days later John was delighted by the arrival of his navigator, Jimmy Robinson, and shortly thereafter Boyd Reagan, an American airman from Walters, Oklahoma. During a bombing operation to Schweinfurt on August 17, 1943, Reagan's plane had been shot down near Münster. He wandered around undetected in Germany for three weeks, hoping to make it safely to Belgium or Luxembourg. He survived mostly on the fruits and vegetables he was able to find, and finally hid in the forest "Grotestan" between Grevenmacher and Manternach, from where he was taken to the home of Father Robert Maroldt, a Roman Catholic priest in Grevenmacher and Pierre's brother.

Margot recalls:

When Reagan came, we had all three of them, and that was difficult because they were all in one room. We had a housemaid who came every morning and left each evening, but the bathroom was beside the bedroom where these three were hidden. If any one of them had made a noise, the maid would have heard them, but she never knew they were there! I talked to her after the war and she said she had no idea there were three men hiding in that room. They were quiet for a whole week — imagine that! I don't remember how I arranged a toilet for them, but something was worked out.

Getting food was easy because Pierre's business was with farmers and they gave him eggs, butter and bacon. I think John was with us for about a week. One day somebody came and said there was an alarm and we would have to get out because the Germans were searching the whole area. I took John with me because he couldn't speak the language, and we went to a family where I told the lady of the house that John was deaf and dumb. But she knew who John was because her husband was also in the Resistance. We went into their dining room where their young son had covered the whole wall with pictures of British planes! I had to remind John to be silent and not let on that he knew all about those planes! Some hours later Pierre came and told us the alarm was over and we could go home again.

In the evenings, after the maid had gone, we would have our dinner and talk. I could speak some English and that's how we communicated. Sometimes other members of the Resistance would come for conversation.

You see, when you are involved, at that moment you have no more fear; you must act, you must do it. From the moment I became involved I had no more fear: I was taken up by the things I had to do and had no time to think that the Gestapo might come. We trusted the people we worked with, except for one. He was a good man, but I knew his character and feared for what he would do if the Gestapo got him.

Pierre was not involved with sabotage. His main activity was in hiding young people — first young Luxembourgers and then Allied airmen. He found families to hide them and helped organize their escape by providing false passports, identification cards, couriers, clothing and food.

After about a week, John Dix, Jimmy Robinson and Boyd Reagan were taken by Nicole and Hubert Glesener. The plan was that they were to travel by express train from Luxembourg non-stop to Brussels, where they would be passed on to another link in the escape chain, later to be known as the Comet Line. Of the group of three airmen and their two helpers, only John Dix was to escape back to England.

Hubert Glesener returned to Luxembourg City after the fateful trip to Brussels. Within three weeks of his return, Glesener was arrested along with twenty-two others, including Leo Koob and Pierre Maroldt. They had been betrayed to the Gestapo. By someone working inside the local resistance movement? By someone else who sold information to the Germans for some purpose? Somebody betrayed them, and that person may still be alive and living in Luxembourg City. But no one was successfully brought to trial and convicted for that betrayal.

John Dix, in the next chapter, offers one theory about the identity of the traitor. Margot Maroldt has another suspicion.

At this point two observations must be made. The first is to repeat that these doubts and suspicions about who remained loyal and who was a collaborator continue to this day and can now never be removed. As well, there is still, almost half a century later, very great sensitivity about talking about one's suspicions, as one can detect in Margot's comments:

My opinion — and it is difficult to be sure — is that there was a Luxembourger who worked for the English and also for the Germans. The day Hubert Glesener and others were taken by the Germans there was a meeting of the Resistance in our house. This was about two weeks after John Dix and the others had gone. This Luxembourger was there; he was a go-between between the people in England and the local Resistance. My feeling — I have no proof, mind you — is that he was a double agent. I think he had been arrested by the Gestapo and they forced him to become a double agent by threatening to kill him if he didn't.

There are many things that combined to point to his guilt. He was in our house this time with other members of the Resistance, and someone came to the door — I was in the kitchen — and said: "Margot, tell Pierre that the Gestapo is now arresting people who are close friends of your husband. Tell him he must get away."

A memorial picture of Pierre Maroldt, who was executed in February 1944. COURTESY OF MARGOT MAROLDT

A LA MÉMOIRE
DE
PIERRE MAROLDT
ÉPOUX DE MARGOT FABER
NÉ A BIVANGE-BERCHEM, LE 29 JUIN 1916
FUSILLÉ AU K-Z. HINZERT,
LE 25 FÉVRIER 1944

MORT POUR LA PATRIE!

I went into the room where the Resistance was meeting and told my husband. This Luxembourger said in a gruff voice, "Be quiet, Madame; there is no danger!" How did he know there was no danger when all over the city our friends were being arrested? What did he know? Did he know that the Gestapo was not planning to come to our house that afternoon? The meeting broke up shortly thereafter and they all left, including my husband. The Gestapo came about six o'clock that evening, but, of course, there were no men here by that time.

They didn't get my Pierre that day. He went to a farm of a friend outside the city, where it was safe for him to hide. But then this Luxembourger came and said that this was not a safe place to hide, and he insisted that Pierre accompany him to a "safer" place in the little Belgian village of Léglise just across the border. My husband had confidence in this Luxembourger, so he went with him to Léglise. The family who took him in said they were in trouble also and that they were afraid to hide him just then. However, they agreed to keep him until the following morning at which time he would have to go.

The next morning, October 15, 1943, the Gestapo came. It is very strange that this Luxembourger would take him to that place. My Pierre jumped out of an upstairs window and tried to run but they had the place surrounded. He had a false passport, but he couldn't remember the name on it so they took him away.

I never got to say goodbye to him. As soon as I found out that Pierre had been arrested I went into hiding and remained hidden until the Americans liberated us on September 10, 1944.

After the war this Luxembourger was brought to justice. Jimmy Robinson came back from England to testify, but it couldn't be proven that the Luxembourger was a traitor so he went free. He lived among us quite openly until he died a natural death some years ago.

Pierre Maroldt was held for a time in a prison in Luxembourg and then taken to the German concentration camp at Hintzern.

On Friday, February 26, 1944, Margot Maroldt of Luxembourg City picked up this newspaper to read. Her husband had been arrested and imprisoned the previous October but Margot had recently been assured that the Germans would not execute him. Then she read this account, a translation of which appears on page 42.

I remember very well one Friday evening in February 1944. One of Pierre's brothers came to me. He had good relations with a German who knew the Gestapo but was not Gestapo himself. This German had gone to the Gestapo to see if there would be any more executions and he was assured that there would be no more. My brother-in-law came and told me that I could relax now and be hopeful that Pierre would survive.

The next morning the newspaper came, and with mounting horror this is what I read [English translation from German]:

"*LUXEMBOURG WORD*, FRIDAY, FEBRUARY 26, SATURDAY FEBRUARY 27, 1944

JUSTIFIABLE EXECUTION OF INSTIGATORS AND CONSPIRATORS

THE ATONEMENT FOR ABETTING AND AIDING IN DESERTION, REFUSAL OF CONSCRIPTION, SUPPORT OF THE ENEMY AND TREASON

PUBLIC NOTICE

As a result of abetting and aiding in desertion, refusal of conscription, support of the enemy and treason, the following were executed on the spot:

1. BASSING, Ludwig: Official inspector, Vianden.
2. BARBIEUR, Edgard: Professional soldier, born in Quarignon, Belgium, res. Grainheim, Brussels,
3. BENZ, Lutz: Physical education teacher, Luxembourg,
4. BRISTIEL, Leo: Steelworker, Esch-Alz.
5. CHRISTOPHE, Adolf: Machinist, born in Kreuswald/Lothr., res Crusnes/Nancy.
6. DAL ZOTTO, Matthias: Steelworker, Schifflingen.
7. EVERLING, Georg: Office worker, Luxembourg.
8. GLESENER, Hubertus: Fitter, metalworker, Luxembourg.
9. GRZONKA, Robert: Construction worker, Luxembourg.
10. HEYARDT, Raymund: Barber, Rumelingen.
11. KOOB, Leo: Baker, Luxembourg.
12. KUHN, Julius: Businessman, Luxembourg.
13. KUENSCH, Emil: Electrician, Luxembourg.
14. LAUX, Emil: Office worker, Mersch.
15. LEMMER, Johann: Plumber's assistant, Diekirch.
16. MANNON, Theodor: Manager, Diekirch.
17. MAROLDT, Peter: Businessman, Luxembourg.
18. MICHEL, Arthur: Painter, Dalheim.
19. NOESEN, Anton: Farmer, Diekirch.

20. PAULY, Konrad: Shoemaker, Differdingen.
21. SANDT, Josef: Wine merchant, Schifflingen.
22. SCHOOS, Josef: Steelworker, Schifflingen.
23. STEINMETZER, Josef: Engineer, Rollingen.

The public announcement of the executions surprised no one in Luxembourg. They were simply the inevitable consequences of a long-standing, clearly established fact and the enforcement of its strictest measure, as announced unambiguously by the *Gauleiter* for the district:

> For a soldier who becomes a deserter there can only be a lawful death according to the laws of all nations on earth. This is none other than the self-preservation of a people, who in wartime must defend themselves against the enemy. The death penalty is even more justified for those who through their words and deeds try to invoke the thought of desertion in other soldiers who may themselves not even have considered it previously; these very same who support deserters by every possible means may even have developed a system. Even though desertion is the worst crime that can be committed by a man during the crises of a nation, the dimension of a crime committed by instigators and conspirators cannot even be discussed. They not only have the death of the deserters on their conscience — a shameful and disgraceful death to befall a soldier — but they are also responsible for the fact that brave and upright soldiers had to die or were wounded critically simply because the deserters didn't take their place next to them. Furthermore, they bring immeasurable suffering to countless families. It would be absolutely irresponsible if those wouldn't be punished by death who have on their conscience the death and serious injury of many soldiers; who try to undermine the firm belief in honour and loyalty of men in wartime, especially a war threatening the very existence of the European nations and in which the most barbarously destructive weapons are deployed against civilians. Of no one of those executed due to abetting and aiding in desertion, refusal of conscription, support of the enemy and treason can it even be remotely stated that he didn't know what he had done. Those who are familiar with the details of this process know that the list of those who thus forfeited their lives could be much longer than it actually is. The lawful bullet only killed those instigators and conspirators who were indeed responsible for the disgrace and shame of young soldiers.
>
> No one who can think clearly can escape the predetermined logic of the punishment that was executed here. With the betrayal of a nation or even that of an entire continent there can be no manner of inconsistency. Just as during the aerial bombing on civilians it would be utter madness not to extinguish immediately and quickly the fire caused by a single fire bomb in order to prevent the destruction of the entire house, so also it would be totally insane for a country not to punish by death men who undermine military

discipline, whether as deserters or conspirators. Lack of consequence would be the suicide of a people. This consequence must therefore be so strictly and so extensively enforced that even the smallest spark scattered from the fire of betrayal be vigorously stamped out. As previously stated, no one can claim that he wasn't warned clearly in advance. Now these drastic measures have become reality as announced. After these lawfully carried out executions have taken place there will no longer be any doubt that there is enough power and will to safeguard and enforce the only possible consequence on the entire line, pertaining to the question of desertion.

The prisoners had been forced to kneel facing a mass grave that Polish slave labourers had dug. Each prisoner was shot in the back of the head and their bodies were buried in this unmarked grave outside the camp perimeter.

After the war someone traced the whereabouts of one of these Polish labourers. He was brought back to Hintzern and identified the exact location of the mass grave. With loving care the bodies were exhumed and brought back to Luxembourg City and placed in a beautiful setting adorned with a memorial.

Each year, on All Saints Day, the Bishop of Luxembourg gives a blessing for those who are buried there.

A memorial in Luxembourg to the twenty-three members of the Resistance, including Pierre Maroldt, who were executed in March 1944.

Margot Maroldt being presented to Queen Elizabeth in Luxembourg, November 8, 1976. COURTESY OF MARGOT MAROLDT

When I read in that newspaper that Pierre had been executed, I couldn't cry. I didn't accept he was dead; I couldn't accept it. Something closed up inside me. It took me weeks to accept that he was gone, and then I could cry. Then the war was over and I was alone.

At first I tried to operate my husband's business, but I was not a businesswoman. I had no profession and it had not been common before the war for girls to be educated beyond high school. For a few years I was housekeeper to Pierre's brother-in-law, the priest in Grevenmacher, who had also been sent to a concentration camp but had survived. I was there five years and those years were a quiet time for me, an interval.

Then the minister of education in Luxembourg, another survivor of the camps, arranged for me to be accepted in a school of social work in Brussels. I worked as a social worker with troubled adolescents for twenty years until I retired. I get a pension for my years as a social worker and I also get a pension as Pierre's widow.

I was decorated by the Americans, the British and my own government, but I'm not sure what they all are. In 1976 Queen Elizabeth II visited Luxembourg to thank those who assisted Allied airmen during the war, and I met her on that occasion.

In every country there are good people and bad people. If Pierre had come back he would have carried on business with the Germans he respected.

Margot Maroldt lives alone now in a comfortable apartment in a newer section of Luxembourg City. She assists Abbé George Vuillermoz, the chaplain to the royal family. In 1980 the Royal Air Forces Escaping Society, Canadian Branch, brought Margot to Canada. One of the highlights of her visit was a trip to the highlands of Haliburton, Ontario, where the fall colours were in their full glory.

John Dix and Margot Maroldt were closely associated for no more than seven days in 1943, yet the intensity of their experience in that time has forged a life-long bond between them that the rest of us cannot fully grasp. John puts it this way:

"A lot of people here have no way of understanding our feelings for these people. 'After fifty years?' they say. I don't care if it's a hundred years."

Chapter Six

I DON'T CARE IF IT'S A HUNDRED YEARS

It was Nicole who had brought John Dix to Pierre and Margot Maroldt, and it was Nicole who came to help him on the next stage of his journey to freedom. He was very sad at having to say goodbye to his hosts; they had done so much for him and had been so kind. However, the prospect of being with Nicole raised his morale considerably.

She was a beautiful young woman who spoke almost perfect English. Prior to his stay with the Maroldts, John had been in another safe house where his hosts and Nicole had celebrated his twentieth birthday. The meal, the candlelight, the champagne, and most of all the companionship, had all combined to make this the most memorable birthday of John's life.

In the days that followed his departure from the Maroldts, John and Nicole spent much time together. She did all her work as a helper after her daily shift in a factory in Shifflingen and she travelled the fifteen to twenty kilometres back and forth by bicycle. She spent many hours with John, taking him for walks in the evenings, even past German military headquarters. Arm in arm they would stroll like young lovers as she pointed out that he had little to fear from the ordinary German soldiers; the ones in civilian clothes were the threat and they had a network of spies and informers to help them. Nicole took John and Boyd to a photographer, and his identity card with new picture attached identified him as Paul Clausen, a veterinary student, studying in Brussels.

As they spent time together, John wondered about this young woman.

> We talked about the problems we might encounter, the dangers involved, the necessity to act without causing suspicion, and I wondered how a girl of about our own age could have become involved in these dangerous activities and how she was so able to help us overcome our fears. She explained that most of this was new to her also, but much of it was common sense and local knowledge.
>
> I was taking every opportunity to be alone with Nicole. To all outward appearances we were young lovers. We enjoyed each other's company, had many earnest discussions on life in general and spent many hours telling each other of our hopes for the future. It was seriously mentioned by our hosts and friends that used to visit from time to time that I should marry Nicole and take her back to England with me. They explained that she was very much afraid because of her activities in helping us and wanted to get out. Older and saner heads were brought to bear on the subject, however, and we were advised to "cool it." Personal wishes could not interfere with the serious business at hand. For the few days remaining to us, however, we continued to make the most of our opportunities to talk and be together.

In order to make contact with the Comet Line, of which John had no knowledge at the time, it was necessary to cross the border from Luxembourg into Belgium and then catch the express train from Arlon to Brussels. The three young airmen, Reagan, Robinson and Dix, escorted by Hubert Glesener and Nicole, made the dangerous crossing successfully and found their way to Arlon. Along with the risks of detection, especially at checkpoints, another disturbing event had occurred. An eighteen-year-old boy had pleaded with Nicole and Hubert to be allowed to join the group. He explained that he did not want to be recruited into the German army and was on the run. Much against her better judgment, Nicole relented.

The group arrived at Arlon station, and Hubert and the young boy went ahead to buy tickets while the others went into the station canteen. John remembers that the young boy disappeared for a short while at this point. It was arranged that John and Nicole would sit together, with Jimmy Robinson close by. Boyd and Hubert were together in the same coach but some distance away and the young boy close to them. Nicole and John sat opposite each other right next to the door of the coach and an elderly couple came in and sat next to John. Nicole leaned across and whispered to John that he should put his raincoat on the rack above his head, light up a cigarette and relax!

Because it was an express train to Brussels, no stops were anticipated. It was, therefore, with mounting apprehension and fear that they sensed the train slowing down as it entered the station at Namur. When it came to a halt John noticed that the platform was deserted except for a line of German soldiers about twenty feet apart the full length of the platform on both sides of the train. Controlled panic beset the group of evaders and helpers; there was going to be a search; had someone informed them? John wondered.

> Nicole whispered to me that she had felt all day that something would go wrong, and she was now certain that we had been betrayed. She held my hand for a moment or two and said that this may be the end of the journey. We did not know each other any longer and it would be everyone for themselves. This sudden and obviously dangerous situation seemed to change my outlook completely. Up to now I had been frightened at the rapidly deteriorating circumstances around me, but now I realized that this was it. I decided I was going to make it somehow and that I was on my own. My false name and birthplace were repeating themselves over and over in my mind. I became Paul Clausen of Brussels.

While John was coming to terms with this new and dangerous situation there was a commotion outside the train. Everyone rushed to the windows to see what was going on. A shot rang out and three German soldiers carried the limp body of a man back to the platform and laid it on a bench.

Two men in civilian clothes entered the carriage accompanied by a German soldier. One of them went to where Jimmy Robinson was seated and the other came to John.

"*Carte d'identité, s'il vous plaît.*" John handed him the papers. The German studied them for a few moments.

"*Vous êtes Belge?*"

"*Oui, monsieur.*"

In the meantime the other Gestapo official asked Jimmy for his papers. Jimmy did not respond, so the soldier grabbed him by the arm and stood him up while the civilian searched through his pockets.

"Are you English?" Jimmy was asked. No reply. The three Germans surrounded Jimmy at this point and searched his raincoat on the overhead rack. They found assorted badges and souvenirs that Jimmy had collected, so the game was up for him. He was marched off the train and made to stand facing the station window with his hands over his head. It was almost a duplicate when they came to Boyd and he, too, was marched off the train and made to face the wall with his hands over his head. It was now quite obvious that the Gestapo had been informed and were looking for three young men, for they spent little or no time examining the papers of others on the train. Did they now have the three?

> We must have been at least an hour at Namur station until the whole train had been checked. The tension was so great that one's judgment of time and events became blurred. I can remember a sense of great weariness and sadness, and I know that I prayed. Mostly, I prayed that the Germans would not search the train again and that Jimmy and Boyd would be safe. Nicole was sitting with her eyes closed and I saw that she was holding the arm of her seat so tightly her knuckles were white.

The two Gestapo men went to the body of the young man who had been shot, which was now lying in a pool of blood. The young man's papers were removed and shown to Jimmy and Boyd, who shook their heads. Jimmy's face was reflected quite clearly in the window he was facing, not more than twenty feet from where Nicole and John could see him.

> After a few minutes orders were shouted along the platform and I heard the whistle of the train's engine and, with a great puffing and lots of noise, the train slowly started to move. I was leaning out of the window with Nicole, looking at Jimmy's reflection and as we started to move, he lifted his head, looked right at me and winked. I watched the two of them as the train pulled away and my thoughts are not now remembered. I was never to see either of them again.

Nicole and John sat back quietly and tried to regain their composure. For John Dix, the events of those last few hours were to invest in him an ability to hide his true feelings which to others appeared unfeeling. He was to learn some years later that Nicole's life was also unalterably changed, and whether it was for better or worse only she knows.

While the train had been allowed to proceed, it appeared that the Gestapo were not entirely sure that they had the three they were looking for, because the two civilians and the soldiers were still on the train looking at everyone closely. However, the rest of the journey was made without further searches.

Nicole told John that when the train reached Brussels she would leave first and he was to follow her about fifty yards behind, being careful all the while to see that they weren't being followed. If they were, he was to make his own way around the area and return to the station and wait for her to come for him. John remembers how he felt:

> As the train slowed down through the suburbs of Brussels, I tried to get my thoughts in order and shake off the fear that would not seem to go away. The train pulled into the station and I saw immediately that it was a much busier place than any I had seen up to now. The train stopped and Nicole left while I hesitated a few seconds before trying to follow her through the crowds.
>
> As I was trying to keep her in sight, I heard a commotion behind me and somebody calling out, "*Monsieur, Monsieur!*" Instinctively I turned around and was horrified to see that the old man I had been sitting with was running through the crowd waving my overcoat over his head! I was too frightened to go back to retrieve the coat and almost ran through the crowds of people trying to lose myself.
>
> I got to the barrier, handed in my ticket and saw that this man was still after me with my coat. I glanced to one side and was terrified to see that some German soldiers had now noticed the commotion and among them were the Gestapo men from the train. I walked past them without daring to look in their direction, left the station and found myself utterly alone, Nicole nowhere in sight.
>
> I remembered she had said she would cross the street and walk slowly away from the station. At last she spotted me and immediately picked up her pace. I followed her into a small square with gardens and a few small shops. She sat down on a bench and signalled for me to join her. We both lit cigarettes and held hands tightly. She said the past eight hours had been the most terrible that she had ever been through and that she could never again stand such tension. I implored her to let me go my own way and asked her to show me the way to the nearest church, where I would seek help from a priest. She refused, and insisted that she would take me to the contact in Brussels first.

After a street-car ride and more walking, the young couple found the safe house, where a man of about forty seemed to be in charge. He invited John into his office and began questioning him until John became a little concerned about the type of questions being asked. As John was about to discover, he was now with the famous Comet escape organization and they had ways of communicating with England to verify his credentials. Then it was time to say goodbye to Nicole:

> She came to the room where I was sitting; I could see she had been crying and she looked completely exhausted. She said in a few minutes I would be picked up by a young couple and taken to their apartment, where I would be hidden until the next stage of my journey. How do you say goodbye under such circumstances?

I don't know what we talked about, but I do know that it was a very sad few moments. We held hands, kissed each other on both cheeks — and she was gone.

The young couple arrived and John was introduced to Auguste and Jose, who took John to their apartment on a quiet back street in the southeast suburbs of Brussels. They poured a glass of brandy into him and John fell into a deep sleep that lasted many hours.

When I woke up I found something breathing into the back of my neck. It was their dachshund puppy curled up on my pillow and it really took to me. I don't know whether it sensed I was in trouble, but we had a ball for six weeks. Except for one occasion, I never went out, so the puppy and I charged around that apartment having a great old time.

Once or twice John was visited by people from the Comet Line, who explained to him that the reason he was being kept so long was that the Germans had broken the Line, and a lot of its senior people had been sent off to Germany. It was therefore necessary to link up the broken pieces again. John has fond memories of the one occasion he was allowed to leave the apartment, even though it was a foolhardy risk:

After about five weeks they said they were going to take me to dinner in a little café on the outskirts of Brussels that belonged to a friend of theirs. There were about fifteen of us, and this was a risky business. Friends are friends, but sometimes they can't be trusted not to talk. This restaurant was closed except for our group. We had wine and a four- or five-course meal, with a lot of singing. We sang English war songs like "Tipperary" and "Show Me the Way to Go Home," quietly of course, because we didn't dare make too much noise.

We left late that night and could not possibly make it home before curfew at ten o'clock, after which only people with special permits could be out. As far as I knew, none of these people had a pass, so we had to be pretty careful getting back home. Because we had had a lot of wine to drink we were all rather merry when we got on the street-car. It was full of people rushing to get home before the curfew. Every seat was full except for one next to a great big German soldier who nobody would sit next to. When we got on, I was dared to go and sit next to him. I was just brazen enough to do it. I sat down beside him and was as quiet as could be, but my friends were in fits of laughter. All the while, this great round German sat stolidly reading his paper. My friends thought it was hilarious. Finally, we got off the street-car and made our way safely home through the back streets.

By this time it was getting on towards the end of October 1943, and John was getting restive, although the whole thing still seemed like an adventure. Finally, word came that he was to be moved, and the morning after another evening of food, drink and laughter with Auguste, Jose and their friends, a woman from the Comet organization came for John. After further interrogation by a senior member of the organization, he was taken by local train to the Belgian–French border.

Even though the Germans occupied both countries, the borders were still fairly rigidly controlled. John was taken to a farmhouse on the Belgian side of the border and what followed was a most unusual experience for any evader:

We arrived at this farm and there were two Americans there already. We were to travel together as far as Paris. We sat down to a meal during which a farmer entered the room with a great big German police dog. He made the dog sit in the corner and then joined us at the table.

"It's too dangerous for us to cross the frontier with you," he said. Then he pointed to the dog and said, "There is your guide."

We looked at the dog and asked, "What do we do with this?" The farmer replied, "He has been trained to go from *A* to *B*. This farm is *A* and a farm on the French side is *B*. He knows the route backwards and forwards and he has taken many resistance people across. You must not touch the dog or try to make friends with it. When you have finished your meal we will put a white handkerchief in the dog's collar so you can see to follow him. Don't touch it either; just follow it."

He gave us each a bit of white cloth to put on the back of our coats and said that we would be walking in pitch darkness along little country cart tracks, among hedgerows and through fields.

"If the dog flattens down in the grass ahead of you, scatter and hide. He will do that only if he senses something unfamiliar to him, but he will not leave you. When the dog gets up and starts looking for you, you all can get up too. He will take you to the back door of a farmhouse on the French side of the frontier. When he gets there, he will bark; people will come out, give him a bone or a piece of meat and the dog will come back here."

We walked two or three miles, keeping our eyes glued to this white cloth on the dog's neck. He trotted along with no sign of friendliness, but we got to the other side and people came to the back door, threw their arms around us and, with a bone as a reward, shooed the dog away. He turned around and trotted away and we never saw him again.

Early the next morning John and his new companions were taken to the railway station at Lille and placed in the care of Michou, well-known in Comet history, and another girl from Comet. They made the journey to Paris without incident, got through the barrier safely and were met by a beautiful young blonde woman, who took them to their safe houses.

It wasn't until after the war that I found out that she was also a collaborator. Two or three weeks after I left the house in Paris, she gave my helpers away to the Germans. The husband was tortured to death and his wife survived the war in the concentration camps at Ravensbruck and Belsen. The blonde woman was executed by the French after the war.

John was in Paris for ten days, then Michou took him and some others by train to a place outside Biarritz. After a long bicycle ride, the party arrived at a little smuggler's hut in which lived one of the most legendary figures of any escape organization.

His name was Florentino. (I found that out after the war.) He was a big man and a real tough character. His peacetime occupation was smuggling. I don't know what he used to smuggle across the French–Spanish border, but he knew those mountains backwards and forwards. He didn't speak any English or any language other than his native Basque. The only word he seemed to know was *"Doucement, doucement!"* — "Quietly, quietly." He carried a goatskin wine flask with him and would give us a little squirt every so often.

It was pitch dark when we started off, so we had these little white markers on the back of our necks so we could follow each other. There were two Americans, Michou and myself. It was winter by now and we had to cross a very small but fast-flowing mountain stream. As we approached the crest of a ridge that was supposed to be near the frontier, he gave us the frightening command, *"Doucement, doucement!"*

We flattened ourselves in the tall grass and he made us crawl through it towards the skyline. It was an hour or two before dawn, but the top of the hill was quite distinct in the first light. At the top of the hill we saw, to our great consternation, the silhouette of a German sentry. We thought it a bit strange to have a sentry way out here in the middle of the mountains, but Florentino made us lie down in the grass and be still. He made hand signals to us that he was going to crawl up behind this sentry, and with a dramatic cut of his hand across his throat, indicated what he was going to do to that German.

He crept ahead of us, snaking his way up to the sentry. Then he stood up and charged, emitting a great bellow of laughter. This "German sentry" was nothing more than a tall sheaf of corn with a rake stuck through it to look like a rifle on its shoulder. He came down to where we were sprawled in the grass laughing his head off. For him it was a great joke, but for Michou and the rest of us, it was a bit less than hilarious.

The whole difficult journey across the mountains to neutral Spain took the group about eight or ten hours. One of the Americans had been in hiding for quite a long time and was badly out of condition. He begged the group to leave him, but that would have been much too dangerous for the entire Comet organization, so he was dragged and carried for part of the way.

Safely down the other side in Spain, having said goodbye to Michou and Florentino, the trio were picked up by the Spanish police and placed in the filthy attic of a police station. Three days later, a representative of the British Consul in Madrid arrived. Apparently he did a regular tour of the frontier police stations and, while he was not permitted to take the group away, he could make arrangements for them to be taken on the next stage of their journey. Three more days elapsed, then bus tickets arrived and there followed a nerve-wracking ride on the roof of a crowded

John Dix joined the Royal Air Force before he was 18. Here he proudly wears the white flash in his hat signifying that he was training for aircrew.

mountain bus. The driver let them off at a hotel that the consulate had arranged. During the stay there the young Americans introduced John to the wonders of the game of poker:

> I never had a *peseta* to spend for the rest of my time in Spain. They took every penny from me. If I wanted to buy a packet of cigarettes or a drink I had to borrow from them; they thought it a great joke!

Eventually a station-wagon arrived from the British Consulate and they were off to Madrid, a pause for two more days and then the last leg of the journey to the frontier at Gibraltar.

> We drove all day. I can't remember whether we stayed somewhere another night, but I do know that we arrived in sight of Gibraltar late one evening. The driver said he couldn't take me across openly, so I had to get in the trunk of the car. It was only ten or fifteen minutes later that the car slowed to a stop and I could hear British voices. The trunk opened and I was free.

After a near-fatal flight back to Britain in a Liberator bomber on top of a pile of mail from the Eighth Army, during which he had no oxygen and nearly froze to death, John was interrogated by M.I. 9. After some time in hospital and a bit of leave he was sent out to Burma, where he did a couple more tours before the end of the war. The return of peace led to work with an Indian maharajah, then British Airways, which brought him eventually to Canada, where he now lives.

Epilogue

Somebody betrayed that small group in 1943. As we learned in Chapter 6, Margot suspects a Luxembourger. John Dix wonders about that young boy. He found out after the war that the Gestapo had arrested the youth on a minor charge.

The Germans had many ways of putting pressure on people — for instance, by threatening their family and friends. It would be a very difficult thing to battle, and only a few people had the courage to fight it. Apparently the Gestapo had picked him up in connection with some minor infraction that had to do with the black market. Perhaps that young fellow was forced to choose between sacrificing his family and giving information about us. Perhaps he chose to sit around the bars and cafés, keeping his ears open and letting out the story that he was on the run from the Germans and needed to get out of the country. One thing led to another and someone put him in touch with Nicole and Hubert. Who knows for sure? At any rate, he returned to Luxembourg after the war and lived there for the rest of his life, always suspected by those who knew him, but there just wasn't enough evidence to bring him to trial.

John Dix in 1945. Still only 22, he had survived being shot down, narrowly escaped being arrested by the Gestapo, and had been escorted down the Comet Line, across the Pyrenees through Spain to Gibraltar. Following his return to Britain, he flew on operations in the Far East.

John Dix has been in contact with Margot Maroldt and Nicole ever since the war. It was only after the war that Dix discovered that Nicole's chief in Brussels had been a Nazi collaborator. When Nicole found out about his treachery a few weeks after she and John had parted, she suffered a complete collapse. Friends rescued her and saw her safely to Switzerland, where she spent the rest of the war. After Luxembourg was liberated and she was able to return home, she began what turned out to be a most distinguished career in her chosen profession. She has told John that she has achieved all of her ambitions except one — she would like to have married and had children.

CHAPTER SEVEN

A HELPING HAND

Ray DePape stirred in his sleep, then woke. For a second or two he wondered where he was, buried, fully clothed in his battledress, in a pile of straw in a strange barn. But where? And why? Then it gradually came back to him. Five nights before, on October 3, 1943, he had been in the briefing room of 431 Squadron based at Tholthorpe in Yorkshire. The briefing dealt with that night's raid on the ball-bearing works at Kassel.

He had assembled his crew, converted on Halifaxes and was ready to go on Ops. As was then the custom with a newly formed crew, Ray as pilot went on an "orientation trip" as "second dickey" with an experienced crew for one trip. As it turned out, it was his only trip. (In a curious twist of fate, Ray's crew was then attached to another pilot, Fred Reain of Ayr, Ontario, and on their first trip they were also shot down!)

Ray picks up the story:

> I didn't plan on being shot down that night, so I had only socks on under my flying boots. We took off for Kassel just before 1900 hours, dropped our load, and on the way back got hit by a stray burst of ack-ack that knocked out our two starboard engines. Then a nightfighter, probably attracted by the fire in the starboard wing, came up underneath us and stitched us from nose to tail. How those of us in the nose of the aircraft weren't hit or killed, I don't know. There were shells bursting all around us in the cockpit and the smell of gunpowder was overpowering!"

Since the starboard engines were on fire and the controls were severely damaged, the pilot gave the order to bail out and Ray jumped. He had learned from lectures on escape and evasion that the Germans immediately threw a cordon around the area where a plane or a parachute came down in order to capture the crew. For that reason, it was essential for him to get out of the area as quickly as possible.

> I landed near a haystack, hid my parachute under it and started to run. I ran till I was played out, rested and ran again, and alternately ran and rested till daybreak, hoping that I was beyond the sweep of the cordon. That day I hid in a thick clump of bushes and had time to take stock of my situation. It is unlikely that many of us gave much serious thought to the possibility of being shot down and having to evade. Oh yes, we had attended lectures on the subject by successful evaders, but this was something that happened to others, not you.
>
> Yet all of a sudden, I'd come to earth, literally, via parachute in enemy territory. Almost automatically the do's and don'ts of the evaders' lectures sprang to mind.

Form 6106

CLASS OF SERVICE DESIRED

DAY MESSAGE
DAY LETTER
NIGHT MESSAGE
NIGHT LETTER

PATRONS SHOULD MARK AN X OPPOSITE THE CLASS OF SERVICE DESIRED; OTHERWISE THE MESSAGE WILL BE TRANSMITTED AS A FULL-RATE TELEGRAM

CANADIAN NATIONAL TELEGRAPHS

W. G. BARBER, GENERAL MANAGER, TORONTO, ONT.

Exclusive Connection with
WESTERN UNION TELEGRAPH CO.
Cable Service to all the World
Money Transferred by Telegraph

RECEIVER'S NO.	TIME FILED	CHECK
		35/34 GB 2 exa report delivery via Wpeg

Send the following message, subject to the terms on back hereof, which are hereby agreed to

RCAF   Ottawa,Ont. 555AM Oct.6th.1943

C.L.Depape,   Swan Lake,Man.

M 9003 Regret to advise that your son R one five two eight seven

five Sergeant Raymond Alphonse George Depape is reported missing

after air operations Overseas Oct. fourth stop letter follows.

RCAF Casualties Officer

922

The kind of telegram that parents dreaded. During the war such messages were hand delivered to 40,000 Canadian homes.

I immediately resolved to evade capture, reach safety and return to action. This determination seemed to unleash an inner strength, a forming of purpose which I believe has been part of my makeup ever since.

I lined up a few landmarks with the aid of the little compass provided in the escape packet. I visualized a southwesterly direction and set out again when evening came. We had been advised not to travel in the daytime and not to follow roads, railroads or pathways unless necessary and to always listen for sounds and voices. I remember hearing voices deep in a wood one time — they sounded guttural to me. I thought that I might be in Germany, but I realized that along the border German was spoken on the Belgian side as well.

All this came back to him as he lay in the straw. He remembered picking this particular barn before dawn because it was on the outskirts of the village and there was no sign or sound of dogs about to warn the residents of a stranger.

His thoughts were interrupted by more immediate sensations. He was stiff and his feet were sore. He was dirty, hungry and unshaven. And he had not spoken to another human being for five days. But what was that he smelled? Something much more appealing than the odour of farm animals, that was for sure. He got to his knees and peered out the open loft door.

I saw this big outdoor oven and in front of it there was a lady baking pies or pastries or something. The smell reminded me of my mother's delicious apple pies back home in Swan Lake. When the pies were taken out of the oven she put them on an outdoor rack to cool, high enough so that the cats wouldn't get them. I had slept late and, when I awoke mid-morning, I realized that I had to remain hidden till dark. I watched those pies all day. They were still there cooling when it got dark, so I went over and took one and made off in the darkness.

It took Ray seven days and about sixty miles of walking to make his first real contact, which he discovered later was well inside Belgium. In those seven days he had savoured the energy tablets in the escape kit and any fruit and vegetables that he could "borrow" from local gardens after dark, and of course that tasty apple pie. From brooks and streams Ray collected water in the little rubber pouch also supplied in the escape kit, and purified it with the chlorine tablets provided. His Interrogation Report, completed on his return to England on December 20, 1943, contains an outline of his first seven days as an evader:

As long as I was in wooded country I kept walking both day and night, only pausing to rest a few hours at a time. I had on ordinary flying boots which made walking rather difficult.

On Oct. 4, when I came to an open space (in the forest) I opened up my escape purse and took out my maps, but I was not able to locate my position. That day I only stopped for about an hour, and at dusk I slept in an old stable.

I set out again about an hour before dawn on Oct. 5. I saw a good many Germans in uniform and also heard labourers speaking the same language. I kept walking all that day and spent the night in the open in some straw.

The next day (6 Oct.) I set off early. By this time my feet were covered with sores making walking very painful. I stopped at every stream to bathe my feet and ease the pain. I continued walking all that day and skirted around a town, where I was told later there was a German rest camp. . . .

During the next day (7 Oct.) I spoke to some farmers in my high school French and identified myself, asking if they would help me. They would not help me but told me that I was in Belgium.

I kept on walking, stopping frequently to bathe my feet and late on that day spoke to another farmer with the same result. About 2200 hours I stopped walking and slept under the stars.

The next morning I saw LAROCHE written on a milestone and walked through the town. I saw a number of Germans in lorries and walking in the streets. . . . I continued walking southwest until dark, and then after a short rest I went on all through the night.

Almost fifty years later, Ray clearly remembers those first times he asked for help and how he was rebuffed each time with a gruff *"Parti, Parti"* — "Leave, Leave." But he also remembers with gratitude that the third time was different.

At midday on October 9, I started off again and made for the forest where I could walk in safety in the daylight. Later that afternoon I skirted the village of Grune. About a kilometre from the village I had circled there was an older gentleman alone in a field digging potatoes. By this time I was walking cautiously in the daytime when cover was available. During the day on several occasions I had heard voices and I was positive that they were French. I had taken three years of French in high school and I tried to recall my Flemish because Mother and Dad had been born in Belgium and we had spoken it at home. I said to this man in my best French that I was RAF and needed help. He replied, *"Parti, Parti!"*

This was the third time I had been turned down and I had begun to wonder why. I was dirty and tired. I didn't know where I was or where I was going. I was hungry and I hadn't spoken to anybody for a week. My socks had holes in them and my feet were a mess of sores and I didn't know where I was going. If at any time the thought of packing it in had entered my mind, it might have been then.

As a parting shot, again in my best high school French, I asked the gentleman if there were any Flemish-speaking people in the village I had just passed. He pointed to a white house at the edge of the village. I thanked him and walked off in the opposite direction from the house.

Safely over the nearby hill and out of sight, Ray circled around through the woods and waited till dusk behind a hedge near the house that the old man had indicated.

A few men passed by, then two more came out on the road between the house and the hedge behind which I was hiding. Soon they were joined by two more and they chatted and waved their hands. Then another man joined the group while one of the originals left in the direction of the village. At about the same time one of the remaining men pointed right at me and I realized that they had been aware of me all along. I scrambled to my feet, hoping that the man whose house I was headed for was amongst the group. I spoke to them in Flemish that I had rehearsed. I asked them to recall the man that was headed for the village if he was going for the *gendarmerie* or the Germans because I wanted no part of either. They took me into the house and I'll never forget what happened next.

I was still in my battledress and it was stuffed with apples. The lady of the house could see I was hungry and dirty. She wanted to prepare a meal for me but first she took me upstairs and showed me how to use the bath and then went back to her cooking. Oh, what a glorious bath it was! I shed a week's whiskers and dirt. My, it was wonderful to be clean again! And then the meal. There wasn't much meat but it was wholesome, nourishing and a real treat — my first meal in seven days.

Ray learned many years later that he was with Mr. and Mrs. Van der Haegen. Mr. Van der Haegen was obviously willing to help, but he was afraid. So at about 2:00 A.M. Ray was blindfolded and taken across the village. He certainly didn't like the blindfold, which gave him a real sense of foreboding, but he was in their hands and had to assume they were friends. He was taken to the home of a man who was thought to be active in the local Resistance.

Ray stayed there for almost a week. While there, several interrogators came to question him: From what squadron? Where had he trained? What had been the target? The type of aircraft? The names of the crew? and so on. Finally they were satisfied. Ray was provided with false papers and was ready to travel. Through his connections, Ray's benefactor was able to provide the false papers. In fact, he had a contact at the Town Hall. He got the proper identity card, brought it home, attached Ray's photograph (which all aircrew carried) and took it back to be "franked" (stamped).

From Grune, Ray was taken by motorcycle to Nassogne, three or four miles away, where he stayed with Edmond Leroy's family.

> I stayed with the Leroys for five days. On the morning of my departure I was treated to a breakfast of bacon and eggs, something I hadn't had since I left Canada. The elder Mr. Leroy took me for a leisurely walk in the woods east of the village and at the appointed time we came out to a road where Emile Benoit was waiting with his motorcycle.
>
> "If we are stopped," Emile said, "you are to keep quiet. I will do the talking. You are my supervisor and we are going to inspect the labour camps nearby."

It was Sunday morning, and as Emile drove slowly through the town of Marche-en-Femmen, mass had just finished and people were pouring out of the church into the square. Among the churchgoers were German soldiers, and this was the closest Ray had come to the enemy.

> Perhaps my imagination was in overdrive, but I thought there were dozens and dozens of soldiers pouring into that square. Fortunately we were not stopped and we wound our way out of town. Emile briefed me on our drive beyond the town.
>
> "When we get close, there will be a young man dressed in dark clothes on the right-hand side of the road. We will pay no attention to him. Three hundred metres further on there will be a young woman dressed in a blue coat and a red hat; pay no attention to her either. A few hundred metres further on there will be another man on the right. You are to follow him."

When they approached the second man, Emile slowed his motorcycle so Ray could jump off. Emile waved goodbye and drove off. Ray was not to see him again, but he learned later of the tragic fate that befell this brave young man in 1944. Ray followed the man as instructed and soon met a small group of young men, all armed.

> They were young Belgians who had been "invited" to go to Germany to a labour camp, but had declined the invitation and were hiding out in the forest. I must say that we lived rather well because they were out almost every night on forays, stealing from anyone they had heard was co-operating with the Germans. They would raid

their home, give them a warning, take their ration coupons, money, food — whatever. If they happened to encounter a German — well, they would take care of him, too. They had accumulated quite a little arsenal in their shack. Until my identity had been verified there was always one of the men with a revolver on his hip within five metres of me.

After several days' stay in the camp, Ray was taken by tram to the railway station at Marloie. He was warned by his guide that there would be German soldiers on the tram:

"Here's a newspaper; pretend to be reading it. I will not be far behind you and I will pick up any conversation if necessary. When we get to the railway station there will be a man sitting in a booth in the station café. We will join him and he will have ordered three beers. I will leave and you are to follow this man."

It happened exactly as his guide had described. Having safely negotiated more checkpoints, the pair arrived at Namur where they had to change trains. His guide this time was a Brussels policeman in civilian clothes.

It was there that I first saw a soldier in German uniform with Belgian insignia sewn on it. I drew this to the attention of my guide at an appropriate moment.

"Yes," he sighed, "there are traitors among us and you will meet more of them, unfortunately."

From Namur they continued by train to Brussels. Before they arrived at the Midi station, Ray had been told to be on the lookout on the arrivals platform for a lady with a dark blue coat and a light-coloured hat with a flower in it.

With that, my guide was gone and I was left alone on the station platform. The crowd was dispersing and I couldn't find this lady. I was standing there trying to look nonchalant and then I noticed that there was a lady looking at me. I looked away, pretending not to notice her while at the same time trying to check her out. A few seconds later I looked in her direction again and with a slight nod of her head she headed for the exit. But she wasn't dressed in a blue coat and light-coloured hat! What to do? I decided to follow her anyway. I had no choice; there was no other lady on the platform.

I never did find out why she was not wearing the outfit I had been looking for. I followed her at a discreet distance and we successfully negotiated the *Feldgendarme* who controlled the exits. I followed her out on the opposite side of the street until she went into a restaurant, then I too entered and we seated ourselves at a small table.

The waiter came over to the corner where we were sitting and my guide asked in English what I wanted to drink. It was only 11.30 in the morning, but I said that I bet they didn't have my kind of drink. With a smile and a wink he brought me rye whisky. Obviously he too was in the "know."

After a short visit and another briefing we went to another house not far away. I was to watch her go in, wait a few moments and then give a special knock on the door: ____.____, ____.____. That's the way it happened. I didn't know it then, but I was now safely in the hands of the famous Comet Line.

Ray found out after the war that the policeman who had brought him to Brussels was a Comet member. The other people who helped him get this far were like thousands of others in villages, towns and cities all over occupied Europe. They did what they could to help but, for their own safety, they often had little or no knowledge of any larger organization that existed to help evaders. They were like links in a chain and they only knew the links on either side of them.

It was in Brussels that Ray met one of the key members of the Comet Line. Her code name was Michou, but her real name was Lily Dumont. Twenty-two years old at the time, she dressed in a short skirt and her bobbed hair made her look like a fifteen-year-old schoolgirl. She spoke in a soft, child's voice. Her face was round and artless. When she sat in a tram, her feet barely touched the floor. Who would have supposed that she was one of the foremost couriers of the Line?

Ray remembers a typical example of Michou's audacity:

I was taken to a big house in Brussels, where there were a number of American airmen being cared for. One of these airmen had a piece of shrapnel in his thigh. Michou took him down the street, they got on a tram, went to a doctor who was obviously a friend, had the shrapnel removed and were back within an hour and a half. Michou frequently played the role of a naïve schoolgirl and used this to great advantage in her dangerous adventures.

The Germans knew that Allied airmen were provided with a picture of themselves in their escape kit to use on a false identity card. It seemed that these pictures were always of either the right or left profile, Ray doesn't remember which, but he does remember that the Germans, in an attempt to trip them up, were now demanding to see the opposite profile on the identity cards. Thus it was necessary that a proper picture be taken.

I was taken to the home of Raymond and Solange Vignoble. Raymond was one of the photographers for the Comet Line in Brussels. They could both speak English, and when they found out that I was of Belgian extraction they asked the Line if I could stay with them for the night.

When my wife and I went back in 1972 to visit them, among my many questions was where they had hidden the negatives of the dozens of photographs they had taken of evading airmen. I knew and they knew that to be caught with them would mean certain death. Mrs. Vignoble opened the oven of her stove and showed me a place behind the asbestos insulation. The negatives were all there.

Crossing borders was always a risky business because of the barriers, sentry posts and guards. All papers were checked and suspicious people were detained at those points. Ray's experience in crossing the Belgian–French border is remarkable for its simplicity.

> Reginald, the RAF chap I was travelling with at the time, and I were put in the back seat of a French doctor's car under a pile of blankets. Sitting in the front seat with the doctor was a Belgian border guard and our crossing was timed to coincide with the time when this guard had to report for duty on the Belgian side. The doctor was going home after doing his rounds in Belgium and was well known to the Germans on guard there. So we just approached the barrier, the guard got out of the car, a bit of small talk followed between the civilian guards and the German guards, and the doctor and he were waved through.

The trip to Paris involved changing trains twice. Ray's guide was now Monique Thomé, another Comet member. At one point they had to go from one station to another, and that meant going through a potentially dangerous checkpoint.

> Monique dropped back to let three or four passengers get in line between her and Reginald and me. The ticket-taker was on a sort of elevated podium, and we had to hand our ticket up to him. I tried to be very casual as I looked to the other platform. Instead of just punching my ticket he grabbed my hand in his. My immediate reaction was to look up at him. He winked, punched my ticket and gave it back to me. I didn't say anything until we got on the other train, and then I asked Monique: "Who was that?"
>
> "Oh, yes, he is one of ours," she replied. And then she said: "Here is a package of cigarettes."
>
> Surprised, I said, "Where did you get those?"
>
> "When we were walking on the crowded platform before boarding the train, a gentleman brushed by me and handed me the cigarettes and said they were for the Englishman."
>
> He had spotted me. I was told a number of times to let my whiskers grow, open my collar and slouch; I was too military in my bearing and if he could spot me, chances were pretty good that the Gestapo could spot me too.

The Comet people had originally planned to escort Ray and the others from Paris to the Spanish border on November 11, 1943 (incidentally, the same day that Ray's name appeared in the RCAF Casualty List back home). However, that was Armistice Day, and it was felt that there might be demonstrations in the so-called unoccupied part of France that could complicate their safe travel. And so the departure was delayed by one day.

The evening before they left, a Free Frenchman who was to travel with the group took them to a fine restaurant where the waiters were formally dressed, the food excellent and the clientele included many senior German officers. Ray was somewhat alarmed at this turn of events.

> We left the ordering to our Free French companion and for the first course he ordered oysters. By the time the oysters were served there were four German

officers at the table next to us. We were so close to them that I could have reached out and touched them. The presence of uniformed German soldiers so close to me made me so tense that I gagged on the oysters! It was years afterwards before I could even look at an oyster, let alone eat one.

The group made it safely to the train and were on their way, this time in the charge of a middle-aged woman. She stayed in another compartment close by.

As we expected, the Gestapo came through and we had to produce our papers, but there were no real problems because by this time we were old hands at this sort of thing. Our guide came by at one point when we were crossing into so-called Free France and no Germans were around and gave us all new identity cards and retrieved the old ones. I asked her: "Where do you keep all these cards? Isn't it dangerous to carry them?"

"In my bloomers," was the reply.

Along the motorway just south of Dax, the four evaders and their male guide, now on bicycles, were joined by Janine. She was the teenage daughter of the redoubtable Tante Go, the Comet's organizer for the Basque end of the Line whose real name was Elvire De Greef. They travelled by bicycle through Bayonne, St Jean de Luc, Urrugne and up into the hills before continuing on foot.

We holed up for the night in one of Tante Go's safe houses and continued our journey the next day. As we climbed higher and higher it started to rain on and off and then steadily. We had no umbrellas or rain capes and so were soon soaked to the skin and cold. Eventually we were escorted into a sheep barn. While our Basque guides slept in the farmhouse in relative comfort, we were comforted only by wet sheep and a leaky roof. However, we were out of the wind. We had nothing to eat that night and nothing to eat the next day except for a small piece of smelly old cheese.

The group crossed the Bidassoa River at night and now were in the hands of the indomitable Florentino, who had guided John Dix and his comrades over the same route a few weeks earlier.

Crossing that river at that time of year could be rather dangerous. It was rain at first, then it turned to sleet and snow. The second night we had to leave the Free Frenchman behind in an abandoned barn, because he couldn't negotiate the hills. He was a big man and not in the best physical condition. We had to stay off pathways and trails and go across country. Reginald played out too, but we got him going again. However, he quit on us that night and just sat down and wouldn't or couldn't move. We tried to convince him that he had to go on so as not to jeopardize the whole group. We were able to leave the Frenchman because he had money and could speak the language, but there was no way we were going to leave Reginald. We tried to motivate him in every way that we could think of. In desperation we tried to ridicule him by saying, "We come over here and fight your bloody war for you and all you can do is sit there and moan?"

That didn't move him, either. I guess he was completely exhausted. Finally, one of the guides took out his revolver and told him to go on or he would shoot him. That got him going, but the Dutchman and I had to practically carry him up to the summit. Once we started down the other side we could roll him along. We probably saved his life because when we got back to London and were interrogated by M.I. 9, they said: "Yes, and those guides had our permission to shoot. We could not jeopardize the Line for one man."

Ray crossed into Spain on his twenty-first birthday. No sooner was the group in that country than they were arrested by the Spanish police and taken first to a police station, and then to a military post in Irun, for interrogation. From there they were escorted to an inn, where the innkeeper was paid by the British Embassy for keeping them. There were servicemen and civilians from many countries there — like a real United Nations — and all of them headed for the United Kingdom.

The innkeeper provided us with whatever clothes we needed: shoes, underwear, and so on. Also shaving equipment and a bit of pocket money. We found a little café that made good pastries and hot chocolate. We would go there about 9.30 or 10 o'clock in the morning, always to the same table. Four German soldiers in full uniform with sidearms were also regular customers there. Certainly they recognized who we were. One morning we arrived at the café and there were these four Germans sitting at *our* table, and each one had a package of Lucky Strike cigarettes. They didn't do anything except sit there and taunt us with their looks, and we had to take another table.

We vowed revenge. We speculated about the source of these cigarettes. They could have been loot from the North African campaign or they could have come from the local black market. If the latter, we would have our revenge. It took us all day to find the black market and it cost us almost a week's spending money, but Lucky Strikes we had!

Next morning we were at *our* table half an hour early, waiting for the Germans with our purchases. They came in and saw our cigarettes and took another table. We had no further contact with them.

Ray teamed up with an Australian airman called Stan who had heard that a contingent of the fascist Spanish Blue Division that had fought with the Germans in Russia was coming home, so Stan said: "Let's go down to the station and have a look at these guys."

So we went down and there was a regular little ceremony welcoming the conquering heroes back home. We noticed that many of them were wearing German military decorations. I even spotted an Iron Cross. At one point in the ceremony everyone but us raised their arms in the fascist salute. Darned if we weren't tapped

Form 610¢

CLASS OF SERVICE DESIRED	
DAY MESSAGE	
DAY LETTER	
NIGHT MESSAGE	
NIGHT LETTER	

PATRONS SHOULD MARK AN X OPPO-
SITE THE CLASS OF SERVICE DESIRED:
OTHERWISE THE MESSAGE
WILL BE TRANSMITTED AS
A FULL-RATE TELEGRAM

CANADIAN NATIONAL
TELEGRAPHS

W. G. BARBER, GENERAL MANAGER, TORONTO, ONT.

Exclusive Connection
with
WESTERN UNION
TELEGRAPH CO.
Cable Service
to all the World
Money Transferred
by Telegraph

RECEIVER'S NO.	TIME FILED	CHECK
		23 GB 2 Exa report delivery

Send the following message, subject to the terms on back hereof, which are hereby agreed to

RCAF Ottawa Ont 355PM Dec 17/43

C.L.DePape
Swan Lake,Man.

M 9970 Pleased to advise that your son Sergeant Raymond Alphonse
George DePape has arrived safely at Gibralter stop letter
following

RCAF Casualty Officer

325PM

This telegram of December 17, 1943, was the first indication that Mr. and Mrs. DePape had that Ray was safe. How he got to Gibraltar would be a mystery to the family for many more weeks, but at least they knew that Ray was safe and would have a story to tell.

on the shoulder by the local *carabinierie.* ''When in Rome, do as the Romans do,'' was the clear message. We went back to our inn with our tails between our legs.

But a day or so later Stan heard of another contingent coming home the following Friday, and he wanted us to go again. I declined: ''Let's not get into trouble.'' He insisted that he had a plan that would save us from harm. So we went again; same routine, bands, speeches and, when everybody gave the fascist salute, we raised our arms and gave the ''V'' for Victory sign, and we got away with it.

Soon after that incident, the military members of Ray's group spent four days at a resort courtesy of the Spanish Air Force. Here they enjoyed clean sheets, private rooms, meals that were served — a real treat for them, and an indication of a much friendlier attitude than that shown by the Spanish military up until then. Following their pleasant stay there, the group was escorted across the Spanish border to Gibraltar and freedom. It was December 14, 1943.

On December 15 in Winnipeg, dawn brought promise of another fine winter day. In spite of wartime restrictions in this, the fourth year of the war, there were still good things to welcome the festive season.

In the Grill Room at Eaton's one could enjoy a dinner of juice or soup, celery and pickles, and a choice of roast turkey, prime rib of beef, roast buffalo or grilled ham with dessert and beverage for seventy cents. Over at the City Meat and Sausage

Company, Grade A turkeys sold for thirty-eight cents a pound; Nova Scotia oysters were thirty-eight cents a dozen.

If one tired of Christmas shopping there was always the Metropolitan, where George Sanders and Marguerite Chapman were starring in a thriller called *Appointment in Berlin*, with an added feature *Let's Have Fun*.

Christmas was approaching sure enough, but the war was never far away. The front page of the Winnipeg *Tribune* carried the headline "Canadians Cut Vital Road," and there followed an account of an attack on a road near Ortona, Italy. And there were the Casualty Lists. The RCAF published its 753rd Casualty List with the names of those killed and missing. There was also this statement: "Cowan, Stewart Frances, F/O, previously reported missing, now reported safe." Those interested in what lay behind that simple statement are referred to his story in *Forty Nights to Freedom*, by his sister, Gladys E. Smith.

Ray's father, Charles L. DePape of Swan Lake, Manitoba, didn't need to look at the List to feel the pain again. Ray's name had appeared in the List published on Remembrance Day, but of course he had received the fateful telegram in October saying that Ray was missing.

Mr. DePape had come to Winnipeg on business. Having completed his affairs for the day he returned to his hotel and tried to sleep. And he had a dream. He dreamt that when he got back home his wife would greet him with the wonderful news that Ray was safe. He hurried home the next day, but, alas, the telegram of his dream had not arrived. He said nothing about his dream to his wife that night.

The telegram came the next day.

As he looks back on that time, Ray remembers:

I was helped by a multitude of people (Belgians, French, Basque, Spanish). A lot of them were young and many of them were women. While they were all volunteers, they realized the risk they were taking. Every move they made could cost them their lives, while for the evaders, the worst would probably be a prison camp. The Escaping Society was formed in 1945 by the RAF to pay tribute to these people, and to assist them in any way that we could. This is why we bring some of them to Canada each year to attend our Annual General Meeting. We thank them for what they did, but they say, "Don't thank us. You liberated us. It is amazing that you Canadians have come over more than once to help us."

As I reflect on my experience, I recall a visit to Belgium with my wife in 1972. This was my first opportunity to go back and personally thank those courageous men and women who helped me in 1943. Michou held a reception for us where we met many Comet members.

It was here that I learned the fate of Emile Benoit, the young motorcyclist. The Germans caught on to his Resistance activities in the spring of 1944 and arrested him. He was ordered to take a German officer as escort on his bike to headquarters for questioning. Knowing what the end would be, Emile purposely drove his bike into a low stone wall in the hope that it would catapult the German over the wall and he could escape. However, the officer read Emile's intentions and shot him.

Among those at the reception was Georges Martens, who had been involved in the Resistance, in espionage as well as Comet. He told me that on all particularly dangerous exploits he carried on him a strychnine pill. The Germans were not about to take him alive. They made him look on while they shot his wife and son. To this day he hates all Germans and will not even step on German soil. I admire the man for his exploits and I respect his views.

On the other hand I have heard Michou, and others, say: "The war is over; let's put the past behind us. Bitterness and hatred accomplish nothing."

And Michou had good reason to be bitter. Her father had died in a concentration camp; her sister Andrée, alias Nadine, barely survived imprisonment in Ravensbruck and Mauthausen and her mother had also been imprisoned. I honour Michou's heroism and I admire her attitude.

Florentino was the most decorated Basque guide, and yet it wasn't until 1977, almost thirty-five years after the war, that France also decided to decorate him. The post-war Comet Committee had organized a two-week bus tour for evaders

ADDRESS REPLY TO:

The Secretary,
Department of National Defence for Air,
OTTAWA, Canada.

OUR FILE 1040-D-552 (R.

REF. YOUR ....

DATED ....

ROYAL CANADIAN AIR FORCE

R E G I S T E R E D

S E C R E T

C O N F I D E N T I A L

A I R   M A I L

OTTAWA, Canada, 14th December, 1943.

Mr. C.L. DePape,
Swan Lake,
Manitoba.

Dear Mr. DePape:

      The Royal Canadian Air Force Casualties Officer, Overseas, has advised me that a confidential message has been received concerning your son, Sergeant Raymond Alphonse George DePape, previously reported missing on Active Service.

      The message states that your son is safe although his whereabouts cannot be disclosed. I cannot stress too strongly the importance of treating this information as secret. I must ask you not to divulge this information as the safety of your son and others might be jeopardized.

      As soon as further advice is received at these Headquarters it will be communicated to you immediately.

      Yours sincerely,

      (W.R. Gunn)
      Squadron Leader,
      R.C.A.F. Casualties Officer,
      for Chief of the Air Staff.

R.C.A.F. G. 32
3000M—5-43 (3277)
H.Q. 885-G-32

This registered secret confidential letter to Ray De Pape's father from the RCAF Casualty Officer brought the good news that Ray was safe. Note the instructions in the second paragraph: Did anybody really think that such wonderful news would not be shared with the other members of the family or the neighbours in Swan Lake, Manitoba?

The indomitable Basque guide Florentino, who took scores of evaders across the Pyrenees, stands between his brother and Ray DePape on the occasion of a presentation to him by the French government in 1976. Ray DePape had the honour of being the medal bearer on that occasion. COURTESY OF RAY DEPAPE

and helpers following the general route they had taken in their evasion. There were thirty-six Comet members and an equal number of Canadian evaders and their wives. Michou was president of Comet at the time and was responsible for this fantastic tour. She asked me to be the medal bearer at the decoration ceremony for Florentino. What a thrill it was for me to meet Florentino on that occasion.

The experience has helped me broaden my own outlook. I've developed an easier acceptance and tolerance of people and situations — a flexibility and objectivity, and the ability to see the other side.

Although I have always practiced my religion, I had not considered myself a particularly religious person. However, my faith was strengthened as a result of this experience.

Why was I the only member of the crew to successfully evade? Who was guiding me, encouraging me, giving me hope through the entire journey to safety? I know my mother and all the family were praying for my safety. But there is no doubt in my mind that the God I called upon during my escape through enemy territory helped me find the strength and courage to persevere. There was a Helping Hand.

Having seen the circumstances and conditions in which people under rigid domination existed and survived against a common enemy makes one appreciate and understand others more fully, especially those who constantly risked their lives to help us in our evasion and escape. This was their contribution to the Allied cause and eventually to their own freedom. When I consider how these ordinary people were prepared to take such extraordinary risks for a cause in which they believed, I marvel at the human spirit. Would that we were all capable of such heroism.

My evasion and escape have had a profound impact on my values and approach to life. The experience has also made me appreciate the privilege of living in Canada.

CHAPTER EIGHT

ANOTHER SYMBOL OF FRANCE

Saturday, April 28, 1990, Paris — a day fit for poets and lovers. A bright spring sun warmed the Champs du Mars. The Eiffel Tower stood out against an azure sky; at the other end of this great park there is another magnificent symbol of the spirit of France — Les Invalides and the majestic tomb of Napoleon that it contains.

Children and lovers played their games on the grass or under the trees, seemingly unmindful of the grandeur of their surroundings. No doubt they were unaware also of the dark stain in memory that older people carry: the picture of a jubilant Hitler standing before Napoleon's tomb in 1940 as part of his triumphant entry into a conquered city, or the recollection of German soldiers crawling around the Eiffel Tower like schoolboys.

The children and lovers this day were oblivious to all this. They were also unaware of the stranger sitting on a bench under a tree talking with an elderly woman. She had never been very tall, not much over five feet, and advancing years had slowed her step, and bent her slightly as though walking into the wind, but her memory had not dimmed, nor had the passion with which she felt some things. She remembered the Nazi conquest of her city; she remembered the degradation Parisians felt as they watched the Germans trample their streets, their pride and their freedom. And she remembers with unabashed glee what she and other French patriots did to obstruct and fight the Germans.

> I know of ten or twenty women who were helpers like me. I did what I did because I was fighting the Germans. It was a sport. [And she laughs.] I was ready to kill them. [And laughs again.] Those Germans, they did too much mischief!

Her name is Simone de Cormont. Born in 1915, she was three years old when her father was killed in the First World War. By 1918, she had lost seven more close relatives.

Her sister, Marguerite, and Marguerite's husband Olivier Lamoureux were arrested by the Gestapo in June 1944 and were deported to camps in Germany. Marguerite died in a camp in April 1945, and Olivier died on a train going to Germany as a result of the torture he had received. Olivier had been responsible for a section of the Centurion Escape Line in the west of France. Simone's brother, an officer in the French army, was taken prisoner in 1940 and spent five years in a German camp. Six other relatives died in German hands in the Second World War. As she recounts her life before 1942, the stranger can detect a strength, a fierceness of spirit, as well as a remarkable ability to laugh.

When Simone finished high school, she went to the Beaux Arts for courses in drawing and painting. When the war came, she left school and enrolled in the Red Cross. She worked in a refugee camp in Paris that had been set up to feed, house and clothe people fleeing from the eastern part of France.

Until February 9, 1944, when she was arrested, Simone lived with her mother in a large apartment in Rue du Rocher near Gare St. Lazare. From time to time before 1942 she had used her house to hide young Frenchmen to save them from being sent to Germany as forced labour.

By 1942 the Comet Line was sending increasing numbers of Allied airmen into Paris, where groups of evaders were formed to continue their journey south to Spain. Members of the Underground contacted Simone to ask if she would provide a safe house for some of these men, and on August 18, 1942, she became an active member of the Resistance, using the name Susan Lacombe. What she did not know then, and discovered only after the war, was that she was one of those thousands of links in the chain that formed the Comet Line. In 1942, however, the only people she knew were the "chief" to whom she reported and the young Allied servicemen who spent varying periods of time in her care. Nameless guides and couriers would come and go, but she knew only one of them — a sixteen-year-old boy, the son of a friend, who came one night to guide an evader from her home to a train station. He was later arrested, sent to a concentration camp and never came back.

I would get a phone call from somebody telling me that another "parcel" would be sent to me in two or three days or that evening, and usually a young girl or boy would arrive with one or more airmen. I made them comfortable in our apartment. If they needed medical attention I would take them to a doctor I could trust. Some of these young men were close to a nervous breakdown and needed medical help.

We got food from the black market and we also had false ration cards. In addition, people sent us food from the country, so finding enough to eat was no problem. Getting civilian clothes was more difficult.

Some of the evaders behaved nicely; others refused to go out, even at night. We played cards and they gave me English lessons, and we had a piano we played sometimes, but it was boring, boring, boring for them.

One night it had become so boring that I told this Captain Harris-Brown and Stephen Jezercak that I would take them to the cinema. It was a German movie, crowded with German soldiers. That night there were also two clowns on stage as part of the program and they did some very funny sketches. I was sitting between these two men, when all of a sudden one of them laughed uproariously and said in a loud voice, "My God, these guys are funny!" I told them to shut up, grabbed them by the arms and sneaked out of the theatre in the dark. I was mad! [And she tilts her head and laughs as she remembers.]

Between August 1942, and February 9, 1944, she helped fourteen young men, eight of whom were evading airmen. Four were Americans: Charles Winkelman, R. Dillon, Robert Jones and Stephen Jezercak; Captain Harris-Brown and R. Stockburn were from England; J. Chapman was from New Zealand; and Canadian David MacMillan was born in Hamilton, now of Vineland, Ontario.

An air gunner with 9 Squadron RAF, David was shot down on his twelfth trip on July 9, 1943, while on a bombing trip to Gelsenkirchen. He sprained both ankles on landing and was picked up by a German patrol near Le Cateau. He was taken to a civilian hospital in Amsterdam, where German doctors treated him very well. He faked poor physical condition, claiming that he couldn't walk or eat, and then one night simply got out of bed, dressed in his uniform and took off. After a week's refuge on a canal barge, MacMillan was placed in the hands of René Sents, a farmer and member of the Resistance who had a travel permit to go to Paris to sell his produce. MacMillan can still recall his ride to Paris:

> I was still in uniform and had to change into civilian clothes. I hid under a tarpaulin in the back of the truck with this great wood burner that somehow produced enough energy to propel the truck. We left after dark and were in Paris just at daylight, when the curfew was lifted. He took me to a house; I got out, waved goodbye and he was gone. Inside the house were three middle-aged ladies, one of whom spoke good English. They fed me and said I would be picked up that evening. In the afternoon two more evaders came, but I don't remember their names.
>
> That evening three men came and asked me a lot of questions to make sure of my identity. Within fifteen minutes three young women joined the men in the next room. They talked in French for quite a while and as they talked I began to notice one of the women. She stood about four feet eleven and was very attractive, very willowy and looked no older than twenty-one. I turned to one of the guys and said, "If I have a chance I'll go with the short one over there." The short one, Simone, turned, walked over to me and said, in perfect English, "This short one is going to take you home."

Simone recalls that David MacMillan was in the apartment for about two weeks, and then someone came for him some time in late August or early September 1943. David eventually made it safely south through France, into Spain and back to England.

Simone's fate was not as fortunate. The Germans were aware of the help thousands of people like Simone de Cormont gave to evaders, and did their utmost to infiltrate the underground network. It wasn't always necessary for the Gestapo to "plant" a German spy in order to identify and arrest people like Simone. All they had to do was to arrest someone unable or unwilling to resist telling what they knew. So Simone was betrayed by an eighteen-year-old French girl who had been interrogated by the Nazis. Even recalling that horrible day, Simone is able to remember and laugh about one hilarious, if terrifying incident:

I was arrested on the morning of February 9, 1944. We had an evader, Lieutenant C.B. Winkelman, from Seebring, Florida, sleeping in the drawing room in his pyjamas when the French police came. My mother took him by the pyjamas and put him in the water closet, where he stayed all day, too frightened to come out.

I took a few things in a bag and the French police took me to the Gestapo, who interrogated me all day. Then I was taken to Fresnes prison and placed in solitary confinement.

She spent three days alone in that filthy hole with no light and hardly any ventilation. She felt her way around this blackened space and found a straw tick floating in water that covered the floor from a leaky pipe. On the third day she was taken to a cell in which there were three young women. It was well lit, thanks to one large window high up in the wall. The cell measured seven feet by ten.

Our guards were German women; many were more brutal than the men. At night we slept on four mattresses on the floor. At five o'clock in the morning we were knocked out of our sleep by the racket of the "coffee" cart as it rolled along outside the cell. It contained a filthy water mixture, usually cold. At ten o'clock we received about two ounces of bread and at eleven we were served vegetable soup, which could be hot or cold, thick or water-thin, depending on whether you were served first or last. The menu closed at three o'clock with what they liked to call coffee.

At first I was unhappy about being locked up with three other women, but I quickly realized it must be a good deal worse to spend several months alone between four walls. Think of it: young souls to whom life meant freedom and action, closed in and buried alive. Day and night they keep thinking about their case; wondering what the Gestapo had on them; wondering if their home had been searched and if other members of their family had been arrested. Under such circumstances of excruciating mental torture, the physical discomfort was usually forgotten.

There was no ventilation in the cell, no sanitation, and no heat. It was ice cold; the place crawled with vermin and the guards could burst in any time.

How did we spend our time during these long days? Keeping the cell as neat as possible came first. We also mended and read whenever we could get a book from the prison chaplain or from a fellow prisoner who cleaned the corridor. If the German woman guard liked you she would bring German soldiers' socks for you to mend as a reward. The only ones to receive parcels or reading material from home were the few charged with minor offences and those condemned to death.

The chaplain was a German, but he would secretly say mass for the prisoners once a month. The entertainment program for the week consisted of a three-minute ice-cold shower every Thursday and, every other Friday, a fifteen-minute walk in the courtyard.

We would go round in a circle, like lions in a cage. One warm spring day we found a flower, a poor little violet, growing between the stones.

To break the monotony we had a choice of homemade amusements: killing lice, singing, telling jokes, and "phoning" between the floors. We did this by way of talking through the heating vents, which served no other purpose because there never was any heat.

In addition to one's own suffering, one had to bear that of one's cellmates. It was always a terrible feeling when one of us was summoned for interrogation. We would wait in anguish for the return of one who had spent the day with the Gestapo. Often there would be one who did not return, which meant she had been sent to solitary or half-killed by the day's tortures. The principal tortures were duckings in ice-cold water, lashings and electric shock. I wondered if some day I would have to go through this crucifixion; one had to have nerves of steel or the grace of God to get through it.

In spite of all this, we did everything to annoy our guards and we succeeded sometimes. These times were moments of great pleasure and victory of the French spirit over the loggerheaded Germans.

I was interrogated every Wednesday and I never told them a thing. I was lucky enough to keep my head clear, so I never said anything that could mean being sent to the camps. I was always laughing at them! I said that I had never even heard of the Resistance, let alone had anything to do with it, and I told them that they must be making all this up.

Simone's performance must have been magnificent, because on April 7, 1944, she was released for lack of evidence against her.

She returned to her home to find her mother still there. Simone went back to her work with the Red Cross, but a month later the Gestapo came to her home to arrest her again. Luckily, she had already gone to work. She received a frantic phone call at the hospital from somebody who said the Gestapo were at her home. She left the hospital immediately, and as she was getting on a bus, she saw the big black car of the Gestapo drive up to the hospital entrance! Simone stayed with a number of different friends in Paris and in the surrounding country, and survived to see the liberation of Paris.

After the war the French authorities arrested the young girl who betrayed her and the French policeman who arrested her in 1944. They were brought to trial. In each case, Simone says, she asked the courts to be lenient with them.

As I think about that time I conclude that the behaviour of some human beings can be so awful, but on the other side, I found that there was so much charity and so much love. There was a girl in my cell who was an agnostic and she used to observe me at prayer. I prayed a lot because I was ready to die and I asked help from God. Well, after the war this girl came to see me. She said that she wanted to become a Catholic because she was so impressed with the way I lived in that prison. I was so moved that I took her to a priest, who looked after her. She was then twenty-five years old.

Simone de Cormont was decorated after the war by the British, French, American and Canadian governments. She lives alone on a quiet street not far from the Arc de Triomphe. Each year, particularly at Christmas, she gets letters from those men who are still alive that she helped to save.

CHAPTER NINE

PAULA, A GALLANT MEMBER OF THE O'LEARY LINE

As she sits in the reception room of her retirement home in Victoria, British Columbia, this attractive eighty-year-old woman bristles when she recounts what she sometimes hears:

"Oh, those German bastards. They should all be shot!"

"Don't they know that there were some Germans who were on the side of the Allies and who were opposing Hitler right from the start?" Paula also dismisses the notion of her being one of the O'Leary Line's most gallant couriers:

> It isn't true, you know. We must stick to the truth. That Jimmy Langley [co-author of *Escape and Evasion, 1939–1945*], he said that just because I did a favour for him one time. He had come through the Line and had got back to England. But there was a girl in a small town north of Limoges who, with her sister, had given Jimmy Langley shelter in spite of the risks. To show his appreciation he sent a message to me, when I was working with Pat O'Leary, asking me to go to the village and convince this girl to come out through the Line to Britain.
>
> So I went to this village and talked to this girl till I was blue in the face, but she didn't want to leave France! No, it's not true what he says about me; I didn't really do very much except to help Pat.

As she works at discounting her gallant work with the O'Leary Line, the listener is not convinced, and as she recounts the rest of her story, it becomes increasingly clear that Paula's activity as a German opposed to Hitler and as a key member of the O'Leary Line was indeed remarkable.

Paula was born in 1909 in a town of 20,000 that is now called Ennepetal, Germany. Her father was an active union member and also a member of the German Parliament up to 1933. As Hitler and the Nazis gradually began to exert more power, not only in German national politics, but also in the daily life of small towns and villages, Paula's father spoke out in opposition.

In 1933 the Nazis came to power and the future of the Spriewald family in Germany was doomed. One night a gang of Brown Shirts arrived at Paula's home, demanding to know where her father was. He was in Berlin on business, but Paula told them that he had gone to Munich. Her father fled across the border to Holland and Paula was left in Ennepetal with her first husband and her mother. Then one day another group of Brown Shirts arrived at her home:

> These were boys I had gone to school with. We all knew each other very well. They said, "Do you see that tree over there?"

78

Paula Blanchain enjoying a luncheon conversation in Victoria, B.C., August 1991. E.S. LAVENDER

"Yes."

"Well," they said, "that's where we are going to hang your father when we catch him."

And then one of the boys raised his arm and was going to hit me, but another boy stopped him and they went away.

For a time Paula lived with her father in a small village in Holland just the other side of the German border. But when the village mayor, a Nazi sympathizer, suggested rather strongly that they get out, they went to Paris, where they were joined by her mother.

None of us got a work permit. I had to do housework, because it was the only work I could get without a permit. With the help of some wealthy Jewish emigrants, my father found a little workshop where he started making toys. He didn't make a fortune at it, but we could eat. It was a very hard time.

In 1940 the Germans conquered France.

All the German women under fifty living in France were ordered to present themselves to the French authorities. We were brought to an internment camp called Gurs in the Pyrenees by train. At every stop the train was stoned. We were very frightened.

It was an enormous camp built by refugees from the Spanish Civil War. It was well built, but there were no beds and we had to sleep on straw on the floor. The camp commandant was very understanding. There were some well-known anti-Hitler German political women in the camp and they pointed out to the commandant that if the Germans got control of the camp they would all be deported and killed and that would be on his conscience. So he let us go and that's how I got out of that camp!

With the help of a group of Americans called the Fry Committee, Paula's father was able to cross the Mediterranean to Algeria. However, he was betrayed there and thrown into prison, where the conditions were unbearable. He managed to get a message to Paula for help, and because she knew the Mexican consul in Marseilles, she was able to get for her father a visa to Mexico, where he spent most of the rest of his life, eking out a living with a few other German exiles making, of all things, rosaries! Paula was to see him one more time. In 1948, he suffered a stroke and came back to Germany. It was one of the most painful experiences of her life.

I was in England at the time and went over to see him. He had suffered brain damage and it was only to get worse and worse. He lived two more years and then he died. Mexico was good in a way, but . . .

In 1941, Paula was in Marseilles, training to be a secretary. By this time she was fluent in French, English and German. She lived with a couple who were always taking in anti-Nazi people. There was always a lot of whispering and she knew that something was going on. One day a nice young man came to lunch.

He was a very good talker. He said that he was a Canadian, had been a prisoner of war and had escaped. He told a lot of stories. I asked him where he had been a prisoner and he said near Cologne. I said I knew Cologne very well, and so we talked and talked and he came again and again.

At that time I had no job but I was learning stenography and all those good things. One day he took me aside and asked, "Have you finished your course?"

"Yes, just."

"You can take shorthand?"

"Yes, I can, in French."

"Would you like to work for me?"

And do you know who that was? Pat O'Leary! He called himself Joseph something. So I said, "You know I'm German, don't you?" "Of course I know," he replied.

"But how can you ask a German to help you do this sort of work?"

"I have observed you all this time. I know your story and you can work for me if you would like to."

Whenever we had a minute to talk, I would say, "Tell me about Canada. Where did you live?"

"In Quebec," he replied. He spoke French, you see.

"Is it nice?"

"Oh, it's beautiful," he said.

"But it must be cold."

> "Oh, the winters are very cold, and there's lots of snow." And then he managed to change the subject.

What Paula didn't know at the time was that this man was not a French Canadian at all, nor was his name Pat O'Leary. He had come ashore on a skiff from HMS *Fidelity* on the night of April 25, 1941, near Etang De Canet, a few miles north of the eastern end of the Pyrenees. By October of that year he had taken over control of this major escape line through France and it became known as the PAO Line, or the O'Leary Line.

Paula started by writing O'Leary's reports, which he sent to England in code by wireless. She learned to code and decode. O'Leary thought Paula was already risking her life, so did not send her on dangerous missions, according to her.

> The first mission I had was the funniest of all. There was this Dr. Rodocanachi, who had an office in Marseilles.

The Vichy Armistice Commission had established a medical board to examine Allied prisoners of war being considered for repatriation. Dr. Rodocanachi was the "American" representative on this Board. In fact, he was one of the most trusted members of O'Leary's organization.

> Well anyway, we got this new wireless operator from England. He only took the job so he could get back to France to be with his wife, who was still there. When this man arrived in Marseilles I was asked to take him to Dr. Rodocanachi's flat, where he would meet his wife. I went with him and there was his wife and they embraced for half an hour. I thought it was so romantic, and that I had done something wonderful!

Having got his wireless set to Marseilles, this man completely lost his nerve. He just vanished.

> Sometimes I would take airmen from one place to another in Marseilles, and once I took some airmen to Toulouse by train. This was before the German occupation of the south of France, but there were controls on the train and you had to have papers. I was identified on my false papers as Paulette Perrier; I don't remember what my occupation was.
>
> I remember only one thing about that trip. Pat used to deliver these false identity cards to us, and when he gave me mine, it said, "brown eyes," and I thought, "Damn it all, he hasn't even looked at me!"

And her blue eyes sparkle as she tells it.

On one occasion Paula was on a night train to Toulouse with Francis Blanchain, who was later to become her second husband.

> He was with a convoy and he really taught me a lot. I was talking to a man in the corridor when Blanchain saw me and made a sign for me to follow him.
>
> "Who were you talking to?"

"I don't know, just a passenger."

"You are not to talk to anyone on the train because people will know that you are not French."

As Paula got to know Francis Blanchain, she discovered that this young, dark, strongly built man was one of the chief guides for O'Leary from Marseilles to the Spanish border. In April 1942, Blanchain escorted Airey Neave to the Spanish frontier. After his return to London, Neave became one of the senior officers of M.I. 9, "Escape and Evasion."

Francis also played a key role in the escape of Whitney Straight from a French prison hospital on the Mediterranean coast. Francis knew a nurse in the ward where British "repatriates" were kept. The nurse gave Straight a powerful sedative that he slipped into the guards' luncheon wine when their attention was diverted. When they dozed off, Straight went out the window, jumped from a low roof and walked out the gate to meet Blanchain, who saw him safely down the Line.

The year before, Ian Garrow, a captain in the Seaforth Highlanders and the first chief in charge of the escape route in southern France, was arrested. For a time he and Blanchain had been in the same prison, but Blanchain had been released because they could not prove that he was working for the Underground.

One day Pat asked Blanchain to go up to the concentration camp where Garrow was a prisoner and make contact in order to arrange an escape.

So he took the train to Limoges, the big town nearest the camp. There he made contact with a member of the Resistance and sought his help. This Frenchman was very co-operative but made Blanchain promise to take a letter with him and see that it got to London. Francis took the letter, but he shouldn't have, as you will see. There was a firm rule that one never got mixed up in the business of another group. He put the letter in his travel case, which he left in the station at Limoges. He walked to the camp, but was searched before he got there. His identity papers said he had been born in London, and that made them suspicious. They found his case with the letter in it at the station and arrested him.

He was handcuffed and put in a car between two policemen. The journey was long and the policemen got tired because it was very late at night. He begged them to release his hands so he could smoke. They agreed and in this way they arrived at the police headquarters. The police got out and stretched their limbs. While they were diverted, Francis got out the other side and ran for his life.

It was late at night, but there was a full moon, which gave lots of light, and he saw the terrace of a café. This terrace had barrels with little trees in them and he hid behind one of those barrels in the black shadow that it cast. He heard some dogs bark and then the car drove off, but he just lay there.

When he heard nothing more he went back to the house where he had got the letter and they hid him. He sent a message to Pat, who replied that he should stay there for a time, grow a beard and wait for a sign to come to Marseilles.

Alex Wattebled, who worked with O'Leary, remembers the incident well.

One day Pat got a message that there was a "parcel" for him, so he sent me to get it. When I got to the house, who do I see but Francis. So we got him a pair of glasses and a false moustache and away we went.

It was too dangerous for Francis to remain in France, because his fingerprints were now on file, so he was put on the next ship for England — an exercise that was fraught with danger.

As the weeks went by, Paula's safety was also becoming increasingly threatened, but she kept going.

What troubled me was that Pat always dictated his reports for London to me and I coded them. In those reports, all the helpers in the north of France were mentioned by their real names because London had to know them. I always wondered whether, if I were caught, I would be able to keep silent. There is nobody who can guarantee that they won't talk — nobody!

Once she went to Limoges to collect airmen. She would often escort them to a safe house when they arrived in Marseilles. There was a little café called *Le Petite Poucet* where they would make their first contact and from where Paula would take them, often to the home of Mr. and Mrs. Louis Nouveau.

What was so extraordinary about the Nouveaus was that they were extremely wealthy people and could have avoided any involvement, but they were always sheltering airmen. They had an apartment on the fifth floor of a building on Quai Rive Neuve, a dead-end street along the old harbour.

One day I was taking some airmen to their apartment. I had one by my side and three were following behind. But when we got close to the building I could see that there was a bunch of policemen right in front of the entrance. I thought, "My God! What am I going to do?"

I didn't know whether I could go in or not, but if I turned around they would get suspicious. I couldn't go by them because it was a dead-end street. I looked back at the three airmen and the one with me. I shall never forget the horrified expression on their faces. I decided to go in.

We walked past them, went in and took the elevator. I thought that if there was something going on in the Nouveaus' apartment, I could not take the airmen there. So I went to the eighth floor and told them to wait, then I went down to the fifth floor and rang the bell. Mrs. Nouveau came to the door and looked at me. I was as white as a sheet.

"You were afraid of the policemen?" she asked.

"Was I ever!"

"Well, there is nothing to be afraid of. That ship you can see tied up to the dock there — there was some sugar on it and some children stole some of it, and that's why the policemen are there."

I went up to the eighth floor and brought them all down. You couldn't run away in a situation like that because you would only attract attention. Some people might call that courage, but I call it a sense of the present danger that you have to deal with instantaneously.

Paula worked for Pat O'Leary until September 13, 1942, a few weeks before the Germans occupied all of France. By that time O'Leary was convinced it was too dangerous for her to remain. He had arranged for a plane to drop supplies, but after confusion about the location of the drop zone the police were alerted and a number of people were arrested. One of those arrested had a notebook with Paula's name and address in it. Even though she had papers that identified her as a Czech, the Nazi occupation of all of France put her life in special danger once more, and O'Leary realized it.

> Pat came to tell me this and said I could not go home. "Why not?" I asked. "Don't you realize that they might send somebody to arrest you?"
> "What am I going to do?"
> I was distraught. Pat knew of a secret apartment he kept in reserve in case there was an extra flood of airmen, so he took me there. That is where I met Mel Dalphond.

Squadron Leader M.H. Dalphond, DFM, CD, lived in Summerland, British Columbia, until his death in 1990. In 1941 he was a sergeant air gunner with 405 Squadron. His was one of twelve aircraft shot down on a daylight raid on the German battle cruiser *Gneisenau* in Brest harbour on July 23, 1941. (According to records in the Department of National Defense, Mel Dalphond was the first air force prisoner of war to escape and get back to the United Kingdom.)

Though slightly wounded, he managed to bail out and evade capture near Lesneven, thanks to the help of a number of civilians. A detailed account of Dalphond's considerable exploits as a prisoner and escaper can be found in Cosgrove's *The Evaders*. His last escape was from Fort de la Révère.

> I just didn't like being cooped up! It was September 5, my birthday. As a matter of fact, I had bribed a guard to bring me a bottle of schnapps, with some cigarettes I had, which he had brought me two days before and I had put under my bed. We were going to have a bash that night. During the dinner hour, when the conditions were right, we got out, so I never did drink that bottle.

Dalphond managed to make contact with a member of the Underground, who put him in contact with "Jacques."

"Jacques" was one of the names used by the intrepid Alex Wattebled. When considering what kind of false identification Dalphond should have, Jacques decided he should be an engineer.

"Why an engineer?" Mel asked.

"Because you look like an engineer," came the reply.

"What the hell does an engineer look like?" Dalphond snorted, but he doesn't remember the reply other than a laugh.

Pat told us to be quiet because neither the people above us nor the people in the apartment below knew we were there. He used to bring us food and we were fed bloody well compared to the camp. I remember one time he came in with a few baguettes and a chunk of meat, which he said was the ration for a family of four for two weeks or whatever. This was all black market stuff. About the third day Paula turned up. As far as we were concerned, she was just Paula and she spoke to us in French.

From there we were taken to the apartment of Louis Nouveau. There were ten or twelve guys already in this big apartment. Another chap arrived and he started walking up and down, up and down, up and down the whole length of the room without saying anything. A couple of guys managed to find out that he had been at Dunkirk and had been hiding with some monks all this time. He had been allowed to stay with them but he had to abide by their rules, including the vow of silence. The guy had not talked for a year and a half or two years — whatever it was. On the second day, he started talking and, by God, you couldn't stop him: he just went on and on. The poor fellow finally came to!

After a day or two the group moved by train to Canet Plage, near Perpignan, from where they were to be taken off at night by boat. They went down to the beach at about two in the morning and O'Leary flashed the signal over and over again for about an hour and a half. No answering signal came from the sea, so they all had to go back to the house. On the second try, Pat flashed the appropriate signal just twice before there was an answering light from a little fishing boat offshore. They sent in a little rowboat to take the men off in groups of four or five.

Paula, meanwhile, was becoming increasingly resolute. Her work was there, with Pat. Moreover she was German: her life with the French had not been all that easy; how would the English treat her? She had decided she would not get into that boat, no matter what Pat said.

Dalphond remembers:

Before we left the house, Pat had come with a few bottles and told me that Paula did not want to go. He knew she was going to argue, so he told me that we were going to feed her some booze. I was sitting next to her because I was the only one in the crowd who could speak French. Pat kept pouring the champagne into her. We got her fairly well loaded, I can tell you, but she still put up quite a scene.

Paula continues:

They took me by force. First they made me drunk. They gave me so much champagne while we were waiting for that ship. I was sitting there quietly crying and then the boat came in and Pat said:

"Now you are going!"

"I'm not going," I said. I was holding onto the sand and then they threw me into the boat.

They were on that little fishing boat for two and a half days. The captain was a Pole and so were most of the crew.

Paula remembers:

> I didn't understand their language, but they often sang together and their singing was so beautiful to listen to.

There were no toilets for women on board and, inevitably, all that champagne was having an effect on Paula.

> So I went to the captain, and he said he always had this trouble with women, but that he would arrange something. He called down to the crew to come up on deck. Then a bucket with a long rope was lowered and he told me to go down below. And everybody was standing around watching this. I thought I would die; it was terrible!

After two and a half days, contact was made with a British corvette near the island of Majorca and the group was taken to Gibraltar. There Mel Dalphond and Paula went their separate ways.

Paula was flown to England and taken to a private house in Devonshire. Because of her facility in French and German as well as English, she was asked to work for the Underground radio at a station outside Bletchley, where she wrote stories for broadcast.

Paula found Francis Blanchain in a hospital recovering from a small operation. They began to see a lot of each other and eventually married. He got a job in the photographic section of the Royal Air Force, and after the war his unit was transferred to Germany, but he said he wouldn't go because he didn't like the idea of living well in a country where the people had nothing to eat. So he was transferred to the War Graves Commission, where his role was to find the graves of airmen who had been killed.

Paula had known for some time that her father was in Mexico. She set out to find her mother, with whom she had lost contact. She had been left alone in Paris and had had a terrible time. The Gestapo had visited her frequently, looking for letters or other information that would lead them to her husband and to Paula. Her mother had become convinced that both were dead.

> When the war ended, Mother found me! It was incredible. She had gone back to Germany, where she met a young man who had been in the German forces stationed in Paris. He said he would try to find me. I don't know how he did it, but he was able to track me down and tell me that my mother was very ill.
>
> I went to this French colonel who was in charge of issuing travel passes and discovered that he was the same officer who had been on that little Polish ship that had taken us to Gibraltar. He said he would arrange a travel pass immediately and he picked up the phone and said to the person he called:

"I'm sending you a young woman who will be there in twenty minutes, and you will recognize her by the decoration that she has in the lapel of her coat. It's a rope with a bucket on it and she will explain its meaning to you." Wasn't that terrible! But I got my pass and I saw my mother. She was quite ill and she died shortly after.

For a time, Paula was blessed with the opportunity to work with Pat O'Leary again — this time in a peacetime role.

He was as good a boss in peacetime as he was in wartime. It was a very pleasant job, with the Awards Bureau. All the French people who had helped during the war were asked to come forward to be recognized and thanked. We had all the documentation from the airmen who had been debriefed when they returned to England, indicating where and when they had come down and the names of those who had helped them. We had all this information indexed with names according to location.

When the French people came forward, we had to establish that they were telling the truth in order for us to give them money. If they had sheltered an airman there were costs for food and so on — sometimes from the black market. It was like a puzzle — we would check the lists and put the pieces together. One time a woman came in and said that she had sheltered an airman — I can't remember his name — for six weeks, or whatever, and he had met her daughter and presented her with a child. That was good shelter, wasn't it!

For her roles in the war the British gave her an MID (Mentioned in Dispatches), and the French the *Croix de Guerre*. When her post-war work with Pat O'Leary was finished, Paula took a number of other jobs until she and Francis decided to move to Canada in 1958. Until Francis died they lived in Montreal. After his death Paula, alone again, moved to Victoria with her cat Jumbo.

She welcomes a stranger with a ready smile and a firm handshake. One gets the impression that she doesn't suffer fools gladly, that she has obviously lived a life in which her very strong convictions have been severely tested, but not found wanting.

My experience in the war led me to believe that there are two kinds of people: those who never get involved and those who do. I am always so sad to get the news of the death of so many that I knew. Dr. Rodocanachi died in a concentration camp in 1944. Louis Nouveau survived Buchenwald — a wonder since he had been badly gassed in 1917. But his health was not good and he died in 1966. Pat is gone too, and now Mel Dalphond.

There are so many wonderful people around. I have met the worst and the best, but I was lucky because I met many more of the best. I have always said that it was the best time of my life: I was young; it was interesting and I had the feeling that what I did was not much, but it had to be done. You know, when you take a tiny wheel out of an alarm clock it might not function anymore.

CHAPTER TEN

"JACQUES"

Pat O'Leary and "Jacques," whose real name is Alex Wattebled, watched the little boat slip away in the darkness of the Mediterranean night. Mel Dalphond, Paula and the others in that boat were on their way to safety and freedom. A very different fate lay in store for Pat and Jacques.

As they trudged back to the Hotel Tennis in the darkness to organize another evacuation of evaders, Jacques reflected on the relationship that had developed so quickly between them. Each trusted the other with his life and Jacques' loyalty to his leader was unbounded:

> I have never seen a man so clever but so nice with his men. He really was a friend and when he asked us to do something, no one argued.

Ane yet, neither man knew much about the other. One thing was for sure: Jacques knew that Pat O'Leary was not his leader's real name, nor was he a Canadian, no matter what he said. On the other hand, Jacques knew that O'Leary knew *his* real name, but did not know that he, Jacques, had been in another organization before their meeting, and had been active in the French Resistance since the fall of France in 1940.

When he was demobilized in August 1940, Alex served as an elevator boy in the Hotel Ambassador in Paris — not an evidently auspicious career move. But the Germans used this hotel as their headquarters, and Alex, using the identity of Max Doré, was almost as fluent in German as he was in French. Before the war he had been a tour guide for Cooks Tours, and he could speak several languages.

Equal to his linguistic versatility was his manner. Outwardly he was genial and co-operative with the Germans. His Gallic sense of humour was irrepressible, yet he was capable of instantaneous and audacious action that would save his life many times, though he would say that in his job in the Resistance, everything was a question of luck.

One day in January 1941, three buses arrived at the Hotel Ambassador with high-ranking German officers on board. What Max found especially intriguing was the presence of senior Japanese and Romanian officers as well. They went into a conference room in the hotel. During the day a large German staff car arrived at the hotel and a German soldier rushed in with a message for one of the generals, who immediately hurried to the phone on the ground floor of the hotel. Alex recalls:

> One of the Germans said to me, "Max, they want a general who is in that conference. It's urgent." So I took the messenger up in the lift to the room where that

conference was going on. Of course, the messenger has to get the door of the conference room opened so he could deliver the message, but that soldier cost the Germans a lot! I was in the corridor behind him and he left the door open for two or three seconds, and I saw what was on the wall.

Do you know what it was? It was a big map about five metres long and two or three metres wide. I saw two German officers with batons facing it and I saw the Soviet Union on that map! I said to myself, "My God, the luck of it! They are going to attack Russia!" This is six months before their actual attack. I said to myself, "The war is finished for them," because I guessed right away what that conference was about. So, I went that night to my colonel in the Resistance and told him.

Really, the Germans were not so clever. How could they have fellows like me and other Frenchmen working in that hotel? Do you know that I was talking to one of the porters a few days later and he said: "I know a general in one of the rooms upstairs, and that fool left on the little table by his bed a dictionary of German and Russian!"

A few weeks after that incident, the Gestapo arrested the French colonel to whom Alex reported this piece of intelligence. Alex knew at once it was too dangerous for him in Paris, so he headed south. He arrived at the demarcation line late one evening without proper identity papers. He did, however, have the name of a contact who would help him.

As I was heading towards the place to meet this man, I noticed two men following me, so it was too dangerous for me to make the contact at that moment. I turned a corner and saw a hotel with a German flag on it. So I went in. My God, when I went into the restaurant there were thirty or forty German officers having their dinner. What was I to do? If I turned around and went outside the Gestapo would get me. If I'm in here, we'll see.

So I sat down at a table and a French waitress came and said to me: "Monsieur, this restaurant is only for Germans." I replied in French, with a very heavy German accent, "But I *am* German. Please serve me right away."

So she did, and all the officers eating there were watching me, and I thought, my God, if they come to me, I'm done — finished. But, of course, the girl told them I was German. They watched me a little bit sometimes, but anyhow I finished my dinner. How lucky I was. And I thought, I am going to play a trick on them. I finished my dinner and paid in the Germany money I had, and then I turned to them, clicked my heels, raised my arm and said:

"Heil Hitler!"

They all jumped up, clicked their heels also and said:

"Heil Hitler!"

And then I walked out. This is the truth on the head of my wife and children!

Almost half a century later, Alex still laughs with gusto as he recalls that dangerous moment. But danger was still with him that night, because without proper identification papers he could not go to a hotel. The Germans checked hotel registers every morning and hotel managers had to report the names of all guests.

Alex used another ploy that must have saved countless men — he went to a brothel.

> I said to the madam, "Give me champagne and two ladies." I knew what I was doing. "Look here," I said to her, "I am a married man and just for one night would you mind not taking my identification?" She had to give the names to the police in the morning also, you see. But she winked and said:
>
> "Oh yes, for one night it's all right. How many ladies do you want?"
>
> "Two will be enough," I said.

Madam was impressed, not only by her guest's apparent prowess, but also his generosity in ordering expensive champagne. And so the night passed safely, and probably not uneventfully.

Next morning Alex met his contact, got safely through the line and on to Marseilles. After a number of other escapades, including a time in prison, finally, in March 1942, Alex met and began to work for the man who called himself Pat O'Leary.

All this Alex thought of as he walked back to the Hotel Tennis beside this remarkable man about whom he knew so little, other than that he trusted him with his life.

They both knew their underground activities couldn't last. By late 1943 the Gestapo had become very active in their attempts to infiltrate the Line, and Jacques was becoming increasingly suspicious of one of the Line's newer members. But there was no question of stopping or getting out. As far as Jacques was concerned, his loyalty to Pat was reason enough to keep on.

Pat would send Jacques to Toulouse, where he would rendezvous with evading airmen coming down the Line. He would find them safe houses and food, then escort them either to the Spanish border or to Marseilles.

> When Paula was with us, we would collect twenty or thirty airmen in Toulouse or Marseilles, then she would encode a message to send to London to arrange for a ship. Beginning on a Thursday we would take three or four of them to the Hotel Tennis at Canet-Plage. On Friday night we would do the same, and on Sunday, the night of embarkation, the VIPs would come — intelligence or high-ranking officers who were evading. Then, at midnight, we would take them all down to the beach and Pat would flash a secret signal with his flashlight. If the ship was there, it would send a small boat with two oars that would take four or five people at a time.
>
> I remember the night Pat decided that Paula should get out before she was arrested. I was in charge of getting the champagne and we had a celebration for some reason. We made sure Paula drank a lot of champagne, because we knew she didn't want to leave. She was a wonderful woman and very brave.

Because of the increased number of evaders in northern France, Pat decided he needed someone to help organize the escape route in Normandy. So in November 1942, Alex and Louis Nouveau went there and to the east of France to help with the escape organization there.

I went to Dieppe in November 1942. I saw the beach where the Canadians had landed in August and I said, "Poor boys, I understand why so many died that day." I met some people there who had helped some of the Canadians after the raid and asked them if they would like to help. I went every day with my bicycle to meet people who could provide a house or some food or false identity papers. This is how we worked it.

By February 1943, Jacques was sure that their Line had been infiltrated. He guessed that Roger Leveu, the man known as Roger Le Légionnaire, was the traitor, but he couldn't prove it.

I had talked to Louis Nouveau in Paris. He told me he had a new man working for him. This is very interesting because when you smell something, you guess about people. I met this man and Louis asked me:

"What do you think of this fellow?"

"I don't like him. I will never tell him where I'm going."

And I never did. But a few days before I was arrested I had a rendezvous with one of our men, and he told me that Pat O'Leary had been arrested. I knew for sure then that there was a traitor in our organization.

On March 5 I had a rendezvous with this Roger at the Café Dupont in the Boulevard St. Michel in Paris. When I got there I saw that there were five fellows with him. I said to myself, My God, they're Germans. They're going to arrest me. So I ran across the Boulevard St. Michel as fast as I could go. There were French policemen there and the Germans were shouting at them to stop me. But they pretended not to understand and they created some confusion so I could gain about two or three hundred metres. I kept running and turned a corner, then saw that there was no Metro station there. Metro stations were safe areas because you could easily get away.

So I ran down Rue Hautefeuille, into a house, up the stairs to the attic and listened. Very soon the Germans came and the French woman in the house told them I was in the attic. I could hear their boots banging away on the stairs, so I went up on the roof of this house, which was four floors above the street. I looked down to what seemed like a concrete yard and saw to my horror that there was no way of escape.

I knew that if they found out I had false identity papers I would be killed. So I decided to kill myself. I jumped! It was dark and I couldn't see very well, but what looked like cement was really the roof of a veranda. I went right through the glass and hurt my leg and my head, but I was still alive, so I started to hobble away, but of course they picked me up and put me in jail.

They tortured me. I had a very bad time because they put electrodes on my testicles and I was burned. After the war I needed a lot of medical treatment because I was all burned inside. But I didn't talk, except to tell them lies. I gave them false names and addresses and they would go and check them out. Pat did the same and so did Louis Nouveau. Sometimes they would beat me because I didn't know the identity of the names Pat or Louis gave them.

The Gestapo knew I had worked in Toulouse and in Rouen, so they kept asking:

"Who aided you?"

"A lady."

"But who? Give us her name and address."

"No. I cannot. She is my mistress! I am a gentleman; I will not tell you her name because it will make trouble for her with her husband."

I kept telling them about my mistresses, whose husbands were prisoners of war in Germany and finally they said that I was no Don Juan; I couldn't possibly have that many mistresses.

After about two months the Gestapo got fed up with Alex and put him in solitary confinement. He spent ten months and seventeen days in one cell. He never saw anybody and didn't talk to anybody, but then, as he explains, that wasn't quite right.

Do you know how it works in prison? Prisoners had a code for each letter of the alphabet — one tap for A, two for B, and so on. The man in the next cell would get a message and he would tap it out to me and I would pass it on to the next one. This would go on for hours. Sometimes there would be another method used. We would get down on the floor of our cell near the pipe that brought water in for us to wash. We would unscrew the tap and put our ear to the pipe to listen for whatever anyone might be saying. This kind of communication would go from floor to floor in that prison. This is how we got messages. We were all trying to find our friends and find out what they had said or not said.

In January 1944, Alex and other members of the O'Leary Line were taken to the concentration camp at Buchenwald, then to Flossenberg, which was much worse than Buchenwald, and finally to the camp at Hradiscko in Czechoslovakia, where he was a prisoner until the Russians liberated the camp in April 1945.

The Germans were deliberately killing the prisoners. They would organize work parties to work in the forest. The men would be put in lines with the strong Russians and Poles at the front of the line and the smaller French and others at the back. Every so often the men were ordered to lie on the ground and not look up. Then the Germans would shoot those in the last ten rows.

A German guard by the name of Ettlinger befriended Alex for some reason. He came to Alex one day and said:

"I will bring you some bread when I can. And every time you are in the last ten rows I will come and put you in the front."

The late Mel Dalphond and Alex Wattebled of the O'Leary Escape Line share a happy moment at the Escaping Society's annual general meeting in 1989. COURTESY OF JIM MOFFAT

Alex remembered:

Do you know that Ettlinger saved my life five times! I took his name and on D-Day, June 6, he came and told me two hours after the first landing. I told him I would help him if he was taken prisoner by the Americans or the British or the French, but if the Russians liberated the camp and captured him I could not help him.

Unfortunately, a detachment of Mongols in the Russian army liberated the camp. I saw Ettlinger die. They killed all the Germans. I was watching for him and I saw him die.

Alex survived the horrors of torture and the concentration camps. After prolonged medical treatment and convalescence, he moved to Pontorson, France, where he now resides with his wife, Esther. Like many others, after the war he discovered the true identity of Pat O'Leary — not a Canadian at all, but Dr. Albert Guerisse of the Belgian army. The reunions with Pat, Paula, now Paula Blanchain, Mel Dalphond and the others were sweet indeed.

Alex had been instrumental in organizing the escape of over one hundred Allied airmen and intelligence agents. In October 1942, he helped organize the escape of thirty-six Allied prisoners from a prison near Monte Carlo. In recognition of his contribution, France bestowed on him the *Croix d'officier de la Légion d'honneur* and the *Croix de Guerre avec Palme*; from Britain he received the British Empire

In 1962 Pat O'Leary, seated centre, was a special guest on the BBC television program "This is Your Life." Alex Wattebled, right, has just made a surprise appearance.

Medal, and the United States awarded him the Medal of Freedom with Bronze Palm. He also holds the Medal of Resistance as well as the Order of Leopold from Belgium and the Belgian *Croix de Guerre.*

As the picture above shows, "Jacques" and Pat O'Leary had a happy reunion after the war on the BBC television program "This Is Your Life". This reunion must have been particularly poignant because O'Leary had also survived the worst horrors of the camps. He had been arrested on March 2, 1943, in Toulouse, three days before Alex had been caught in Paris. The betrayals by Roger Le Légionnaire were fatal blows to the O'Leary Escape Line.

After a brief imprisonment in Marseilles he was taken to Fresnes near Paris and later survived the indescribable tortures of the camps at Neuebrenn, Mauthausen, Natzweiler and Dachau. On Sunday, April 29, 1945, the great doors of the death camp at Dachau suddenly burst open at the thrust of an American army tank and those who survived, including Pat O'Leary, were liberated. One of his duties later in 1945 was to identify the body of the traitor Cole, who had been shot by police while resisting arrest. O'Leary was also to learn that the French Maquis had administered swift and fatal justice to Roger Le Légionnaire.

CHAPTER ELEVEN

EIGHT DAYS IN FRANCE

The Shelburne Line

Late in 1943 M.I. 9 dropped two French Canadian soldiers into occupied France. They were Lucien Dumais, a survivor of the Dieppe Raid who had escaped after being captured, and the late Ray LaBrosse. Their mission was to organize the Shelburne Escape line by which Allied airmen and some secret agents would be collected in Paris and then guided to Brittany from where they would be taken off by a Motor Gun Boat of the Royal Navy. Escape procedures and routes had to be worked out. Safe houses had to be found. Supplies had to be provided and, most important of all, scores of helpers had to be recruited as guides, forgers, interrogators and security agents.

These M.G.B.s were small but serious vessels of war. They carried a crew of 36, had three silenced 1,000 h.p. diesel engines and could cruise at 21 knots for nearly a thousand miles. They were lightly armed with one six-pounder, one two-pounder, twin 20 mm oerlikon machine guns and two .303 inch machine guns.

On the moonless night selected for the operation the B.B.C. would broadcast the following message at 7.30 and 9.00 pm:

"Bonjour tout le monde a la maison D'Alphonse."

This would mean that M.G.B. 503 had left Dartmouth.

If for some reason the trip had to be delayed, the B.B.C. would announce, in French:

"Yvonne always thinks of the happy occasion."

And, if the operation had to be cancelled, the signal was:

"Rigoulet has a good head."

Before setting out from Portsmouth the last thing received by Lt. Commander Mike Marchall, the captain of the M.G.B., were the German recognition signals up to midnight. Now we know that this information resulted from one of the great scientific achievements of the war — the decoding of the German top secret code — Enigma. So important was this secret that it was used only on very special occasions because excessive use might mean that the Germans would realize that their code had been broken.

Sailings from Portsmouth were always timed so that M.G.B. 503 would not be within 30 miles of the enemy coast until two hours after sunset. As the craft got closer to the Brittany coast, speed was cut to reduce sound and the phosphorescent wash. Once contact with the shore party had been made the M.G.B. anchored off shore with a grass rope and the landing party went ashore in newly-designed surf boats using muffled oars. No one ever wore headgear lest it should fall off and so leave a trace. Usually the gun boat was at anchor for about an hour and a half, with the sailors ashore for only about 3-4 minutes.

Between January and August of 1948 seven agents and 128 airmen were rescued by Shelburne. Ken Woodhouse was one of them.

* * *

On the afternoon of Thursday, March 16, 1944, fourteen-year-old Marc Rendu was working in a field with his father, Maurice, near the French village of Remerangles. They were doing some farming for Monsieur Petit. It was a beautiful afternoon with a high, clear sky and a touch of spring in the air. Marc was happy to be working alongside his father. And he was proud, too — proud of what he knew his father and grandfather Wilfred Rendu were doing under the very noses of the Germans who occupied their countryside. They didn't tell him much, of course, but he couldn't help being aware of some of their clandestine activities.

Marc liked to watch the skies as he worked, for almost every day now, in this the fifth year of the war, big American bombers flew eastward towards Germany and then, some hours later, westward again to their bases across the Channel. Small fighter planes escorted these huge aircraft on their outward journey as far as their fuel would allow, and they came back like sheep dogs several hours later to escort the bombers home again. On this day the planes were there again — black specks against the sky with tiny dots of fighters circling and searching for enemy aircraft.

Suddenly Marc was aware that something was wrong. He turned to his father and shouted: "Look Papa, there is a plane much smaller than the others that's turning back!"

Father and son watched the smaller plane lose altitude, white smoke trailing from its engine. Maurice Rendu sensed immediately that the pilot was in grave danger and he knew what he had to do, because he had prepared for such an event. He ran to his father's truck, which he kept ready for such an occasion, started the engine and watched with baited breath until a parachute opened. He projected where the landing point would be and set out across the field in the truck.

On the end of that parachute was a young man, aged twenty, from Prince Albert, Saskatchewan. Ken Woodhouse, now living in Saskatoon, was flying his Spitfire in his sixty-sixth operation as a member of 401 Fighter Squadron, based at Biggin Hill. Ken describes what happened that day:

> The Spitfire Nines of 401 Squadron were on a sweep into France to escort American Flying Fortresses home. I had switched my fuel from the extra drop tank to the main tank as we deployed ourselves around the bombers, when suddenly the

mighty Merlin of my aircraft coughed and died; it was as simple as that. I tried pumping the primer to get some life into that motor, but even that proved fruitless. We had been having a fair amount of engine trouble for several months.

So I called up our CO, Squadron Leader Lorne Cameron, from Roland, Manitoba, and said that I was bailing out because of engine trouble. I turned the smoking Spitfire south, deeper into France, pushed the button that destroyed the IFF (a device for detecting enemy aircraft), unbuckled my harness, unplugged the electrical cords of my heated flying suit and tried twice to step out but was pushed back in by the slipstream, then pulled up the nose, sat backwards in the door, pushed the control column with my foot and out I tumbled.

Almost half a century later Ken still wonders if he was responsible for his engine's failure. In spite of the fact that the 401 war diaries record that the whole squadron was grounded on March 17, the day after he went down, in an attempt to discover the cause of these failures, and that the evidence would indicate either faulty drop tanks or defective spark plugs, he still wonders . . .

Ken's engine failure was to be the only piece of bad luck he was to encounter in the next eight incredible days — each marked by moments of near disaster along with acts of courage, ingenuity, quickness of wit and breathtaking audacity by complete strangers on his behalf, and throughout it all there was the timely intervention of benevolent chance.

As he slowly descended, he heard the muffled crunch as his small Spitfire crashed beside a small wood, and he looked down:

I scanned all directions as far as I could see, looking for towns, fields, the enemy, somewhere to run for cover. I spun around in my 'chute to look to the west and saw a small truck raising a cloud of dust and obviously heading to where I would likely land. The ground came up before I was expecting it so the landing gave me quite a shaking up and I hurt my left knee. I had landed in a shallow bowl-shaped depression about six feet deep in an otherwise fairly flat field. Hidden from view, I was able to get rid of my parachute and get ready to run. I saw this truck pull up at the edge of the field about three hundred feet away and a man jumped out and waved frantically at me. If I had landed anywhere else in that field I would have been in plain view the whole time I was trying to bury my parachute.

At first, Woodhouse thought that anyone who would approach him so quickly and so brazenly in this almost totally open region did not have his best interests at heart, so he tried to run away. The sore knee didn't help his speed and soon Ken was aware that the man was still waving at him and shouting: *"Vite, Vite!"*

I could see that this man was obviously agitated, for he was searching the surrounding area for signs of pursuit. He shoved me into the back of his half-ton truck. There I found a coffin-like box and some burlap sacks. He motioned me to get in and he covered up the box and off he sped.

He had scarcely got the truck out of second gear when he braked and stopped. I heard voices, one of which was obviously German.

"Have you seen a parachutist?" the German demanded.

"Yes," the man replied. "Over there, over there!" And he was obviously pointing to a spot a few kilometres away, where my plane had crashed. Not on the ground ten minutes and already I was within four feet of discovery. Had I delayed a few seconds longer in deciding whether to trust this man, we both would have had a difficult future. I also learned eventually that I had been running directly towards a German radio post hidden in the wood where I had planned to hide.

The truck sped along for no more than a kilometre from where the plane had crashed. The Frenchman backed the truck against a hay shed and indicated that Ken was to get under the hay and keep quiet. The truck sped off and Ken was alone again to consider his next move.

I decided to occupy my time preparing my escape. I broke open my escape kit and examined the contents as well as what I had in my pockets. I had a nail clipper with "Made in Canada" on it, so I filed off that incriminating evidence. My parents had given me a Rolex watch and I put that in my pocket, where it would be less conspicuous. I cut my pilot's wings from my battledress jacket and put them in my shoe in case I needed them later to convince some German that I was not a spy. I also cut the tops off my flying boots, which had been specially designed for the purpose, thus making the boots look like ordinary civilian boots. [Many years later, on a return to Remerangles, the tops were presented to Ken and he still has them with his other mementoes.] Finally, I taped my dog tags to the back of my legs.

Sometime later he heard a car drive close by and stop. German voices followed and it was obvious that there was a search of the farm. Perhaps it was because Maurice Rendu had been so "helpful" earlier in pointing out where the parachutist had come down that the search was not very thorough and Woodhouse was not detected. Soon after the Germans left, Maurice Rendu and his wife arrived with a loaf of bread and a bottle of cider, then left again after some feeble attempts at conversation aided by Maurice's French–English dictionary.

At dusk Maurice returned again to lead Woodhouse to the village of Fay St. Quentin. After very careful navigation of some fields, fences and hedgerows, they came to the small courtyard of a house. Leaving Woodhouse, Rendu entered the house and was soon out again with an older man and an elderly lady. They examined the fugitive very sternly and talked energetically as to whether they should accept this man or not. It was with considerable relief that Woodhouse finally heard the old man explode with laughter and say:

"*Mon Dieu, il est un enfant!*"

The three French people seemed to derive great enjoyment out of a joke that was lost on Ken.

Maurice Rendu, the French farmer who helped to hide Ken Woodhouse on the first night of his evasion, March 16, 1944.
COURTESY OF KEN WOODHOUSE

I don't know what they were laughing at, but a few minutes later I was invited into the house and there I got my next shock. Standing in the living room with the French couple and Maurice were two rough-looking young men dressed in typical French farm clothing. I was apparently to undergo another inspection. These two remained silent but watched me sternly as the others fired questions at me in French. I tried my best to answer them, but how does one prove one is not a German plant?

Unable to contain themselves any longer, the two young "Frenchmen" spoke up at last: "Hi Mac, welcome to France!"

They were two members of an American bomber crew shot down some months previously. They all enjoyed their joke and I was to learn later that the elderly couple were Mr. and Mrs. Wilfred Rendu, parents of Maurice. I also learned that they had sheltered seven airmen including me.

It was important that the three evaders be moved along so, before dawn on March 18, Wilfred Rendu and a gendarme drove them away. At some point the truck stopped and three more American airmen were added to the group, including one who had been operated on by a French doctor for a wound in his leg. By early dawn they were in the village of Roche Condé, where they stopped with the back of the truck against a door in the wall of a building. The door opened and the group was led through a loading chute of a small flour mill and on to another doorway that led into the living room of a house. Waiting for them was a seventh airman.

In the early morning hours the older Rendu and the gendarme drove the group into Beauvais. The truck suddenly stopped, and this time there was genuine alarm. Rendu and the gendarme were very agitated.

When I saw what the problem was, I was very moved but not afraid. Coming toward us was a long column of British prisoners of war escorted by a number of German armed guards. They were a work detail of some kind; we were told later they were probably going to repair some bomb damage at a German air base at Beauvais airport. I wished I could have called out some encouragement to those soldiers, but that would have been not only futile but disastrous.

The truck with its precious cargo moved on again to a place nearby, where they were to get their false identity papers. An anxious delay was caused when it was discovered that not all of the evaders carried a picture of themselves.

While awaiting our identity cards, three of us, moved by nature and the great amounts of strong coffee we had consumed that morning, inquired of the whereabouts of the lavatory. One of the Frenchmen opened the gate of the compound a crack and pointed to a lone building at the far side of the park where the soldiers had just been marching along.

Thinking back on it now I cannot understand why we were allowed to go, but we went: three poorly disguised airmen, in an enemy-occupied city, unable to speak the language, with no identity cards and our heads full of information about escape routes that the Germans would love to squeeze out of us. Like three giggling kids we went, trying to make light of it. We walked across this park to the lavatory and looked for the HIS and HERS. No such luck; we were in France, where men and women used the same facilities. We stood there, immobile, open-mouthed and embarrassed, but recovered ourselves, did our duty and returned to the compound.

It was late that afternoon when arrangements were completed for the seven evaders and their French guides to go to Paris. The Resistance men gave the evaders a briefing on how they were to conduct themselves in their company and what the consequences would be if they departed from these instructions.

We were to catch the train to Paris, but we were to walk to the station spaced out and on either side of the street. No talking, no gawking. If we smoked we were to leave the cigarette in our mouth. We did our best to look like seven complete strangers. One Resistance man had gone ahead to buy the train tickets. As we neared the station we noticed him standing amongst a group of people who appeared to have nothing to do. As we passed through this knot of people, one at a time, our tickets were slipped into our hands and on we went after the leader right onto the train.

The train coach was well chosen; it was one of those with compartments with doors that opened to the platform but no aisle. Once the train was moving, each compartment was isolated from the rest, so there was no way a railway official or a German could check up on us. For this reason we all relaxed, the Frenchmen got merry, and the wounded American could even rest his leg.

As we neared Paris the two Resistance men decided to examine our identity cards. There was a long discussion about them and then, to our astonishment, they tore them up into little pieces and threw them out the window. Their explanation was that the cards were incorrect and it was better to have none at all than cards that were not right, because, with an improper card, we would have to explain when and where we got them. But with no identity card at all, we could at least pretend we were escaping unaided.

And so, on the evening of Saturday, March 18, Ken Woodhouse and his six fellow evaders arrived at the Gare du Nord.

To be successful, helpers and evaders needed to demonstrate a variety of special qualities. Among the more important of these were cool-headed courage, quick wits and audacious ingenuity. And they had to be blessed by the timely intervention of good luck. In his brief stay in Paris, Ken Woodhouse had three experiences that illustrate all of these elements.

The trip from Beauvais to Paris had been relatively uneventful, but tension mounted as the group prepared to leave the station past the ever-watchful eyes of the Gestapo and their collaborators.

As we neared the gate at the end of the platform to enter the station proper I endured one more skipped heartbeat as I saw in front of me a tall, erect Gestapo officer with eyes that I could feel piercing my disguise. I was sure he would pick out the seven of us, but we escaped his gaze. It all seemed like a fantastic dream, but it looked as if we were going to make it, when suddenly, from behind me, came a plaintiff cry that froze us in our tracks:

"Hey, fellas, wait for me!"

In English, it was! I suppose it wasn't too loud, but it hit us like a brick. It was the wounded American, who had been getting further and further behind. Somehow the cry had either been unnoticed in the noise of the station or had not been recognized as English.

We left the station and began circling the block in front of it. Apparently we were being watched by unseen friends to see if we were under suspicion before our new guide took us under his wing. A little old lady appeared from somewhere, a dear old soul, who strutted along without a care in the world, stopped to buy some bread while we waited outside, and eventually delivered us to an apartment — and then disappeared, and we never saw her again.

Woodhouse was moved from place to place and eventually taken up a rickety set of stairs to the apartment of Mme. Genevieve Schneegans and Olympe Vasseur.

This fake travel certificate and the reserved seat train ticket for Car 27 Seat 28, from Paris to St. Brieuc in Brittany, are among Ken Woodhouse's prized mementoes.
COURTESY OF KEN WOODHOUSE

Genevieve and Olympe had sheltered a number of airmen, and Ken was delighted to make the acquaintance that night of one of them — Keith Soutar, of Pittsburg. Olympe and Genevieve were nervous for their own safety and that of their guests, but Keith Soutar was overjoyed to see someone from "home." He had not seen anyone for months who could speak English and he was very lonely. He was to feel more alone the next day when Ken was led away, because, as a pilot, he had priority in the escape line. As they parted, Keith asked Ken to write to his mother in Pittsburg as soon as he got back to England to tell her that he was all right.

Because he did not have proper identity papers, Woodhouse was taken to a high school he believes to have been Lycée St. Louis, in the heart of Paris. There he was wined and dined by Maurice and Marguerite, a couple in their late forties, who would die in Dachau after being betrayed, and was introduced to "two rough-looking peasants", whose English was very good. It should have been, for they were Russel Barnlund, of Sanford, Manitoba, and Ken Lussier of Ottawa, two members of a Lancaster crew that had gone down on its first trip.

Ken describes what happened next:

My guide then displayed the most amazing talent I have ever had the pleasure of witnessing, and it possibly saved my life, and certainly his, not more than an hour later. He called me into a small office at the rear of the apartment that was attached to the school. This man had everything there with which to make up false identity cards, travel passes, restricted zone passes and goodness knows what else.

He had piles of blank identity cards, the proper brown ones about two and a half inches by four inches; legal papers; lists of names of young men who lived in obscure places and whose identity we were to take, because he also had the death notices of these young men; specimen signatures of mayors of hundreds of French villages; and also signatures of German authorities in various areas. There were rubber stamps and seals of various offices in many of the French provinces, numerous types of inks and pens and, oh, just everything imaginable.

He got busy making up the identity cards, and I had the honour of watching this master forger at work. He first chose the name of a young man who lived or had lived in the area for which he had the appropriate signatures and seals. Then he would write in the name he chose using the right pen and ink for the document — I was to become Louis Alphonse Kervizic, an agricultural worker. This was followed by the physical description of the airman for whom the card was intended. Then he would look up the name of the mayor of that town and copy his signature. Next came the seal of office, followed by our photo and our thumbprints. (My thumbprint went on all the cards he made that night!)

Next he made travel permits, all signed by the mayor of the town we were heading for. Because of our destination in the restricted zone in Brittany, special travel passes were required, which he also made. Last but not least, he handed me a train ticket and a reserved seat ticket for the train that was to leave that night for St. Brieuc in Brittany.

This false identity card showing Ken Woodhouse as Louis Alphonse Kervizic was made in a back room of the Lycée St. Louis in Paris in March 1944. It passed very close scrutiny by suspicious policemen less than an hour after it was made. COURTESY OF KEN WOODHOUSE

The travel permit forged for Ken Woodhouse. COURTESY OF KEN WOODHOUSE

So much for ingenuity. Just before going outside, Ken's helper advised him to stamp on his card a few times and rough it up a bit, which he did. Within five minutes of their leaving, both Ken Woodhouse and his helper were forced to exhibit courage of a cool-headed kind as well as quickness of wit.

> We had not gone 150 feet when we walked right into two big Paris gendarmes. There were no smiles on their faces; in fact, they were all business. One of them stopped my guide up ahead and the other came on to intercept me. He said something to me in French that I did not understand. This was, at last, the moment of truth I had been dreading. If I opened my mouth my poor French would give me away; to pretend to be deaf and dumb didn't seem to make much sense either. Common sense came to my rescue. What else could he be asking for? I reached into my pocket and handed him my new identity card on which the ink was hardly dry — and I prayed. He took it and thumbed through it as the other gendarme came up to look me over. Muttering something, he handed the card to me and off I walked. I saw my guide quite a way ahead walking slowly. I expected a shout from the gendarmes, but none came. When we turned a corner several blocks later my guide, who by now was very alarmed, said, "*Run!*" And we did.

Ken and his guide ran for many blocks, stopped for a rest, and then walked to the train station. To his great surprise and pleasure he saw in the crowd Russel Barnlund, Ken Lussier, Keith Soutar and the wounded American. His guide, his task completed, disappeared and Ken never saw him again.

The new guide was a young woman whose name Ken did not know then but, according to information he uncovered after the war, may have been Mirielle Catherine Herveic. Whoever she was, what followed represents audacious ingenuity at its frightening best.

There were at least seven of us and she beckoned us to follow her. We did just that, single file, right through the gate and onto the crowded platform. When we reached coach number twenty-seven, the number stamped on our ticket, we found its aisles jammed with people, some sitting, others standing, and all holding parcels and luggage. Our guide, showing no doubt as to who was in charge of us, pushed and shoved along, stepping over those who would not or could not move, all the time shouting and cussing. We followed her as best we could, fighting our way to our reserved compartment, number sixty-eight.

We found it positively jammed with people and their baggage! They refused to move, in spite of our guide's best efforts. Sensing an impasse but not accepting defeat, she indicated that we were to get off the train. Back we went, pushing, tugging and bumping our way along the crowded aisle and onto the platform. She went off in search of a railway official. Soon she was back, a protesting official in tow, all the time talking a mile a minute and flashing her reserved seat ticket at him.

Again we followed her and the official onto the car, down the aisle past people who were thoroughly irritated by now, to our compartment. The official raved and raved until finally, and grudgingly, the "squatters" moved out. Because any contact with the French people in the aisle would have surely given us away, we kept aloof and quiet in the compartment. As the journey progressed so did the appearance of contempt on their faces. I asked our young guide to explain all this hostility and she replied:

"Who else would have a reserved compartment and who else would have the authority to force a French railway official to see to it that we did get it, and who else would sit aloof from all those others in the aisle? Why, a group of German civilians, that's who."

The train the evaders boarded in St. Brieuc was a far cry from the Paris express they had just left. Woodhouse describes it as a kind of "Toonerville trolley" with a door at each end and seats on either side of a central corridor.

It was almost filled but our guide and most of the airmen were able to find seats among the French civilians and the inevitable German soldiers. However, Bob Sweatt, of Houston, Texas, and I had to stand at the end of the coach among some German soldiers and French civilians. One big German soldier stood just ahead of Bob and me, and we were kept busy turning to face away from any soldier who looked as if he might engage us in conversation.

Finally, it had to happen. The German popped a cigarette in his mouth and started patting his pockets in a futile search for a match. I knew just what was coming and, not knowing how to handle it, I turned and faced the rear. In a few moments I heard a grunt of satisfaction and saw a cloud of smoke; obviously someone had given him a light, so it was safe to turn around. As I did so, I noticed that Bob Sweatt was deathly pale. Upon seeing my questioning look, he reached into his pocket and withdrew his hand cautiously. In his cupped hand was his GI-issue cigarette lighter, so obviously American! Bob had held this up to the German's nose without realizing what he had done until it was too late. Bob and I still enjoy recalling that one. Luckily the German did not recognize the lighter for what it was.

The group was next taken to Guingamp where they anticipated very rigorous security checks, for this was within the fifteen-mile restricted zone. They were all in civilian clothes and had forged papers and, what was worse, each had his head full of incriminating information about escape routes, names of people who had helped them and places where they had been hidden, as well as information about German military installations that had been picked up along the way.

As we approached the gate leading out of the station, nobody stopped us. It was incredible! This is security? we thought. Our guide was standing at the gate as we filed past, indicating without speaking that we were to saunter down the street to a certain doorway. The owner of that house wanted to get rid of us as quickly as possible, so Bob Sweatt and I were led to a large house with an iron gate. A lady came and ushered us in. Her name was Mme. Francine Laurent, a nurse by profession, and she made us feel right at home.

Mme. Laurent fed the pair, gave them soap and water to wash with and showed them where they could sleep. As they were soon to discover, this remarkable woman had sheltered many airmen during the war. She had their names and addresses hidden in a can in the stove pipe leading to the chimney, and she removed it to add the names of Sweatt and Woodhouse. By the end of the war there were thirty-two names on that list.

Not only did Mme. Laurent and her husband shelter airmen; they also used their house to store arms, ammunition, explosives and radios. At one time two young Frenchmen were caught by the Gestapo, just after taking delivery of some radio transmitters. Upon hearing of this, the Laurents fled for their lives, for they feared that these young men would not be able to resist the torture they were sure to endure and so would compromise the Laurents. Two months later, however, the Laurents learned that the youths had died without revealing their secrets so the Laurents returned to their home and their activities. Mme. Laurent was awarded the *Croix de Guerre*, France's highest award for valour. She died in 1954.

Sweatt and Woodhouse spent the following morning watching German soldiers walk by the house; the town was full of them and the two evaders wondered how in the world so many airmen could pass amongst them and not be caught. Towards evening a middle-aged man pulled up in a truck. It was a wood-burning outfit that somehow turned the wood into coke and from that came the fuel to propel the truck. Francis Kerambum, the driver and owner, worked diligently for the Germans during the day, hauling provisions to the various German bases in the area. In the evening he drove Allied airmen to and from places of concealment.

Kerambum once told Woodhouse that he had been picked up by the Gestapo and accused of doing exactly what, in fact, he was doing with his evenings. He just broke down and cried and cried and sat in the corner of the room like a simpleton. His acting was so convincing that the Germans concluded that such a wimp was not capable of any cloak-and-dagger activity, so they released him.

> I remember sitting in the back of this truck with Barnlund, our legs swinging away from the tailgate. There we were, rolling along in this old truck chatting away and swinging our legs, seemingly without a care in the world. I remember telling the guys to shut up because so many able-bodied young men should have been in prison or labour camps in Germany. It was weird, I tell you!

At selected spots the truck would stop and one or two evaders would be handed over to someone waiting in the dark. At one such stop Bob Sweatt and Ken Woodhouse and another man were led off by a young and lovely French girl. She took them quietly and cautiously through fields, along hedgerows, past some darkened houses and then, in a final fifty-yard dash, into a barn, where they were told to be quiet for a while. After some time she seemed satisfied and led the group into a house. Later the same evening they were taken to a farmer's shack that contained a roughly built double bed and a single bed. The young hostess tucked her charges in for the night and warned them again to keep quiet.

She was back before dawn and chided them for allowing her to sneak up as she did. The day passed pleasantly in the company of a very young girl who brought all her farm animals in one by one for the men to admire and kiss. Kissing her cat was tolerable but the duck, the chicken and the rabbit were more of a challenge. The airmen laughingly called a halt to this game when the little girl dragged in a forty-pound pig for them to kiss.

When it was quite dark the group, now joined by other evaders, began their last harrowing walk — through minefields in a restricted area, where the penalty for being found would be death.

> We passed along trails through wooded areas and along hedgerows. It was so dark it was very difficult to see the person ahead of you.
>
> Then something went wrong. We had been following a trail through a wooded area, when our guides stopped to get their bearings or to wait for the all-clear signal from someone ahead of us. After a time we started up again and came to

an intersection, where we discovered to our horror that we had stumbled into a clearing in which there were several houses. People I thought might be German soldiers were walking to and fro between the buildings, and light shone from a few doors and windows.

Panic nearly got the better of us. We all stopped dead to assess the situation. After the initial shock had passed some men disappeared into the trees and others milled about in indecision. I decided to bluff it out and walk right through that camp or whatever it was. As I passed a hedge or a vine-covered rock I noticed our male guide and another airman behind it. I kept on going, expecting at any moment to be challenged or shot. When I had made it through I noticed that the guide and the airman were right behind me. I don't know why we were successful except that perhaps the Germans (or whoever they were in those houses) mistook us in the dark for other soldiers, or were too drunk to care, or thought we were civilians who had the right to be there. One thing I'm certain of: without a doubt we were seen. Nothing has ever been written about this incident as far as I know, but other guys remember it and nobody has ever explained what it was we saw.

We kept going along a sunken trail bordered on the tops and sides with thorny bushes. At frequent intervals we stopped. I learned later that it was customary for one man, such as Joseph Garion, of Morlai, to go ahead and scout for land-mines and to mark any he found with a white handkerchief. Once we had passed and the last of the guides had returned, he would remove the markers so that the Germans would have no indication of any movement through their minefield.

Partway along this sunken trail our guides became alarmed again and told us to scatter. I needed no second warning as I scampered up the seven-foot bank and fell into more thorns on the other side. That was bad enough but another evader landed on top of me driving the thorns deeper into my flesh. Silently, with hearts pumping like trip hammers, we waited while a German patrol passed along the trail and disappeared. Once again we were undetected, but it was a close shave.

We lay there for about ten minutes and then made our way to the ''House of Alphonse.''

The "House of Alphonse" was a code name for the home of M. and Mme. Giguel. It was a typical Breton stone cottage, with two rooms and an attic used as a hay-loft, only threequarters of a mile from Bonaparte Beach. This strip of beach lay within a tiny cove on the northern coast of the Breton peninsula, a little more than three miles from the village of Plouha (see map on page 109). Ken Woodhouse was in for a surprise when he entered the cottage:

When a candle was lit I counted over thirty people standing around, many of whom I had met at various stages of the escape route. Russel Barnlund, Ken Lussier and Keith Soutar were standing among the crowd. And there were French civilians and at least one spy. Now all our eggs were in one basket, a basket that was right at the coast, in a minefield, in a restricted zone patrolled by German troops. Any noise, any light, any chance encounter with a patrol would spell disaster not only for us but for the whole escape network and the many helpers who served it.

At the appointed hour the group began their last nerve-wracking walk, led by their young French guides.

One of the most remarkable was Marie-Thérèse Le Calvez, an eighteen-year-old, remembered half a century later for her youth, beauty and unruffled courage — a courage put to the extreme test as she guided them along the rough cliffs and then down the two hundred feet to the blackness of Bonaparte Beach. The minutes or hours that followed must have been an agony of suspense.

Ken Woodhouse recalls the night:

We were in pitch darkness above the cliffs at Anse Cochat. We were told to follow the man in front of us very closely. When we got to the top of the cliff, we were to sit down and dig in tightly with our heels and hands. If we had slipped we might have taken the whole line with us.

There were about twenty-six of us plus a secret agent. He was carrying two large objects that looked like large thermos bottles. I thought he must have brought his lunch with him. Eventually he came over to me and another airman and gave us each one of these "thermos flasks." He told us that they contained very important papers: we were to hold on to them for dear life and, if intercepted at sea

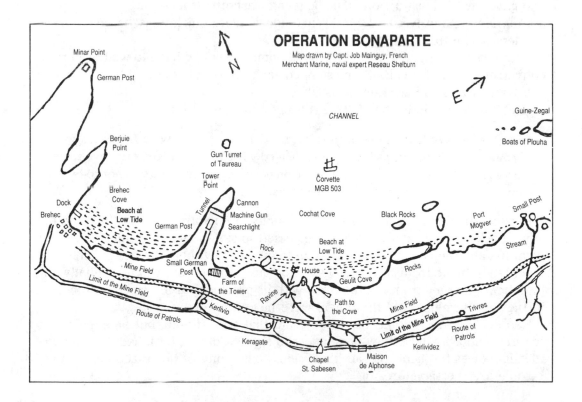

OPERATION BONAPARTE

Map drawn by Capt. Job Mainguy, French
Merchant Marine, naval expert Reseau Shelburn

by the Germans, we were to throw them overboard and let them sink. I never did find out what vital information I was carrying.

Again we were warned in no uncertain terms of the extreme danger of our situation. We had to descend these cliffs to the beach without knocking loose one rock or making any sound whatsoever. Any noise at all could alert the German patrols we had been dodging.

Following their instructions they were able to feel their way down to the beach. Partway down was Joseph Mainguy, whose excellent map of the beach appears on page 109. He was a merchant marine captain and one of Dumais' helpers. His job was to remain halfway up the cliff and signal the incoming MGB using a hooded flashlight. In a small grotto at the base of the cliff Marie-Thérèse pointed a small blue light out to sea.

Ken and his companions huddled in the blackness for what must have seemed like hours. One minute they could see the outline of a rock against the sea, and then it was gone. As anyone knows who has stared into an inky blackness, one can easily begin to see strange shapes and hear disturbing sounds. Anxious young men with frayed nerves and excited fear could hardly contain the tension they felt within them. And there was the silence, except for the quiet lapping of the waves against the shore. Finally, a different sound — a muffled and repeated swishing. They were here! Marie-Thérèse moved among the small knots of gathered men and gave the final instructions. The boat came ashore, its incoming cargo of guns, ammunition, explosives and two French agents were quickly discharged and the evaders began to board.

There were too many for the little boat! Someone would have to wait. A hurried conversation and Russel Barnlund stepped back. Silently, the little surf boat backed away and was swallowed up in darkness.

That surfboat ride to the MGB is still vivid in Ken's mind.

How those navy fellows managed to locate that tiny bay, row to the exact spot through the minefields, pick us up and then row back to the MGB that gave them no signal was remarkable. We scampered on board and again were told not to make any noise as we were hustled below decks.

Excited anticipation soon turned to ominous foreboding. The surf boat did not come back when it should have! Time passed so slowly that it seemed like hours went by, and the captain was preparing to move off without it, because first light would soon make them sitting ducks for the gun batteries on the cliffs. Finally, the little boat emerged from the darkness with its precious cargo; it had become lost in the fog. Barnlund and the others were helped on board.

Ken declined the potent tot of navy rum that was offered, but he circulated a ten-franc note for his fellow passengers to sign. Today, a bit faded and some of the signatures too faint to read, this French bill is one of his prized mementoes. Legible are the signatures of

Russ Barnlund, Sanford, Man.
Gordon H. Bell
John Bouch, USAAF
George P. Buckner
Rudy Cutings
Sgt. Richard C. Hamilton
Sgt. Abe Helfgott
Wm. A. Hoffman
Lt. Robert V. Laux
Lt. Wm. B. Lock, USAAF
Ken Lussier, RCAF
S. Metherwell, Calgary
Chs. H. Mullins, New Mexico
Wm. Sewchuk
R.H. Sweatt
Lt. James M. Thorson
Lt. D. Turnbull, RNVR
Roger Vissert
Dave Warner

On the shore Marie-Thérèse now faced what must have been the hardest moment for her. She stared out into the black night. In a few hours, if they were lucky enough to avoid confrontation with German E-boats, those young men would be safe and free in England. With the other helpers, however, Marie-Thérèse could only turn back to the House of Alphonse.

Ray LaBrosse captured the emotions of that poignant moment, for he had experienced it several times. At his funeral on August 10, 1988, Ray's daughter remembered visiting Plouha after the war with her father.

> I remember walking along the beach at Plouha as Dad showed me how the actual escape of the airmen took place. At one point I turned to him and asked what he felt as he saw the boats slip into the darkness. He put his arm around me and said, "Well honey, there were a few times when I wished it were me going home. This little farewell was always emotional for us, because we had the urge to get in the boat too, and say, "I'd like to rest a while."

Eight days after the engine of his Spitfire died over a field near the French village of Remerangles, Ken Woodhouse was back in the United Kingdom. On March 26, the entry in the squadron's War Diary reads as follows:

> We received a great surprise today when F/O K.B. Woodhouse (CAN.J.18080) walked into the dispersal after having escaped from France, when he baled [sic] out S.E. of Amiens on 16th March. This is considered a damn good show, and "Woody" is going back to Canada for a month's leave.

How did the adventure affect Ken's life?

Tne experiences of those seven days turned out to be the highlight of my life. They have affected me tremendously because I have been on this ever since. My first letter was in 1945. I didn't know the name of the man who picked me up in that field, but I did remember the name on the side of the truck: *Rendu, Fay St. Quentin*.

So even before the war was over, I wrote a letter to that address asking for information about my rescuer. My letter was delivered to Maurice Rendu and I continued to exchange letters with him and his father until their deaths. I have also been able to correspond with Mme. Laurent and Francis Kerambum in Brittany, and I've visited various places along the escape route several times. Every time we go over, we keep admiring their courage. They didn't have to do what they did for us. And some of these people did it day after day. But they turn it around and say we came over when we didn't have to — but, heck, we were only young, naïve guys.

In 1969 there was a real wingding over there, and 120 Canadians and Americans were invited back. Part of the visit was to Paris and there, apart from all the receptions we were given and also gave — for we gave as much as we received — was a visit to Mount Valerien. It's a hill about 200–300 yards high and wooded with pine. At the bottom of the hill and built into its base is a long, low building. In it there are twenty-one coffins, twenty of which contain the bodies of Resistance people. The twenty-first is empty, waiting for the last registered Resistance person to die.

Partway up the hill is a little chapel. It was explained to us that, at the top of this hill, 5,400 Resistance people were shot. On the night before their execution they were allowed to pray in the chapel if they wished. We were shown where messages to loved ones were scratched in the stone and brick of its walls. I tell you, it twists your soul to look at those messages. Then we went to the top and there were posts set in the circumference of this cone-shaped hill and in the middle of the circle was a single post. The Germans tied Resistance people to the posts and stuck a machine gun on the centre post and just went round and round with the gun and mowed them all down — 5,400 in total throughout the war. When those 120 hardbitten Canadian and American guys saw that, we all had tears in our eyes.

You ask what those seven days did for me. It didn't really strike me until a couple of years later that this is what Christ did for us. He died for us. Those people died for us; maybe not all of them were helpers to evaders, because some of them were shot for blowing up trains, but some of them were our helpers. That has really affected me; that is really powerful. It means that I owe them a debt I cannot repay. But I can help other people and I've done it.

CHAPTER TWELVE

NOT BAD FOR A JEWISH GUY FROM WINNIPEG

The Marathon Plan

In the three months that followed D-Day, in June 1944, large numbers of evaders and escapers were hiding out behind enemy lines in France. By that time both the Comet Line and the O'Leary Line had been badly infiltrated, and hundreds of their people had been arrested. Moreover, Allied bombing of key rail centres made travel by rail risky and undependable.

For all of these reasons, a new plan was devised by M.I. 9 in collaboration with the French and Belgian Resistance. It was called Marathon. Evaders and escapers were to be concentrated in areas likely to be out of the way of both the retreating German armies and the eventual advance of the Allies. Three woodland camp areas were designated. One was near Rennes in eastern Brittany; a second was in the area of Chateaudun, including the forest of Freteval west of Orleans; and the third was in the Ardennes, astride the French–Belgian border.

There were two main reasons for this plan. First, it was considered that the safety of these large numbers of evaders would be greatly enhanced if they were away from potential combat areas. More important, such a move would lessen the risks to the helpers. There was real concern about the edgy nerves of the retreating German armies — an anxiety heightened by the slaughter by an SS division of all men, women and children in the village of Oradour, north of Limoges.

In the forest of Freteval, near Cloyes and east of Le Mans, large numbers of airmen were gathered. They were supplied by air drops and the local black market. Arrangements were made with the Resistance to refrain from subversive activity in those areas so as not to attract German attacks.

By August 1944, over three hundred airmen had been liberated from these camps by the advancing Allied armies. Lou Greenburgh was one of them.

* * *

"Corkscrew starboard — Ju-88 on our tail!" the rear gunner shouted. Pilot Officer Lou Greenburgh put the big Lancaster into a dive and was just levelling off when he heard another scream:

"He's under us!" And a burst of cannon shell caught the port wing. "S for Sugar" began to skid. Lou strained to regain control, only to hear Geordie, the engineer, say: "He hit our fuel tank, Skipper. We're losing a lot of petrol."

In spite of the damage, Lou pressed on. "Sugar" seemed to be developing a will of her own and Lou found her tougher and tougher to control. He was flying between

Crew of Lancaster Mk II S for Sugar. Rear row, left to right: "Strommy" Stromberg —
wireless op.; Les "Geordie" Weddle — flt. engineer; Fred Carey — mid-upper gunner;
Pat Buller — navigator. Front row, left to right: Colin Blake — rear gunner; Lou
Greenburgh — pilot; Don Banent — bomb aimer. COURTESY OF LOU GREENBURGH

two layers of orange and red cloud, bursting with shrapnel and tracers. Then he
saw the target, ablaze — Berlin. He spotted the markers, dropped his bombs and
turned for home.

I asked the navigator for a course for the East Frisian Islands off the German coast.
It was taking all my strength to keep the wheel straight, and then the dirty weather
hit us. Propeller ice flew back against the fuselage and I used precious gallons of
fuel climbing through the storm clouds.

The aircraft was shuddering and sliding horribly as we staggered across the North
Sea, but I still thought we had a chance. I'll never know where that FW-190 came
from. It got the starboard engines and that's what finished us.

We were falling like a brick. I could hear the wireless operator tapping out the
SOS messages. The wheel ripped itself from my hands and we began to spiral. I
opened my side-window panel, but I couldn't see. When the altimeter read zero
I heaved the wheel back as far as I could, forcing the tail down.

Then we hit and I was knocked out for a moment. I woke up coughing, still in
the cockpit, up to my chin in heart-stopping cold water. The others were already
in the dinghy when Geordie grabbed me. We both fell into the North Sea, but
somehow we managed to get aboard the raft.

All seven were safe and aboard, but wet through and shivering with cold. The
sea was murderous and the wind cut through their sodden clothes. What a hell

of a way to end our first trip, Lou thought. Not that Lou hadn't been wet, cold and hungry many times before in his life.

He was born in Winnipeg in 1916. When he was three his father walked out on the family and committed suicide. His mother married again and from that moment he was an outsider. He was frequently beaten. He was not even allowed a bar mitzvah. When he was fifteen he left home for good. Like thousands of other young Canadian men during those years he "rode the rods" from coast to coast. There were lots of days when he had no food and many nights spent under a bridge or in a boxcar. In Vancouver he joined the march of the unemployed to Ottawa and was rewarded for his trouble with a stay in a Regina jail.

In 1937 he worked his way across the Atlantic on a cattle boat and managed to join the Royal Air Force as a member of the ground crew. Now at least he would have three meals a day and a dry place to sleep. In spite of his lack of formal education, Lou convinced a selection board in 1942 that he was pilot material, trained in Poca City, Oklahoma, and joined 514 Squadron RAF as a pilot in late 1943.

At the time most boys are discovering girls and hockey, Lou Greenburgh had learned he was not good enough. He had experienced rejection and abandonment. He knew what it was like to need help desperately. Lou could have been forgiven if, from those early experiences, he had grown to hardness and cynicism. Instead, by some inner grace, he developed an inner strength and a compassion for others, and he was determined to be damn well good enough and never, never abandon or reject another's need.

A wartime picture of Lou Greenburgh. COURTESY OF LOU GREENBURGH

Lou's fortitude, compassion and strength of mind and heart were crucial qualities during this cruel, endless night of December 30, 1943. As the night wore on, the dinghy sprung a leak and began to take on water. Brine dribbled from one crewman's mouth, his eyes glazed and he kept screaming and pointing to imaginary ships and planes.

> Yet he was the one who finally spotted the Lancaster that found us. We had used all but one of our Very lights. When I shot off the last one the rear gunner said that he saw a Lancaster. I told him not to be ridiculous, but that's what it was. It was Wing Commander Samson out looking for us. He radioed Air Sea Rescue and they came and got us.

For his skill, fortitude and bravery that night, Lou was awarded the Distinguished Flying Cross.

Three months later, on March 24, 1944, Lou's new plane was attacked, resulting in the loss of two starboard engines and heavy damage to the controls. This time he ordered the crew to bail out. He was preparing to bail out himself when the navigator, in his haste, dropped his parachute out the escape hatch:

> He screamed at me not to leave him. What the hell could I do? I couldn't leave him, so I got back in the cockpit and, at 2,000 feet, tried to fly the thing home. Five hours later we crash-landed on the base.
>   I went to the officers' mess, but I couldn't eat. I went out and threw up. I couldn't sleep either and I didn't know whether I would live or die.

And from that day to the present, Lou Greenburgh has not been able to eat a full meal without throwing up. His son, Edward, recalls that when he was growing up it was a regular morning occurrence to hear his dad retching in the bathroom.

By June 1944 some would say that Lou Greenburgh had had more than his share of luck — most of it bad. In the two and a half months that followed he experienced a number of hair-raising experiences, three of which are recounted here.

Lou's bomber was shot down on D-Day, June 6, 1944. Like many other airmen who bailed out, Lou lost his flying boots getting out of the aircraft, but he landed successfully. He was about ninety miles north of Paris and was lucky enough to find friendly assistance. He was passed from one helper to another until he and another airman, Jock Brown, were taken to the home of M. and Mme. Reant, in the village of Wavignies, Oise. In spite of her fear, Mme. Reant made the two young men welcome and shared what food they had. Most nights Lou and Jock stayed in the basement of the Reants' home.

One night Mme. Reant screamed that the Germans were searching the houses in the village and told Lou and Jock to leave immediately. They had planned to hide in a nearby orchard, but it was full of Germans so Lou ran up to the attic. When he heard jackboots on the stairs Lou dived out the window into a bush of nettles. He lay there frightened and sore from the scratches and watched in horror as M. Reant was dragged out of the house, his hands tied behind his back. They put him in a van and drove off.

Because of helping me, M. Reant was arrested and later executed. For a long time after that I couldn't sleep. I thought, what the hell — they knew the risk they were taking and they took us in anyway. Because of what he did for us he was killed.

From the Reants' home he and Jock Brown were taken to a safe house at 24 Rue des Epinettes, off Avenue de Clichy in Paris. Mlle. Epechere, in her early twenties and a devout Catholic, was their helper. One day she insisted on going to mass and taking the two of them with her.

Not bad for a Jewish guy from Winnipeg, eh?

We went to mass with her and afterwards we were walking along the street — Jock a couple of hundred yards behind and Mlle. Epechere and me in front. I happened to turn around and was terrified to see that two SS officers had stopped Jock. I said to Mlle. Epechere:

"They've got Jock. Let's get the hell out of here!"

"No!" she shouted, and without a moment's hesitation, ran back to the two SS officers and struck one of them so hard that he stumbled.

"How dare you pick on my brother! He has been deaf and dumb ever since he was born, and everybody has been cruel to him. Haven't you Germans done enough to us? You ought to be ashamed of yourselves, picking on someone so defence-less. Do you have to terrify him? Look at him — see how frightened he is? How dare you!"

Such was the force of her action and her words that the German she struck turned to the other and said, "Ah, she's crazy." And they buzzed off. Jock came back to us, and never again did he venture out on the streets. I think she deserved the Victoria Cross for that.

From the Austerlitz station in Paris, Lou was taken to the station at Benneval

I was met by M. Dolphin, a member of the Resistance. He had a number of electri-cians working for him and they were building communication lines for the Germans, so I became an electrician. We were in this van headed for the forest of Freteval when we were stopped at a German sentry post. One of the sentries had a machine gun, which he pointed right at the van. He insisted on examining our papers. Another sentry looked at me and said: "I want you!"

I was just about to get out when the driver panicked, drove off, turned down a side road and ran smack into a barricade. We figured the game was up this time for sure. But then the driver gathered his wits and shouted:

"For God's sake, the Allies are advancing and we have to repair communication lines all over the place and you have nothing better to do than stop us and ask silly questions. Can't you see we're in a hurry?"

One of the officers intervened: "Let them go. And give them an escort!" We drove off, stopped to get rid of the escort and finally made our way to the forest of Freteval in one piece.

More than one hundred and fifty Allied airmen had been gathered in these deep woods. The plan's success depended on a number of factors, chief of which was the co-operation of large numbers of local civilians: farmers for vegetables, butter, milk, eggs, flour; tanners and shoemakers for shoes; a village baker for bread, and a small girl and her horse for its delivery. Tarpaulins borrowed from farmers provided shelter, and chairs and tables were rough-hewn from trees. A local doctor made regular calls on the sick and wounded. Even a barber appeared once a week.

Each day had a regular routine: up at 6:30 A.M. for breakfast, cooked over charcoal so that there would be no tell-tale smoke; then water duty and general cleanup. The makeshift tents had to be covered every morning with fresh grass to make them invisible from the air. Very strict rules were in place to prevent unauthorized visitors from getting too close. A very large man with a huge club guarded the entrance and each new evader was subjected to careful interrogation before being allowed to enter.

Waiting was the hardest part. As July gave way to the first days of August, daily radio broadcasts from London told of Allied advances in the area. Moreover, there was ample evidence of Germans in full retreat along the roads outside the forest.

Finally, the camp commander took a vehicle and drove to Le Mans, where he met Airey Neave of M.I. 9. On August 13, Neave led a team of British commandos to the forest and the airmen were all rescued without loss of life.

Lou was taken by truck to Caen and then by plane to England. In June 1945 he was invited to Buckingham Palace, where King George awarded him the Bar to his Distinguished Flying Cross — a long way, indeed, from that jail cell in Regina.

After further service with Transport Command in the Middle East, and now a squadron leader, Lou took his discharge and came home. He felt about as welcome as a crocodile in a swimming pool; his business failed and his family shunned his English wife, who later left him. He rejoined the RAF and served another six years before returning to Manitoba and service as a probation officer.

> I'm okay now. I still can't eat a meal and I had prostate cancer a few years ago. I'm semi-retired, but I volunteer as a probation officer, and the other day I got a phone call that made it one of the happiest of my life. A twenty-five-year-old fellow phoned me up and thanked me, because he said that if it hadn't been for my report on him he would have gone to jail. That really made me feel good.

As he speaks, a cat wanders through the room. It was a stray that arrived one night, half starved, terrified and badly hurt from someone's blows. Some nights it sleeps at the foot of Lou's bed. That makes him feel good too.

CHAPTER THIRTEEN

SOMETHING INSIDE ME BOILED

The German soldier thanked the young woman and left the post office in Bakel. As he walked down the street of this little Dutch town in the summer of 1942, he couldn't help but reflect on how friendly and co-operative the postmistress had been. In fact, other men at the barracks had remarked on the warmth of her smile and the courtesy with which she helped them. There was, of course, some talk among other residents of the village that she was a collaborator but, as far as he was concerned, she was just a bright and helpful Dutch civilian who realized the advantages of having the German army in her country.

She had been christened Wilemina, but everyone knew her as Mientje Manders. Mientje's father was the postmaster in Bakel and she was his assistant. The Germans who occupied a house nearby didn't have a telephone, but the post office did, so she would frequently bring messages for them from their homes in Germany. In this way she led them to believe she was a friend, and the inevitable consequence of this behaviour was that many in the village were convinced she was a collaborator. She was anything but! By the end of the war in 1945 a succession of escaped prisoners from German work camps and Allied airmen were given shelter by Mientje and her husband, Bernard.

It would have been understandable and prudent for Mientje and Bernard to keep out of trouble and not get involved in any anti-German activity that, if detected, would lead to imprisonment or death. So why did they risk their lives trying to save complete strangers? What was the motivation so compelling that it could blot out fear and drive them to such dangerous activity?

To understand this motivation one must go back to a day in the early part of the war. An Allied aircraft had crashed on the outskirts of Bakel and the Germans had captured one member of the crew. Just a few hours before, this young man had been safe on a bomber base in England. In the short time since his plane had taken off he had seen some members of his crew die and he had experienced the fright of bailing out for the first time and of landing in enemy-occupied territory, not knowing whether he would be shot. He was, to the eyes of the villagers watching, very young and very frightened. Even though he was surrounded by German soldiers, someone offered him a cigarette. In shaking hands he took it and was about to put it in his mouth and light it when a German soldier roughly knocked it away.

Mientje watched this incident with growing fury and determination:

> When I saw that, something inside me boiled, and I decided that I would do something to resist those Nazis!

119

When a large house became vacant, she and her husband rented it and, beginning in 1942, they took in evading airmen and passed them on down what she later discovered was a major escape line, although she had no way of knowing it then.

By the time Bakel was liberated in September 1944, over fifty airmen had found refuge in the Manders' home. Often Mientje and her husband would have several airmen in their house at the same time, and getting food for them was sometimes very difficult because there were never enough ration coupon books for all of them.

> I would go on my bicycle every morning, sometimes at four o'clock, to the farmers in the area to ask for milk, bread, cheese and eggs. I knew they milked very early and I waited for them to finish, and when there was no one else around I would ask for food. I always got some. In a small village like ours not many people had much schooling, and I could help them with forms they had to fill out or mail they got that they couldn't understand. They never asked me why I wanted so much food, but they all knew we were helping Dutch boys hiding from the Nazis. Even our neighbours who lived right in the centre of the village didn't know what we were really doing.
>
> This daily food gathering was dangerous work, because it was before the curfew was lifted at seven o'clock. Sometimes I didn't go to bed at night because I had to clean up everything from the meals we made. Also, some of the boys had stayed so long in haystacks and other places that their clothes were dirty when they came to me and I had to clean them.

In addition to providing a safe house for evading airmen, Mientje frequently acted as a guide for them on trains. That was often very hard, but sometimes there was a bit of humour in it. She would buy the tickets at the station, but the trick was to pass the tickets to the evaders without communicating with them or being observed.

> Once this airman didn't understand what I was trying to do and people started looking at me. So I said to him in Dutch, "You are a very lazy man and next time you are going to buy your own ticket."
>
> He didn't understand what I was saying and they all laughed.
>
> I remember another occasion when I was taking some airmen somewhere on a train. They couldn't speak Dutch and I was afraid some of the people would start talking to them. So I gave them each a newspaper that they could pretend to be reading. That was all right, except one of the boys had his paper upside down!

In early August 1944, Mientje and Bernard were to meet a young airman from Truro, Nova Scotia, a meeting that deepened into a poignant friendship that has lasted for forty-five years. Douglas Jennings was a member of 214 Squadron RAF. Aircraft from his squadron were providing radio countermeasures, positioned every twenty miles in the bomber stream, trying to disrupt German fighter control. On June 22, 1944, his aircraft was on a raid to the Ruhr when it was shot down by a German fighter. He bailed out and landed safely, though he had some shrapnel in his leg. He spent twenty-six days in a German hospital.

The hospital is still there. It is a U-shaped building with three floors. We were on the third floor and wounded Germans were on the other floors. The guy next to me was Ken Forth, a navigator. There was another guy there, Johnny Hodgkins, who had been fatally burned. They tried to keep him alive by bathing him in salt water; they did everything they could with the technology of that day, but Johnny died. The Germans took good care of us and we were treated like gentlemen. We had clean white sheets and a diet that was a lot better than we had on the RAF station back home. There was one American, one Canadian and the rest were RAF guys.

Forth was trying to raise my education a little bit, as Englishmen are wont to do with colonials. He taught me how to play chess. During the time we were supposedly playing chess we had time to do surreptiously what prisoners are always doing — planning to escape. We made a big escape plan, but it was totally fanciful because he was in a body cast up to his waist with a broken pelvis. He wasn't going anywhere.

One day a Dutch male nurse I had never seen before came into the room and began working around my bed. He said, in broken English, that I was going to be interrogated and that was very bad for me. This put the wind up me so, without telling anybody except Ken, I made a plan to escape.

We had a Red Cross parcel, and I planned to put it and other heavy stuff in a pillowcase and use it to hit the guard with as I went to the bathroom. This was total nonsense, of course. I had been walking just two days since arriving. I escaped anyway, which was crazy.

There were big blackout frames on the windows made out of black tarpaper over wooden frames and pressed into place in the window. I woke at two o'clock, opened one eye and found that the guard was dozing. His head finally went down and I made up my bed to look as though there was somebody in it. I then went across the room to the window and tied my sheets around the radiator near the window. I got the blackout down and the window up, which I had previously prepared. It was pretty lax surveillance there. Up and out I went in my Johnny shirt and nothing else.

I got out on the roof of a glass solarium, spread-eagled so I wouldn't break the glass, went over to the wall and jumped into the darkness. I took my bearings from the North Star and headed what I thought was eastwards towards Germany to outfox my pursuers.

I ended up in Rosmalen by four o'clock in the morning, so I hid in a field of high-standing grain and stayed there all day with no food or water. It was cold. There was a scarecrow nearby and I went to take the clothes from it, but there was a shout from a nearby window. I put it back and took off to a ditch, where I stayed because my leg was pretty stiff and painful.

Later people went by, and to identify myself I whistled "God Save the King." Still later, more people came up the road and saw me. They told me not to shoot because they were friends. They brought clothes and a pair of shoes that didn't fit, so I clumped my way behind them, running two or three miles in the darkness until they stuck me in a haystack.

Next day they came for Douglas, dressed him as a policeman, and took him to Bakel, where Mientje and Bernard took him in. Mientje remembers his arrival:

There was a police motorcycle with two policemen — one in the sidecar. But the man in the sidecar was no policeman; it was Douglas Jennings and he was wounded. He had been in a hospital but had escaped somehow. The police who found him were in the Resistance and they brought him to us. The doctor who lived next door was also in the Resistance, so he came and looked after Doug's leg and gave me instructions about how to care for it. Doug was with us for about four weeks, I think, then he was taken away by the Resistance to try to get him through Belgium. But they couldn't because the front line was too near, so they brought him back again.

On one occasion there were three American airmen being hidden in Mientje's house. It had a back room with a door that led to the rear. If the Germans appeared at the front door, Mientje would cough loudly enough for them to hear. This was the signal for them to go out the back door and get away as fast and as far as they could. When the danger had passed, someone would look for them and bring them back. Mientje recalls one such near catastrophe:

There was a knock on the front door and when I opened it, there were several German soldiers. I didn't know what to say, so I said, "Do I know you?"

"No, we don't think so," and then they asked, "Do you ever come to the dances we have at Eindhoven where we are stationed?"

"Oh yes, I do." I never did, of course. "But please, come in." And they came in. I told them to sit down and asked them if they would like a cup of tea.

"Oh yes, we would like that very much, thank you."

We talked for a while about dancing and then they asked, "How will you get to the dance at Eindhoven?"

"Oh, I'll find some way," I said.

"Don't worry about that," they replied. "We'll come and get you."

I said I couldn't do that because my father didn't like it that I would go to a dance, so I would have to come on my own without my father knowing about it.

And then there was another knock on the door. It was another German soldier, who told the rest they had to leave because they had been in my home ten minutes already and they were only allowed three minutes. They thanked me for the tea and left with a friendly wave.

I closed the door. I found I couldn't move or speak. I stood there paralyzed with fright for what seemed like an hour. I had to tell my boys that everything was all right, but for a long time I couldn't speak a word. When, finally, I recovered and was able to tell them what happened, they became very pale and quiet. I am no hero; I did what I had to do, and it was for myself as well as for them, because the Germans would have shot me straight away had they found those boys.

Mientje's husband, Bernard, was very active in the Resistance. Everyone knew him as Bernard von Bakel, but his identity papers showed that he was Bernard Manders, and that saved him from arrest whenever the Germans were looking for von Bakel. One Sunday a plane crashed near Bakel and three parachutes came down. Bernard got the fire brigade and went to where the plane had crashed in flames. He was able to rescue one of the men and bring him back at night to their home.

Bernard was never arrested, but he had some very close calls. The day before the Allies liberated Bakel in September 1944, two secret agents were dropped by parachute with radios in order to relay the location of German troops and gun emplacements. Bernard helped them rig an aerial from the top of the church spire, and Mientje would talk with the Germans in a friendly way to find out what she could about their movements and relay their information to the radio operators. The Germans eventually spotted the aerial and demanded of the priest the name of the men who put it there.

This was a very dangerous situation, because they told the priest they would be back the next morning for the man's name. If he didn't give it to them they would take people out of their houses and shoot them. The priest didn't know my husband was directly involved, but he came to talk to him about it. My husband told the priest to meet the Germans the next morning at a certain corner in the village. Bernard would be partially hidden behind a building in the next block, out of earshot.

At a signal to Bernard by touching his hat, the priest was to point down the block at Bernard and say that he was the man they wanted. The priest touched his hat and my husband ran for dear life in the opposite direction with the Germans after him with rifles blazing.

Our home was nearby and I could hear the gunfire. I didn't know whether they got him or not. Hours went by and I was very frightened. Then I heard the rumble of a tank approaching and I looked out. There was a big American tank coming down the street with Bernard sitting on the front of it with a big grin on his face!

And so Mientje and Bernard and the villagers of Bakel were liberated.

The days were glorious when some of "her boys," such as Douglas Jennings, returned after the war, and they were able to revive old, precious memories and laugh again at some of them. A few years ago Bernard died and Mientje was alone, except for her sisters and the memories of "her boys."

In early 1989 she received a letter from the Escaping Society with an invitation for her to be its guest at their annual meeting in Vancouver.

Mientje Manders and "one of her boys," Reverend Doug Jennings of Truro, Nova Scotia; Vancouver, 1989. COURTESY OF JIM MOFFAT

I didn't think, at the age of seventy-four, I would be able to go. Then I got another message that said I could bring someone with me. I was so pleased. I said, I'm going to do it. I have to do it. So I brought my sister, Johanna, who is fifteen years younger than I am. Her husband said I must go and that it was all right for his wife to come with me.

For the first time in twenty-two years Mientje packed a suitcase to travel. The sisters took the train to the Canadian military base at Lahr, West Germany. There she met other helpers and together they boarded an RCAF plane for Canada.

Now she was in Vancouver with Doug Jennings, a United Church minister in Truro, his wife, the other helpers and all the other "boys."

I see how grateful my boys are. I knew that some of them were, because they wrote to me after the war, and some, like Douglas Jennings, came to see me. I am thankful to those who gave me this opportunity to come to Canada.

I just feel as if I am another person. Back to life again!

CHAPTER FOURTEEN

THE DEAF AND DUMB SANITARY INSPECTOR

Peter Smal wasn't getting any respect from the nurses. There he was, recuperating from surgery on his shoulder, and what did they do? They used his room as a smoking lounge, that's what they did. And they gossiped and complained, which was bad enough. Worse, however, were the personal remarks about him. And his mother! Would you believe it!

> Look at the silly bugger lying there [they said]. Deaf and dumb, they tell us. Probably didn't even hear the air-raid siren or the bombs coming down in that last raid. Didn't even know what hit him!
>
> Have you ever seen anything like his mother? Ploughing down the hospital corridor like a Spanish galleon under full sail — right into his room when he came out of surgery. Wouldn't even let one nurse in the room. I don't know why Dr. Wulffaert tolerates that kind of arrogance. I know one thing, as much as I don't like them, those German doctors over in the public hospitals here in Brussels wouldn't stand for it.

And with one last derisive look at poor Peter, they stubbed out their cigarettes and got back to work.

"Poor Peter" wasn't Peter Smal at all, of course, but those nurses didn't know it. He wasn't deaf and dumb either and, while his cronies now might say he was well cast for the job, he was no sanitary inspector. And the Spanish galleon wasn't his mother; in fact, he had never seen her before, didn't know her name then and doesn't know it to this day.

"Peter Smal" is a Maritimer, the pride and joy of Amherst, Nova Scotia, and his name is Wesley R. Knowlton. To fully understand the circumstances behind Wes's stay in that Brussels hospital in the summer of 1944, we must go back two years.

Wes graduated as a navigator from Course 58, for air navigators, at No. 8 AOS, Quebec City, with twenty other young Canadians. He really wanted to be a pilot but was told, "You will be a navigator, period."

He crewed up in October 1943 with 431 Squadron, first at Tholthorpe and then at Croft. His first trip was on Christmas Eve 1943 — a nice easy one, he says, laying mines in Heligoland Harbour, near the Frisian Islands. The second trip was different:

> It was our first trip to Berlin and we flew over Sweden, then turned south over Rostock to Berlin. Dropped our bombs, came out the same way, back over Sweden. In fact, there had to be a lot of diplomatic tap dancing over that because Sweden was a neutral country. We had to apologize, but I guess the Swedes didn't really give a damn.

The graduates of Class 58 for navigators and their instructors. Wes Knowlton is on the left end of the front row in this picture. Of this group, nine were killed, four survived without being shot down and two, including Wes, were shot down but evaded capture.
COURTESY OF WES KNOWLTON

Just after we arrived at Rostock on our way in, our rear gunner saw a fighter, used the fishpond and blasted him. Fishpond was a type of radar that shows something out back. The wireless operator handled it and if there was an aircraft out there it showed as a blip on the screen. If they were all our aircraft they would be at a constant distance behind us, but anything that was moving up was a fighter, so that's how we picked him off.

But, when we got back to the base, they scoffed: "Oh yeah, another new crew. New crews always get a fighter on their first trip." But we had the last laugh, I guess, because before we were through debriefing it had been confirmed by others who had seen a fighter go down.

Wes and his mates were to make another sixteen trips before they were shot down on April 28, 1944. The target that trip was the railway marshalling yard at Montzen, right on the German border not far from Maastricht, Belgium. A nightfighter hit them, but Wes figured they could make it to the North Sea in about twelve minutes if they could get the fire out. The skipper dived in an attempt to do that, but it didn't work, and by this time they were down to about 6,000 feet.

The bomb aimer, the wireless operator and I went out my hatch. About the time I went out the nightfighter hit us again and the pilot and three gunners didn't get out. We had an extra gunner because we had another gun turret slung underneath with a cannon in it.

As far as I was concerned it was a case of getting the hell out of there. Part of the problem was that we only wore the harness for the parachute, not the 'chute itself, so you had to grab that and put it on and, believe me, you were moving fast.

I have since found it amusing listening to the stories of others who have jumped. Some guys remember every detail of their jump and their descent. Others, like John Watkins and Stu Leslie, and like me, don't remember a thing. I remember getting down to the hatch and going through, but who pulled the ripcord I don't know. I do know that my headset was still on and the cord was still plugged in. And that didn't do me any good at all, as I was soon to discover.

Wes doesn't remember hitting the ground, and he believes that he must have regained consciousness about two hours later. When he started to pull in his 'chute he noticed he had blood all over his ears and his head, caused when the headset was ripped off as he jumped. He noticed also that his right arm was in very bad shape, but he didn't know how bad it was. He managed to bury his 'chute in a small gully and got going, headed south.

In total darkness he walked through a cluster of buildings, which he learned later was a German training camp, and that started the dogs barking, but he kept going. At first, his mind played tricks on him. He was sure the train he saw going by had a car bearing the letters L.N.E.R., for London North-eastern Railway, so he was convinced he was back home.

Then a guy came by on a bicycle and said, "*Kamerad?*" And I knew I wasn't in England!"

This fellow took Wes, now in considerable pain because of his shoulder, to the home of Isidor Verbiest. Contact was made with the Underground and someone came to check him out to ensure he was not a German "plant." He was there three and a half months, in a hay mow over a goat pen.

It wasn't too cold, but I never got undressed. I just left all my clothes on because I never knew when I would have to take off. One of the things I could do was look through a crack in the boards and see the Germans out there training in that camp I had walked through — about five hundred yards away. Sometimes Germans would come into the yard and get water from Isidor's well and spend some time talking with him.

During that three and a half months in the hay mow I had no exercise and was never outside. There was nothing I could do and I was pretty much on my own. I could have left but I didn't know where to go and I didn't speak the language. I figured I was lucky to find somebody who was for the Allies. At one point in my stay I was brought a book in French on the life of Guy de Maupassant. I could read some of it but there were a lot of words I couldn't understand. When Isidor came to visit me we learned to communicate using as a base my indifferent French, amplified by a few words in English and Flemish.

Isidor or his wife, Elisa, brought Wes food, but there were eight children in the family and food was very scarce — his three meals a day each consisted of a cup of water and three slices of black bread. So cautious were his host and hostess that never during all that time did any of the eight children catch sight of him. Isidor wasn't really a farmer: all he had was a bit of land on a hillside, where he grew a little wheat and kept a few pigeons and goats. As Wes recalls it, the meat ration was 500 grams per week for a family of eight.

All this time, there had been no medical examination of Wes's shoulder. It just healed the way it was. Sometime in July, the escape organization in Brussels decided it was time for Wes to move. Some members of the escape organization also held jobs with the German police and the SS, and they knew that Isidor Verbiest was going to be investigated. The hours that followed were the most excruciating Wes had ever experienced.

They put me on a bicycle. Remember, I had been lying in a hay mow for three and a half months with no exercise, because I couldn't go outside or move around. And my shoulder hurt. First, I had to pedal about nine miles on that bike to get to the train station.

Members of the organization had bought the train tickets. They had also arranged a travel permit and a work permit for Peter Smal, the deaf and dumb sanitary inspector. I got on this little train and went to Louvain. They told me to watch for a man in a brown suit and where he went I was to follow. We got off at Louvain and from there it was a case of catching a trolley car to Brussels.

There were a hell of a lot more people waiting to get on this car than it could take. I *had* to get on — there was no question about that — because the man in the brown suit had made it and I had to follow him. As I was trying to squeeze on, a German soldier beside me was also trying to get on. The trolley started to move out of the station so he handed me his rifle, threw his kit bag on and jumped on after it and here I am walking along the platform with his rifle. I handed it up to him and he reached down and helped me on. No words were spoken the whole time. Of course, he didn't know I was deaf and dumb, but he did know that not many Belgians were speaking to Germans at that time, so it was natural for us not to speak.

I got on the car and looked for my friend. I spotted him at the far end of the car and almost immediately fell sound asleep, completely exhausted. A German officer woke me up to ask the time. A girl who was watching and seemed to be aware moved in and talked to him immediately.

When I got to Brussels a woman came along and took me by the arm, and she and I followed another woman who was about two hundred yards ahead of us. We walked two or three miles and finally arrived at the safe house of Madame Heuten and her sister, Georgette. By golly, I fell down in the bed they gave me and I don't think I could have gotten up. The bike ride, the scare on the tram, the walk — all that happened on the same day after three and a half months of inactivity.

Wes was the only evader in that safe house, but it was a very active place in an apartment building. It was deliberately chosen because their movements would be less suspicious in a big apartment building, with tenants coming and going all the time. Mme. Heuten was the leader of this organization. Her husband had been a professor at the university and as soon as the Germans moved in he was shot, so she started her own kind of activity. These activities went far beyond just helping someone like Wes Knowlton. She provided a payroll for people who agreed not to work for the Germans, and about once a month British Intelligence would drop a supply of money for her activities.

Mme. Heuten's organization was quite distinct from the Comet Line. She was very careful not to get involved in other organizations for the very reason that she was not looking for co-operation. The more people involved, the greater the risk. She must have had eight or ten girls working for her, Wes thinks, as couriers or guides or messengers. And it was while with Mme. Heuten that arrangements were made for Dr. Wulffaert, a surgeon, to examine the shoulder Wes had injured almost four months before.

Dr. Wulffaert had been a surgeon in the British Royal Navy in the First World War and, in his younger days, had studied with Dr. Wilder Penfield. Dr. Wulffaert arranged for three other doctors to examine Wes. It was decided that Wes needed surgery. A very small private hospital was chosen, and Dr. Wulffaert would perform the operation. The only other people who knew the true identity of Peter Smal were the anaesthetist and one nurse.

Papers were provided identifying Peter Smal as a deaf and dumb sanitary inspector who needed an operation on his shoulder, which had been injured in the recent bombing raid nearby. So far, so good. The cover story was sound and the surgeon skilled, but there was one problem, as Wes recalls:

> One of the risky parts was when I was coming out of the anaesthetic. They feared that I might start to mumble, and mumble in English! Not a good idea for a deaf and dumb Belgian sanitary inspector who wasn't too bright. They had anticipated this possibility and had this flamboyant woman act as my mother. When the operation was completed, she took over and wouldn't let anybody in my room. Sure enough, when I came out of the anaesthetic I was doing all kinds of talking, but she made so much noise in that room that nobody could hear me.
>
> As I was recovering, the nurses used to come into my room and smoke, and they didn't worry what they said because they knew I was deaf and dumb. I just lay there trying to ignore them. One day one of these girls came in complaining about what a difficult time she was having with another patient and with the stupid bugger here who can't talk. I just about exploded.

Wes was in that hospital about a week. The operation was on the head of the humerus, which had been smashed when he bailed out. Dr. Wulffaert had to break it again, then fasten the humerus to the clavicle, so there is no shoulder joint. Wes has some movement in his right arm but he can't raise it very high.

On September 14, 1944, the British army came to Brussels. Wes went down to a main square with his friends from Mme. Heuten's house to witness their arrival. A soldier in a British tank popped his head out of the turret to ask for information. Wes stepped up and said: "Hi. What kept you so long?"

> The soldier was surprised to hear someone speaking English so well. He went on to say that he believed all the Germans had left Brussels by that time. But they hadn't by any damn means! Within an hour a German car with a bunch of Germans tried to drive through the crowd, and that tank let it have one right there.
>
> That night there were fires all over Brussels. The people knew who the collaborators were and they went into those houses, brought out all the furniture and set it on fire. When Mme. Heuten heard about it, she put a stop to it.
>
> The next day they brought women down into the square, and they were cutting the hair off any woman known to have slept with German officers. But Mme. Heuten put a stop to that, too. She said that women who had been sleeping with German officers last week would be sleeping with British officers next week and all this was crazy, and she stopped it.

Soon after that, Wes was flown by DC-3 to Britain, where he entered No. 9 Canadian General Hospital at Bramshot.

> God, it was marvelous! Canadian doctors, Canadian nurses — everything Canadian! The operation in Belgium had been a success, but now it was a case of physio and occupational therapy to get the shoulder going again.

Almost a year to the day after his first mine-laying operation in the Frisian Islands, Wes was home in Amherst for Christmas of 1944. Then he entered a convalescent hospital, Divadale, in Toronto, in the former home of Sir Joseph Flavelle. Flavelle had given it to the air force, and there was a staff of fifty to look after forty-eight patients. In May 1945, Wes enrolled in the first summer session for veterans at the University of Toronto.

> Looking back on my experience as a member of 431 Squadron and as an evader, I was affected physically, in the shoulder, of course. And I have about a fifteen percent loss of hearing, but that was due to all that noise in the aircraft. I don't think that the experience affected me otherwise, except that it was a real maturing sort of thing. When I got back, more than anything else I wanted to get some education, get established and get things going. I wanted to forget about the war and get on with living.
>
> If it hadn't been for the government giving us those benefits to go to university, I don't know where I would be, because I couldn't have afforded to go there on my own.

"Peter Smal," alias Wes Knowlton, did indeed get things going. After raising a family with his wife, Joy, and a successful career in business, he has retired and lives in Willowdale, Ontario. On most Fridays around ten o'clock in the morning, Wes and several other evaders can be found having a coffee and a chat in the cafeteria of a local K-Mart. Small talk, most of it, but a maintenance of a bond that the rest of us greatly respect, but cannot share.

One of the mementoes Wes has is the program for the December 1942 graduation dinner of Course 58 for navigators, of which he was a member. Opposite the name of each of the twenty-one members of that class, the printed program sported an irreverent comment. Opposite Wes's name, for example, there is the remark: "(To Pilot) 'Where the hell did you learn to fly?'"

In his own writing, Wes added some notes after the war, which read, in summary,

Released/washed out:	3
No information:	3
Survived the war:	4
Missing in action:	9
Shot down but got back:	2

CHAPTER FIFTEEN

WITH THE MAQUIS

By 1943, both the O'Leary Line and the Comet Line had been badly compromised by traitors. Andrée de Jongh, the spirited leader of Comet, was arrested on January 16, 1943, and, with many other compatriots, was sent to a concentration camp. In March of the same year Roger Leveu, Roger Le Légionnaire, betrayed Pat O'Leary to the Gestapo in Toulouse and the gallant Alex Wattebled in Paris. The Shelburne Line through Brittany and across the Channel was not to complete its first successful rescue until January 1944.

Nevertheless, there were hundreds of Allied airmen stranded behind German lines with no intention of giving themselves up. Some, like Lou Greenburgh, were brought together in heavily wooded areas such as Freteval. Scattered throughout the occupied countries of Northwest Europe, many would remain hidden under the protection of their helpers until advancing Allied armies set them free. Still others would cast in their lot with local Resistance groups and carry on the fight in that way. Such was the fate of three young Canadians whose stories are touched on here — Bill Poohkay of Edmonton, Alberta, Fred Richards, of Oakville, Ontario, and Jim Moffat, now of Pointe Claire, Quebec.

Bill Poohkay and Jim Moffat were both members of 427, the Lion Squadron, but they may never have met because Jim went down on March 31, 1944, almost three months before Poohkay. On June 28, somewhere over France, Poohkay's plane was attacked and the pilot ordered the crew to bail out. Poohkay recalls:

> As the 'chute opened, I asked myself, What were those instructions about correcting the swing? Oh yes, it depended on which direction you wanted to go. But it was night — pitch black! I didn't know what was on the ground so I said to myself, "The hell with it; let it swing, let it swing." I knew I could live off the land: I was a farmer; I was from Alberta and I knew how to survive. I made my way into some woods nearby and saw tracks on the ground. Deer tracks! And I thought I would have meat for my supper.

At a farmhouse not far from Rheims, he was cautiously allowed into the kitchen, seated at a table in the middle of the room and offered some food. It was only a few weeks since D-Day, and the French were very careful of strangers. Soon, a fair-sized group of people came into the kitchen to see the Canadian airman who claimed to have been shot down. They sat on benches around the room: the mayor, the chief of police — about twenty all told, and all watching and waiting.

Two days later some Maquis people came to look him over. They followed him everywhere. A few days later, reassured that he was a genuine Canadian and not a German spy, he was welcomed into the local Maquis group and joined their underground activities.

Bill Poohkay chuckles as he remembers capturing two Germans:

I captured two Germans in a potato patch! Our Maquis group was in a little village recently vacated by the retreating German army. I was alone near a field of potatoes. Two little children came running up to me, hardly able to contain themselves:

"There are *Boches* hiding in that field!"

I shouted in the direction they indicated and told the Germans to come out with their hands up. The scared Germans, bristling with sidearms, grenades and bandoliers of ammunition, slowly stood up, raised their hands in surrender, and walked out of the potato patch. I gave the two kids strict orders to take the prisoners into town and warned the Germans not to do anything foolish. I said to the kids: "They have surrendered and are now prisoners."

Fred Richards is a tall, lean, quietly spoken Canadian. He was a Spitfire pilot with 412 Squadron. Early on the morning of January 20, 1945, his Spitfire Nine was hit by anti-aircraft fire.

I knew I had been hit. We were flying through a dense snowstorm at the time, but I knew I was too low to bail out. I had already pulled the coop top out and the next thing I knew the plane was down and I was hanging upside down in the straps in the cockpit. I seemed to be okay except for my knees. But there was a strong smell of gasoline.

That's the first thing that entered my mind — that the whole thing was going to go up in flames. I could see half a dozen people milling around while I was hanging there upside down. I was afraid that someone would light a cigarette and the whole thing would go up, including me. I didn't know where I was at the time, whether in German-held territory or on our side. Anyway, I started shouting in my high school German, "*Verrochne sie nicht!*" I thought it might mean "No smoking."

I still couldn't get out, so they got a long pole and pried the cover off the cockpit and that got me free of the plane. One fellow called to me, "Come, come," and I tried to follow him. I was still picking up snow to wipe off the blood. We walked quite a way, the falling snow covering our tracks. The Germans were apparently only half an hour behind us.

Finally, in the early hours of the morning, we got to a house. They washed my face, put me to bed and I fell asleep, exhausted. About dawn they woke me up and I tried to talk to them in my German. The man got a map from a kid's schoolbook and pointed to a map of southern Holland. It showed me we were in Giesbeek on the south bank of the Isle River. The fellow was a miller named Kuijpers. He took me into another bedroom; only about six hundred yards away was my downed Spitfire. I could see I had come down in a small orchard. Coming down in the trees had sheared off both wings. Several days later I saw a party of German soldiers come along with a flatbed truck to take the plane away. It was the last I saw of it.

My host showed me into a little room — the "safe" room. It was a space between the walls of two bedrooms, about three feet wide and ten or twelve feet long. On the end wall there was a louvred insert that gave me air and a hidden view of the yard outside. There was an old radio, two or three rifles and an old bicycle in there. The door into this room was a piece of half-inch plywood set flush into the wall. Wallpaper, carefully matching the seams, hid evidence of the entranceway.

A Red Cross nurse came a couple of days later. She brought me a Bible, Shakespeare's *Midsummer Night's Dream* in English, and a deck of cards. I read every day, and I must have played ten thousand games of solitaire. I watched out the window, and kept a log of all the German trucks and troops that passed by.

I exercised inside the house every day. My knees were healing, and I picked out the little bits of metal shrapnel until they healed over. My head was a little more troublesome. That first day a pro-German Dutch paramilitary group, *Schwartzjungen*, searched the house but didn't find me. When they left I got a little pin, and made a very tiny hole in the wallpaper — in the centre of a flower where it couldn't easily be spotted — so I could see what was going on in the hallway. When the Germans came to search the house next day, my spyhole brought me within breathing distance of the Gestapo: I had a close-up view of the officer's face. I was scared, I can tell you.

One morning I was in the kitchen, when a German soldier walked in with a bar of soap and a towel. He said something to me and I just pointed to the sink and got out as soon as his back was turned. It turned out that the troops were just there late at night and got out first thing in the morning.

Richards was put in touch with the local Resistance group. They referred to the leader as "Walkie-talkie" because he was so proud of his apparent ability to get in touch with his headquarters and with London and Paris. He didn't appear too military, but he could speak a bit of English. The first thing he did was take my dog tags and escape kit, with the chocolate bars, the foreign currency and my maps.

In that particular Resistance group there were three other foreigners. A French Canadian sergeant air gunner had been captured twice and escaped twice. The third time on the loose would be his last if he were caught again. There was also a Romanian who had escaped from a concentration camp; he spoke no English, German or French. And there was an American, Colonel Glenn Duncan, a Thunderbolt pilot who had been shot down and had walked out of Germany.

Walkie-talkie's great idea was to dress us in German officers' uniforms and for us to somehow stay there until the British army came. Another of his bright ideas was to bind us up in bandages and take us near to the front to lie there until an advance got us out. We thought he was nuts.

Group Randolet was a Resistance group operating near the Franco-Belgian border. For a hard-rock miner turned air gunner from Timmins, Ontario, the journey to active participation in that group began in the skies over Belgium on the night of March 30/31, 1944. Jim Moffat was the only survivor of a mid-air collision between two Allied bombers returning from a disastrous raid on Nuremberg.

Nuremberg: a picturesque medieval city that traces its charter back to the thirteenth century. The artist Albrecht Dürer was born there in 1471, and by the sixteenth century it was a well-known centre of culture and the arts. With the coming of the twentieth century the city was a growing industrial centre, but during the war it had a darker significance as well.

It was the centre of the Nazi Party and each August and September it provided the ideal backdrop for nationalistic pageantry. To the music of blazing Wagnerian

The crew of a Halifax bomber from 427 Squadron. From left to right they are: Sqdn. Leader George J. Laird, DFC, from Winnipeg, the pilot; F.O. W.E. (Red) Soeder, navigator, Saskatoon; P.O. Joseph Corbally, bomb aimer, Toronto; Flt. Sgt. W. Pat Clapham, W.A.G., Yorkshire, England; Flt.Lt. Paddy McLure, Dublin, Ireland (he was replaced by Jock Morrison before the Nuremburg raid), P.O. L.H. Smith, M.U.G. Sturgis, Saskatchewan; and F.O. Jim Moffat, rear gunner from Timmins, Ontario, and the only survivor. A peninsula in Frobisher Bay has been named after Sqdn. Leader Laird who, with the rest of his crew, is buried in the British military cemetery at Hotton, near the Belgian–Luxembourg border. COURTESY OF JIM MOFFAT overtures and stirring martial songs, enormous Nazi flags adorning the city's facades, vast torchlight processions, marches and rallies in the huge stadium Hitler built, the city swelled to the fervour generated by the oratory of Hitler and other Nazi leaders.

While not yet a major industrial centre, Nuremberg was the hub of a number of main highways. It had been bombed by the Allied air forces several times during the war as part of their overall bomber offensive against Germany, but the raid of March 30/31, 1944, was different from all the rest.

It has been described as the greatest air battle of all time. From their bases in England, 1,008 Allied aircraft took off on the evening of March 30, 1944, for the long and perilous trip to targets deep inside Germany. For 782 of these aircraft, Nuremberg was the target.

In the bomber stream were fourteen Canadian squadrons, including 427, the Lion Squadron, based for a time at Skipton-on-Swale. Squadron Leader G.J. Laird, DFC, of Winnipeg, was the pilot in Halifax LV 923 that night, and Jim Moffat, from Timmins, Ontario, was the tail gunner.

On October 23 the previous year Laird's aircraft had been attacked over the Zuider Zee by an unidentified and unseen aircraft, which raked it from the left and below, completely destroying the rear turret and badly holing the fuselage and bomb bay. The rear gunner and the wireless operator were killed instantly and Sergeant W.H. Cardy, the flight engineer, was so badly wounded in the right arm and eye that he was unconscious for most of the trip home.

The plane's hydraulics had been shot away, so that the landing gear could not be lowered and locked. And the man who could help solve this crisis, the flight engineer, was unconscious. By some act of guts or grace, Cardy came to long enough to instruct other members of the crew, including Moffat, to grab the axe and chop away at the pipelines that contained the glycol. If they could get rid of the glycol the wheels would lower. If they failed, a belly landing in a plane so crippled could be fatal.

As they approached the station, the control tower advised Laird to gain altitude and bail out with the living members of the crew. He refused; Cardy had suffered a serious loss of blood and the skipper feared that his engineer would not survive a parachute jump and a painful time on the ground until he was picked up.

Moffat and the others hacked frantically at the lines, trying not to think of the consequences of failure. Finally, the glycol lines were severed, the wheels went down and locked in place. Laird landed the plane at 10:40 P.M. It was promptly written off as scrap. For their actions that night Cardy received the Conspicuous Gallantry Medal, Laird the DFC. When the crew was brought up to strength, and they had another aircraft, Moffat was asked to move from his mid-upper turret to the rear turret — no medal, but a move that was to save his life on the night of March 30/31, 1944.

Date	Aircraft Type & Number	Crew	Duty	Time Up	Time Down	Details of Sortie or Flight	References.
3-10-43.	Halifax V- LK637	J-1696 F/L Laird, C.J. R143989 Sgt. Lockhart, G.S. R100526 Sgt. Corball, J.C. 196417 F/O Bowerman, J.T. J41919 F/O Moffatt, G. J64132 F/O Findlay, J.C. R70148 Sgt. Cardy, W.H.	Capt. N.Av. B/A. AG MU/AG R/AG F/Eng.	1810	2240	Target - KASSEL. Bomb load 1 x 2000 lbs. H.C.M.I. +56 x 30 lbs. Inc. +510 x 4 lbs. Inc. +90 x 4 lbs. "X" type Inc. While on the inward journey aircraft was attacked over the Zuider Zee by an unidentified green enemy aircraft which raked the Halifax from port and below and sprayed the whole length of our aircraft, shooting to pieces the rear turret with cannon, and badly holing fuselage and bomb bay. The rear gunner and MU/AG were instantly killed and the F/Eng. was critically wounded. No further attack was made. The 2000 lb. bomb fell through the starboard door, live, somewhere between enemy coast and English coast while the remainder of load was jettisoned over the Zuider Zee. Abandoned task after this action and returned to base.	706
5-10-43.	Halifax V- DK226	J18508 F/O Countess, R.B. J15199 F/O Solmundson, K.A. R147843 Sgt. Azua, H. 1387614 Sgt. Biles, J.C. R180038 Sgt. Thomson, T.A. R182093 Sgt. Lawson, V.M. 1684805 Sgt. Ready, A.P.	Capt. Nav. B/A. AG MU/AG R/AG F/Eng.	1837	0213	Target - KASSEL. Bomb load 1 x 2000 lbs. H.C.M.I. +56 x 30 lbs. Inc. +510 x 4 lbs. Inc. +30 x 4 lbs. "X" type Inc. No clouds - visibility, good. Attacked primary target at 2128 hours from 21,000 feet aiming on centre of T.I. green ground markers in bomb sight. Green T.I's well concentrated. Observed heavy concentration of fires running N.W. to S.W. concentrated around markers with pall of smoke rising up to 5,000 ft. Very successful prang if markers accurate. Glow of fires could be seen from a distance of 150 miles away.	707
4-10-43.	Halifax V- RB241	R15843 F/S Holland, H.K. R135936 Sgt. Price, M.M. R142710 Sgt. Pochkay, A.H. 1198337 Sgt. Danks, S.A. R96914 Sgt. Lebel, J.L.L. R159623 Sgt. Lebel, J.M.K. R80209 Sgt. Matchett, T.H.	Capt. Nav. B/A. AG/AG MU/AG. R/AG F/Eng.	1755	0119	Target - FRANKFURT. Bomb load 1 x 2000 lbs. H.C.M.I. +600 x 4 lbs. I.B. +30 x 4 lbs. "X" type. +48 x 30 lbs. I.B. Nil cloud - visibility very good. Attacked primary target at 2130 hours from 20,000 feet bombing on T.I. red and a ground detail. Bombs seen to explode in built-up areas, and resultant fires were beginning to take good hold. At 2138 hours an orange red explosion in target area was seen. Although bombing run was comparatively early, effort seemed quite efficacious.	708

An excerpt from the Operational Record Book of 427 (Lion) Squadron. It records the events of October 23, 1943, in which Halifax V LK 637 was attacked, two members of the crew were killed and Sgt. Cardy, the flight engineer, seriously wounded. For his leadership that night, Laird, the pilot was awarded the DFC. He died with the rest of his crew except for Jim Moffat in a mid-air collision over Belgium five months later. Jim Moffat's account of this night's events appears below.

The trip to Nuremberg was Laird's thirteenth operation. Despite the knowledge that the moon was up and the skies clear for most of the outward route, making the bombers easy prey for nightfighters, the raid was not cancelled. In addition, strong winds compounded the navigational difficulties when, because of the curvature of the earth, the bomber stream moved beyond the range of the British-based oboe guidance system.

In less than two hours, 108 Allied aircraft and ten German nightfighters were lost in the skies over Nuremberg and its approaches. Eighty-three bombers were lost on the way to the target and the rest fell on the way home. As for the target, one Nuremberg factory was half destroyed and three others damaged. One hundred and twenty-nine Germans were killed.

Six hundred and four Allied personnel were killed that night. Fifty-nine were civilians in German-occupied countries. Five hundred and forty-five Allied airmen died, including 109 Canadians. In fact, more Allied airmen were lost that night than in the whole of the Battle of Britain. It may have been the greatest air battle of all time but, from the Allied point of view, it was a disaster.

Enemy action accounted for almost all of the bomber losses. Those who wish to follow the straggling bombers back to their bases, and to read a comprehensive analysis of the raid should turn to Martin Middlebrook's *The Nuremberg Raid*. This narrative will describe just one tragic accident, which resulted in the death of fourteen young airmen.

30.3.44.	Halifax III."W"	J.4896	S/L Laird, G.J. DFC CAPT.	22:00	:: ::	Target — NUREMBURG. Bomb load: 480 x 4 lb. I.Bs. + 60 x 4	9. K.
	LV.923.	J.13272	P/O Soeder, R.R.P. NAV.			lb. "I" type I.Bs. + 56 x 30 lb. I.Bs. This aircraft did	
		J.19835	P/O Corbally, J.G. B/A.			not return from the operation. Operational record of crew	
		1622894	W/S Clapham, W.O. WOAG.			as follows: S/L Laird DFC 13 1/3 Trips. 96:25 HOURS.	
		C.18075	P/O Smith, L.H. MU/AG.			P/O Soeder 26 1/3 168:05	
		J.27919	P/O Moffatt, J. R/AG.			P/O Corbally 10 1/3 73:10	
		159666	P/O Morrison, J. R/NAV.			W/S Clapham 9 1/3 73:15	
		R158503	W/S Stainton, A.J. CO-PILOT.			P/O Morrison 15 1/3 104:25	
						W/S Stainton NIL NIL	
						P/O Moffatt 10 1/3 75:10.	
						P/O Smith 19 1/3 140:30	

*An excerpt from the Operational Records Book of 427 Squadron showing what
happened to four of its Halifax bombers on the night of the disastrous raid on
Nuremberg, March 30/31, 1944. When this report was written no one in the squadron
was aware of the tragic end to Halifax "W" LV 923 and all of its crew except for Jim
Moffat.*

We got to the target okay: we had a good navigator. But there were something
like hundred-mile winds and everybody was off course. We counted off twenty-
two aircraft going down in the space of twenty minutes until finally the pilot said:
"Okay, no more. Don't tell me any more."

We had a couple of attacks from nightfighters, but we got through to the target. There was only one other aircraft over the target that I could see. It was
a Halifax and he was going in — and an Me-109 came down to attack him. Whether
he was shot by the gunners or whether he miscalculated, I don't know, but he
dove right into the Halifax and cut off its tail. I thought, Isn't that funny — it's
going down in a flat spin. I had never seen that before. He was falling tail down,
with the tail end of the aircraft on the inside of the spin.

We had been flying back from the target for about twenty minutes when the
navigator said: "I'm sorry, Skipper. I've made an error. We'll have to turn forty-
five degrees to port to regain course."

As the Halifax cut across towards the main route, a Lancaster from 622 Squadron was also altering course. Then Moffat heard the pilot yell: "What the hell?"

Immediately there was a big bang. The Lancaster brushed over the top of our aircraft and its propellers tore into the fuselage, sheared off the mid-upper turret,
where I would normally have been, and I thought later that our pilot, second dickey
and the mid-upper were probably killed instantly.

At first I thought we were okay. The plane seemed to be flying level. We had
been shot up before and had come through. I tried to signal the skipper, but there
was no reply. I looked out to the right and saw the big rudder. Then I looked to
the left and there was nothing. I thought, "My God, even if he is alive he won't
be able to do anything, because even with both rudders a Halifax was not stable."
We were going down in a slow spin, tail in, just like that other Halifax I had seen
a few minutes before.

I tried crawling forward, but the hatch was jammed. Then I noticed a big hole
in the fuselage about the size of a table and I crawled out there. My waist was

<u>REPORT NO. K</u>

Aircraft type: Halifax III , No: Letter: W   Squadron: 427

Date of Loss: 30/31.3.(45)+4   Target: Nurnburg

Cause of Loss: Collision with bomber   Base: Skipton

Bomb Load: Incends. only.   Special Equipment: H2S (U/S).   Fishpond (U/S)

Crew:

Name	Rank	Duty	Experience	Fate
Laird DFC	S/L	P	15	Killed
Soeder	F/O	N	27	"
Corbelly	P/O	B	12	"
Morrison	P/O	F	20	"
Clapham	F/S	W	9	"
Smith	P/O	M	22	
X Moffat	F/O	R	12	
Stainton A.J.	SGT	2nd Pilot	1	Killed

<u>NARRATIVE:</u>

H2S U/S on way to target. Target bombed and 10 mins. late. On way back got off track to stbd. Nav. gave turn 60° to port. Course held 15 mins. before collision. Vis. very bad, pilot ordered watch to port for other a/c.

Pilot said "what the hell" then impact. R/G saw a/c going past to stbd. rear slightly below. A/C went into spin immediately. Stbd. fin and rudder torn off and large hole forward of rear turret on port side of fuselage slightly up. Height 21000'. R/G got out of turret easily, could not find chute which was caught in broken control wires. Got chute on, trouble with one hook, left hook on harness turned wrong way round, necessitating taking off gloves. Intercom. u/s. Baled out of hole. Height 4000'. Landed 1 km. west of Batancourt. Both a/c landed near Rachecourt. Baled out with helmet and oxygen connection from turret, no trouble with these. Landed hard on back, no injury. One a/c burnt on ground. French said 14 bodies were found. Hazy, no moon, very dark.

Same night a/c brought down by flak in same area (Halifax B). W/OP Sgt. William Jones (Wolverhampton) taken prisoner, shot in leg. 3 other POW in crew, one evading.

Did not see a lot of a/c before collision. Saw collision between bomber and fighter over target. Bomber lost tail, went down tail first spin. Fighter also spun down.

Jim Moffat's report of the loss of Halifax ZLW from 427 Squadron in a mid-air collision on the night of March 30/31, 1944. It must have been taken after he was liberated in the summer of 1944. The recorded date of the loss is wrong. Also note that both pieces of electronic defensive equipment, H2S and Fishpond, were not working. The aircraft was at 21,000 feet when it collided with the Lancaster from 622 Squadron. Jim bailed out at 4,000 feet.

out of the aircraft and I was trying to put my 'chute on. There was no breeze
or anything. I tried to hook one side of my 'chute but the hook was turned the
wrong way so I took off my gloves, turned the hook around, snapped it, put my
hand on the top of the 'chute and then pulled the ring to open the 'chute before
I realized that I was still half in the plane. I kicked against the side of the fuselage
two or three times to force myself away from it. I didn't count then; I just pulled
the ring, swung two or three times and hit the ground.

Moffat was down, alive and unhurt. Exhilaration mingled with relief and apprehension, but, by God, he was down! Unlike most downed airmen, he didn't bury
his 'chute and run. It was four o'clock in the morning and he was tired, so he rolled
up in it and slept till dawn. When he woke, he didn't know what country he was
in, but he thought it must be Germany and there was no hope of evading, so he
just about decided to give himself up. He walked down a hill towards a little village
and saw a teenage boy approaching him.

"France?" Moffat asked.

"*Nein*," was the reply. "*Nein!*" That word, even for an airman who did not understand German, roused strong emotions and got the adrenalin flowing.

That "*Nein*" seemed to turn a switch in me and I decided right there and then:
To hell with the Germans, I'm not going to be captured, I'm going to get away.

I saw a crossroads in the distance and went to it. The sign said Halanzy. I knew
that wasn't French, therefore I must be in Germany. The best bet was to get into
the woods and look at my escape map. But I had to go through Halanzy, because
if I started taking off through the fields I would attract suspicion.

So I walked through the village. I still had my uniform on and I had my overkit
under my arm because it was snowing and I thought if I were sleeping in the open
at night I would need something to sleep in. A postman went by me two or three
times on his bike, and I thought he knew who I was. At the end of the street three
or four fellows stopped me. I was sure they were going to turn me in, but that
wasn't the case. They were trying to explain that I should hide. Just then, a man
of about thirty rode up on his bike and said: "I am from Birmingham, England. I'm
here to get you back as fast as possible, but you must get behind that hedge because
the Germans are looking for you."

Marie-Claire, wife of Vital Paul, well remembers the night Jim Moffat was brought
to her home. While he was the only evader they helped, resistance to the German
occupation was not new to the Pauls. Albert, a policeman from Étalle, and Vital,
his brother, a railroad accountant, were members of a very active Resistance organization. By happy coincidence, Albert was visiting his brother in Halanzy the day
Jim walked through the village.

Sabotage was Albert's prime function, while Vital provided London with weekly
reports on train movements and their cargos in co-operation with a radio operator
in the group. The third man was an engineer from the local mine. The year before

Jim's arrival Vital, Marie-Claire and the mining engineer co-operated in a venture that helped Albert blow up a rail line. The engineer provided Vital with dynamite from the mine, but two problems were immediately apparent.

The first was that, because some French Maquis from across the border had also stolen some dynamite from the mine, the Germans were doing a search using trained police dogs to sniff out the dynamite. By great good fortune the dogs didn't discover the dynamite hidden in Vital's backyard shed. The other problem was how to get it to Albert, some twenty kilometres away.

Marie-Claire thought it was much too dangerous for Vital to take it on the train, and in any case any man would be under more suspicion than a woman. Good Friday, April 23, 1943, was chosen as the day for delivery. Marie-Claire sent Vital to mass, stowed the dynamite in her large handbag and boarded the train, surrounded, as it turned out, by several German civilian workers. The dynamite was safely delivered to Albert.

Marie-Claire was remembering all this as she hurriedly put her children to bed, with a special prayer for the fourteen young flyers who had died so tragically. In her heart there was also a silent prayer for the unknown survivor, about whom it was much too dangerous for her to say anything to the children. When she had completed the prayers and kissed her children goodnight, she peeked through the shutters that opened to the rear of the house. With a shock, she saw four men: Vital, Albert, the mine engineer and a tall young stranger. They had gone to the other end of the village, out into the fields and around out of sight to the rear of Vital's home to avoid detection.

Does she remember what Jim looked like at that moment? Marie-Claire laughs: "Oh yes, he was such a tall man, and he had such big feet!"

It is Marie-Claire's recollection that Jim Moffat was with them for only one night. Vital wanted so much for their nine-year-old son to meet Jim, but again Marie-Claire convinced him it was too dangerous. It was decided that he should be taken to Albert's home in Étalle. Since Jim still did not have false identity papers, a train journey would be too dangerous. Albert contacted a policeman in Arlon who had a car; they borrowed it and drove without incident to Albert's home with William Jones, another RAF evader. Jim Moffat remembers:

> I stayed in Albert Paul's home in Étalle for a month with Jones and a young Belgian, the brother of Albert's wife, who was also hiding from the Nazis. Albert lived in that house with his wife, Cecile, and baby daughter Monique.

April passed in relative quiet, with the pleasures of learning French and playing with Monique. The three young men had planned what they would do if the Germans suddenly arrived. If there were only two or three they would shoot them and then run. If there were more than three they would forget about the Sten gun, jump out the window and take off across the fields. They would go straight along these long and narrow fields rather than cross them, because there were hedges lined with barbed wire along the edges that they would have to crawl over or under.

Some days they would spend in the solarium at the back of the house, which was surrounded by frosted glass that shielded their presence. They could look up and see the American bombers flying east in neat formation and then, some time later, watch them headed west again, ragged and scattered. Once or twice they heard a whistling sound and saw Spitfires on a low-level attack.

One dark night in April, Albert Paul, leader of the local Resistance, took them out to a cowshed in the middle of a field. Inside the shed was a planeload of arms and explosives that had been parachuted to the Resistance. Albert was proud of the fact that the revolvers and some of the other material had been made in Canada.

After the strain of operational flying and the emotions stirred by the loss of his aircraft and, for all he knew, the other members of his crew, Jim Moffat found rest and relative tranquillity in these quiet days of the spring of 1944. Arrangements had been made to move Jim and Jones on to Brussels, but the night before they were to go, a bombing raid on the rail yards at Brussels obliged them to the postpone their travel plans. Time passed while they waited for other arrangements to be made.

These uneventful days of April came to a sudden and frightening end early on the morning of May 1.

"The Germans are at the door," Cecile hissed. Jim Moffat could hear them battering at the front door. Cecile's brother went out the window followed by Jones and Moffat. They ran across the field in their bare feet, not having stopping to put on their shoes.

> As the Germans were shooting at us, I thought we had better try for the hedges, which would give better cover. Unfortunately, at the second wire fence that I went under I lost my pants! I had never liked braces, and in the air force you had to wear them. I had torn the braces apart and made a belt out of them, but when I put my pants on that morning I couldn't find the belt so out of the window I went without it. I just took off and went through three or four fences and hedges and into the woods, but there was very little undergrowth to hide in. I ran until I was about ready to drop, then I noticed this big bush and dived in and crawled into the centre of it. In my haste I didn't notice it was a thorn bush!
>
> The German soldier who was chasing me ran right past my hiding spot — within ten feet of me. I was breathing so loud I thought he would surely hear me, but I guess he was breathing hard too. About an hour later, several Germans came looking for me with a dog, but the dog must have been following the first German's tracks because he went right by me in the same direction that first soldier took. I stayed in that bush until dark and then tried to crawl out.
>
> I just had a shirt and a waistcoat on — no shoes or pants. My feet were cut and the thorns had torn up my body pretty badly. Getting out of that bush was twice as hard as getting into it!

Jim crawled painfully out of the bush and made his way to a big tree about half a mile away. He sat up against the trunk of the tree, covered himself with leaves and slept in spite of the cuts and the cold.

Moffat's morale was sinking. He was very, very unhappy and didn't know what to do. At one point during the day he ventured near a highway and saw five or six gendarmes on bicycles. He called to one of them and explained that the Germans were after him. The gendarme told him to wait until dark and someone would come for him.

Nobody came. It wasn't until much later that he learned that all of the gendarmes had been rounded up shortly after leaving him and the cache of arms and explosives that he had seen in the shed had been seized. He was on his own again. Later that day he heard someone chopping wood. When he discovered the man was alone, he decided to approach him from the rear.

> I got to within thirty feet of him and said, "*Bonjour!*" The man turned around and almost had a heart attack. Here he was, facing a guy with no shoes and no pants!

Soon the man was back with some clothes and a sandwich of black bread and bacon fat. Jim walked south all night and arrived at the Belgian village of Virton. Here luck was with him again and by some strange coincidence he made contact with Desiré Paul, the brother of Albert from Étalle. Desiré lived not far away in Torgny, but it was too dangerous for Jim to stay in their home so they made a bed for him in the bell tower of a little memorial chapel.

> I would spend the night on a pallet in the bell tower. Bright and early in the morning I would crawl out of the steeple and along the back of the church roof, into the attic and down and out a window and into the forest. I would stay in the forest and walk all day. I was in that bell tower on June 6, D-Day, and I was also there when the buzz bombs started falling on England. Desiré came with the news:
>
> "They have pilotless planes going over to bomb London." I thought, Well hell, they have possibly won the war, and my morale really went down that day.
>
> I would see Desiré Paul every morning and sometimes in the evening as well. He used to collect beetles with Professor Fouss and I would go with them. I thought that when I got back to Canada I might become an entymologist. Professor Fouss would come about once a week and bring me English books to read. He could speak very good English, but Desiré and his wife couldn't speak English at all.

The effects of a poor diet and the infected scratches caused by the thorns were making life miserable for Jim Moffat by this time. He had scabies, his lower body and legs were covered with boils and he was quite sick. A few days later he was loaded onto a truck and taken to the village of Dampicourt. There an English lady who had married a Belgian cared for him. She had been a nurse in the First World War and was a real Florence Nightingale. She made it possible for Jim to have his first hot bath in months.

He was then taken to a Resistance camp. A doctor who travelled from camp to camp by motorcycle came and gave him a shot of something. Jim promptly passed out. It was realized that he was sicker than first thought, so arrangements were made to take him to a safe house in Couvreux, where he stayed for three weeks with Mme. Germaine Autphenne, whose husband, Major René Autphenne, was a prisoner of war in Germany.

Recovered somewhat, Moffat was taken back to this same Belgian Resistance camp deep in the woods, where he stayed until July. There were two Russians in that camp and the three of them decided to try for Switzerland. They got into France and travelled for two or three days. Water was plentiful, but food was scarce.

> I remember one time we were going through a field and it looked like cabbages so started to eat the stuff and found out that it was tobacco. It was awful. Because we were so hungry we decided we had better get in touch with somebody. We approached a farm worker in a field who turned out to be an Italian.
>
> He gave us one raw egg and his bottle of tea and a bacon grease sandwich. We punched a hole in the egg and passed it around three times before it was dry. We were each afraid of taking more than the other fellow. When we were finished, the Italian fetched Lt. Louis Paul, of Baalon, a member of the local Resistance.

Louis Paul took Moffat to his home in the village with the assurance that he could arrange safe passage to England. They were in the house no more than five minutes when Paul's wife screamed: *"Les Boches!"*

> I went out the back door and crawled to the edge of the garden and hid. Looking out, I could see a pair of German jackboots and a rifle butt. There was a truck there and this soldier was guarding it. When it was dark I crawled into a farmer's field and stayed until midnight. Cows kept coming up to me and I kept shooing them away. I thought I could remember the way we had come along the road from the camp and I was fairly certain I could find my way back to it.
>
> About midnight there was a bright, bright moon. It was quite cool as it was getting on towards late August. I got to the woods and walked along the trail that I had remembered led to the camp. They were all lying on the ground like they were sleeping, but they weren't covered or anything. I thought that was strange, then I touched one of them. He was ice cold; he was dead. They were all dead! The Germans must have killed them all that afternoon.
>
> I lost my cool then. That is the only time I remember losing my cool. I just went crazy. I ran and ran until I dropped. The next morning I discovered I had run the wrong way.

Alone again, dodging along the edges of forests, Jim Moffat walked with a heavy heart. At some point he heard voices in the woods and saw machine guns hanging from the trees and men walking around. He had stumbled into the Group Randolet, another Resistance group near Montmedy, France. Again suspicion greeted him and he was warned that they would hang him if they discovered he was a German "plant."

While staying with the Pauls in Étalle in May, Jim had hidden his dog tags in the soles of his shoes. Because he had jumped out the window without the shoes, he had no proper identification. They regarded him with a good deal of suspicion and kept him prisoner for three or four days until his identity could be verified. When they were satisfied, they allowed Jim to continue using the identity he was given in Étalle — Charles LeBrun, a woodcutter, from Étalle.

On August 6 Jim's birthday was celebrated in the camp with nothing more than a kind of blancmange — a mixture of flour and water with no salt or sugar. This Resistance group was very poor and seemed to have little or no support from the local area. Its members had been in the French army and were demobilized after the surrender in 1940. In the summer of '44, de Gaulle announced that all officers and NCOs were now back on active duty, wherever they were. They knew they would be rounded up by the Germans so most of them took to the woods. In charge of the group was Lieutenant Randolet.

There was nineteen of us in this group. Life as a farm boy and a miner in the Timmins gold mines prepared me for the rough and tumble of resistance life so I enjoyed it more than I suffered. They were short of food, but on one occasion we made a special arrangement with a truck driver who delivered groceries from place to place. We arranged to lie along the side of the road and jump out and stop the truck when it came by. We all had a cigarette and we talked with the guy, shook his hand, robbed him and went on our way. He went back and said that the "terrorists" had robbed him again and got the supplies reissued by the Germans.

Usually the group would operate forty or fifty miles from our base. One of our main duties was to attack retreating Germans on the highways. We would position ourselves at a bend in the road near some forest and conceal machine guns on both sides of the road. We would wait for a German convoy to pass and then attack a lone truck, car or motorcycle.

There was a radar station near our camp. I had explained to them that radar stations are what the Germans track aircraft with. Was there a way we could blow up the station or put it out of commission? We had no explosives so what we had to do was cut telephone lines and power lines to the radar station. The Germans would repair the lines the next morning and we would move our camp about twenty miles away, because the Germans would go into the nearest wood and throw hand grenades around trying to kill us.

We had no beds, no blankets — nothing. At one stage we had a German staff car, just an ordinary camouflaged car. One of our fellows could speak German fluently and he would pose as the driver. Four of us would hide in the back covered with a blanket and we would go down the highway forty or fifty miles looking for Germans. Usually there was a German in control of every town. If we shot anyone the Germans would look for us in the local area, not where our camp was.

On September 2, 1944, the Group Randolet heard that there were twenty Germans in the village of Quincy, in a valley near the Chiers River, who wished to give themselves up to the Americans. The decision was made to go and capture them. But the "twenty" Germans turned out to be about two hundred seasoned veterans of Rommel's Afrika Corps, and in the ensuing fight three members of Randolet's group were killed and a number wounded, including Randolet himself, but again Moffat escaped unscathed.

The men could now hear the sound of American guns in the distance. Every two or three days a runner would come from one of the villages with news of the American advance and the most recent location of German troops. In early September someone arrived with news that either Germans or Americans were in the next village.

> The lieutenant said that because I spoke English, I should go with three other fellows to find out whether they were German or American. We went to the village and, sure enough, there was an American jeep parked on the street and Sergeant Ellis, from New Jersey, with his feet on the windshield having a snooze.

A few days later Jim was in Brussels at the Metropole Hotel, then back to England for a stay in hospital. Almost six months after being shot down, Jim Moffat was free.

And what of the rest of the participants in his story? William Jones, the English airman in the Pauls' home in Étalle, was captured and became a prisoner of war.

The Gestapo arrested Albert Paul the same day Jones and Moffat jumped out the window. Seven days before the liberation of the city of Liège, on August 14, 1944, Vital took a chance and went to the Liège prison to visit his brother. When he arrived at the prison gate he saw a sign that said that Albert and several other Belgian patriots had been executed. Marie-Claire remembers that for Vital it was as though he himself had been shot in the heart, and she is sure that the burden of that tragedy hastened Vital's death from a heart attack in 1961. A square had been named after Albert in the town of Torgny. Cecile, his wife, survived the war, remarried and lives in Namur.

The doctor who treated Jim for scabies and boils in the Resistance camp was shot by the Germans two days later.

Jim returned to Canada on the *Queen Mary*. After the war he did not become an entomologist but went to Ryerson Polytechnical Institute, graduated and worked for Bata Shoes, then for Household Finance Corporation until he retired as branch manager in Montreal in 1984. He now lives in Lachine, Quebec.

He has served a term as president of the Canadian Branch of the Royal Air Forces Escaping Society. Each Christmas he and Sergeant Ellis exchange letters. In May 1988, Jim and his wife, Ann, returned to Belgium for the first time since the war. They visited Jim's old friends in Étalle, Virton, Torgny and Baalon. As a result of Jim's visit, the survivors of the Group Randolet and the mayor of Quincy arranged for the erection of a large stele in memory of those who died in that September 2, 1944, attack.

Jim Moffat and a member of the Belgian Resistance standing in front of the stele erected in memory of the airmen who were killed when their two bombers collided on the night of March 30/31, 1944, returning from Germany. Jim Moffat was the only survivor of that collision. COURTESY OF JIM MOFFAT

In March 1990 Jim Moffat returned to the community of Aurange, of which Rachecourt is a part, to participate in the dedication of a memorial plaque honouring the crews of the two aircraft that had collided on March 30/31, 1944, and from which Jim was the sole survivor. Marie-Claire says that the whole community turned out for the ceremony, and it was a time of very deep emotion for them all.

Nuremberg suffered heavy damage from Allied bombing raids in 1945. In September of that year the surviving Nazi leaders returned to that city once more, this time to stand trial as war criminals in a court convened by the Allies in the city's Palace of Justice. The Nazi Party stadium lies broken and abandoned on the outskirts of the city. Weeds cover the massive steps leading to the podium and the last echo of a hundred thousand "Sieg Heils" have long since gone, except as a fragment of frightened memory.

CHAPTER SIXTEEN

LUCKY JOHN NEAL

He should be called "Lucky" John Neal, for Lady Luck watched over him and at critical moments she intervened to prevent disaster. Circumstance, timing and unpredictable forces played a larger role in determining his future than calculated planning or dedicated action by him or his helpers.

Throughout his career, John Neal had been lucky. Even the high point of his adventurous life was influenced by a lucky break. He had agreed to join a particular crew as their regular bomb aimer, but first he had one final flight with a crew heading out for Laon. The crew he was about to join went out sometime during the summer and never returned. Neal later called this incident "a double lucky dose for me."

John is an optimist, with a frank facility for relishing life's illogical, humorous and ridiculous moments. When asked why he decided to join up, he chuckles as he describes the events in Montreal in 1942.

I was an eighteen-year-old machinist apprentice in the CNR locomotive yards. One day, a bunch of us were sitting down inside a locomotive boiler we had been ordered to clean out. We should have been working! Instead we were inside the boiler, chewing the fat. Then one of the domes on the locomotive opened: the works manager's angry red face appeared. It was not a pretty sight.

"I want you guys in my office within half an hour." Down went his head, and slam went the dome. We were in for it.

At the appointed time a bunch of contrite-looking young apprentices were lined up in the manager's office.

"I know what you guys were doing!"

"We were talking about the war," one brave soul volunteered.

"Talking about the war doesn't get my engines repaired" came the irrefutable response. "So there's only one answer for it. Any guy who is not down at the recruiting office by 7:00 tomorrow night is fired."

I decided on the RCAF: the glory of flying, I guess, got to me. Once signed up, I had to come home and tell Mom. That was the hard part.

What motivated me? The works manager at the CNR was my motivation!

Once in, Neal opted for pilot's training. He was sent on a special course to bring his high school credits up to air force standards. His training began in Victoriaville, Quebec, but detours along the way were not unusual in the service. He was transferred to Gunnery School at Jarvis, Ontario, for training as a bombardier. In Hamilton, a few miles from Jarvis, he lost his heart to an Eaton's department store salesgirl.

I was buying Christmas gifts for the family when I saw her. But the manager of her department wouldn't let us go out together. He didn't have a romantic bone in his body! He protected "his" girls.

(In parentheses, John claims that although the manager never gave him a chance to lose his heart that time, "I have lost it many times since, the latest being last Wednesday!")

Neal got his bombardier's wing and his sergeant's stripes in April 1943. While on leave he was notified that he had been given a commission: he was now Pilot Officer John A. Neal. A few weeks later he was posted overseas. The trip to Halifax was not without its problems, and Lucky John ended up in hospital. Why Lucky John this time? He missed his ship, a small vessel sailing in a convoy to the United Kingdom. "The ship left without me, but with seventy-five other airmen. It was torpedoed. There were twenty-five survivors."

In Halifax, on March 25, he boarded the *Pasteur*, a high-speed ship that sailed without escort. Bedded down on the floor of the main salon, with a mattress and a few blankets, Neal slept the sleep of the lucky. The worst that he suffered on that crossing was the acquisition of a few lice from his bedding, which had been used by a shipload of Italian POWs on the previous, westbound trip.

By the end of April he was in England. Operational Training Units and Conversion Units were followed by a dull period at a holding unit awaiting operational duty. At one Yorkshire posting, airmen were taken by truck into the wilderness, dropped off by ones and twos and told to find their way home. This was supposedly to practice the skills of evading capture should they be unfortunate enough to come down in enemy-occupied territory. The British Home Guard (a unit of older, part-time militia men) lurked in the drop-off area representing German troops on the look-out for "enemy" airmen. "We were warned to avoid capture. It was rumored that if caught, the Home Guard would take all our clothes, leaving us bare-assed naked to find our way home as best we could."

Waiting to join an operational squadron was not unusual. Often men were sent on seven days' leave, but these vigorous, healthy activities were looked upon as a waste of time. Later, for many who *did* come down in enemy territory, the practice proved useful.

On January 21, 1944, John flew his first operation with 419 "Moose" Squadron, a Canadian formation proudly flying the RCAF flag. Many of the squadrons had mixed crews of Canadians, Brits, Aussies, New Zealanders and other Commonwealth and Allied airmen. Crews changed — were reorganized or split as losses, promotions, sickness or a variety of other circumstances dictated. In John's case, personality differences led to a split-up of his crew after the ninth op. For a while he was a spare bombardier assigned as needed to one crew or another that was short a position.

When I was shot down, I was twenty years old. On April 22, after two trips with a crew that bombed Lille and Ghent, I was assigned to Lieutenant Chuck Thomas's crew. He was an American from Florida, who had joined the RCAF, then later switched to the US Air Force after Pearl Harbour. For some unexplained reason, he stayed with a Canadian Squadron, although he wore a US uniform.

Our target was the railroad marshalling yards at Laon in northwest France, roughly halfway between Brussels and Paris. At about 11:00 P.M. our Halifax bomber was shot down by a Messerschmitt 110. We were hit just as I was ready to drop my bomb load.

There was a tremendous flash. I jumped out of my prone bombardier's position to see what had happened. The pilot shouted, "Get the hell out of there. Bail out."

"Wait," I said, "I've still got my bombs on board. Let me get rid of them." I went forward as everyone sat tight and the doomed Halifax roared earthwards, dumped the load and we all bailed out.

Almost immediately below the plane, I could see the German fighter still following us. He whipped right across my 'chute. Why I didn't get tangled up in the propeller I'll never know. We bailed out at about 6,000 feet and it took approximately fifteen minutes to hit the ground. There was no wind, no moon — just a beautiful night. I landed in the middle of a ploughed field.

At first, I worried that I might have been close enough to our target to get hit by shrapnel. Some of the planes that had gone in a few minutes before us had hit an ammunition train — we could hear the explosion and even the shrapnel whistling through the air. I stayed where I landed for perhaps half an hour. Then I heard voices: one male, one female. I couldn't understand the language, but it wasn't hard to tell that the couple were making love. An incongruous situation!

When the last of the planes were out of earshot, I buried my 'chute, ready to head out of the area. Still wearing my battledress and flying boots, I set forth in a southwesterly direction, using my little button compass to keep me on course. I was headed for Paris.

A mile of walking brought me to a little wooded area. I kept on. Without knowing it I walked across the runway of a blacked-out German aerodrome. There were trip wires along the edge of the runway: I stumbled over one, but the alarm didn't seem to be working. After I got across, I saw a fighter plane take off. That was a shocker. (I later learned that it was Couvron airfield, just south of Laon.)

Lucky John Neal.

John was now hungry. His escape kit contained only a few water purification pills and some Horlicks tablets. He tried the Horlicks with some water, and found it less than satisfying. But he kept on his way, sleeping under cover of the wooded areas by day and walking at night. By the third night he was desperate.

Hunger gnawed at my insides: I would take a risk! I knocked at a small cottage door and waited. After a bit, a lady cautiously opened the door just wide enough

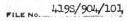

IN REPLY PLEASE QUOTE

FILE No. 419S/904/101

ROYAL CANADIAN AIR FORCE
OVERSEAS

No. 419 (R.C.A.F.) Squadron,
"MOOSE SQUADRON"

28th April, 1944.

Dear Mrs. Neal:

I regret having to confirm the telegram, which you have already received, notifying you that your son, Flying Officer John Arthur Neal, is missing from operations on the night of April 22nd, 1944. The mission from which he failed to return was an attack on an important objective in enemy occupied territory but, unfortunately, nothing has been heard of the aircraft or crew since take-off. There is still quite a possibility that all or part of the crew may be safe or prisoners of war but news of this could not be expected for some considerable time yet.

Your son was with us for 3½ months and had successfully completed ten operations against the enemy. He seemed to be a very happy lad who was quite content in his duties as a Bomb Aimer and, as a result, became quite popular with the remainder of the lads of the Squadron.

If any further news comes to hand, you may rest assured you will be notified immediately.

F/O Neal's kit and personal effects have been collected and forwarded to the Central Depository, Colnbrook, Slough, Bucks., who, after completion of necessary details, will communicate with you as to their disposal.

May I convey my sincere sympathy to you in your great loss, and hope with you that better news may follow.

Yours sincerely,

(W.P. Pleasance) Wing Commander,
Commanding 419 (RCAF) Squadron.

Mrs. W.E. Neal,
99 5th Avenue,
Verdun, P.Q. Canada.

"Missing" letter received by Mrs. Neal the day John was liberated.

to peek out. She was scared. "Je suis Canadien," I said. Her face lit up in a big smile. The door opened wide, as I walked in, she called the people from next door to join us. In a flurry of activity the table was set for one, food produced, and people poured in to watch a lone Canadian wolf down a meal. The crowd was made up of women and small children: there were no men. They told me that the able-bodied men had been hauled away to forced labour camps.

My hostess and her guests were Polish refugees who had come to France in 1939. Caught up in the German invasion of France a year later, they were again refugees, fearful of every knock on the door, hardly daring to hope they would find a place to rest and rebuild their shattered lives.

Everyone watched, encouraging me to eat heartily. They had done their very best to make my meal a celebration. Though extremely poor, they had pooled their meagre rations, even providing me with a bottle of wine. Then they prepared a package of food to take with me: boiled eggs, limburger cheese and the pathetic delicacies of the poorest of the poor.

After the goodbyes, John continued on his way, southwesterly, through a wooded area he later learned was the Forêt St. Gobain. He was on a back road where traffic was light, but every so often the sound of a motor forced him to dive into the ditch for cover. He suspected that German troops would be patrolling the area. As night fell, a heavy fog rolled in, blinding him to dangers that might be in his path. The approach of footsteps sent him into the cold, wet ditch. It was a slow progress he made that night, trudging along the side of the paved road, unsure of the darkness on either side.

When the thin light of morning bleached the black sky, he realized he was skirting the edge of the forest. He blessed the light of morning but was wary of being seen. For a moment he recalled a phrase he'd read somewhere — *naked to mine enemies.*

Looking for a place to hide that morning, he came into a village called Suzy. At the very edge of the place there were two farmhouses, one on either side of the road, each with a haystack beside it. Which to choose? The nearest one was on his right. He headed quietly for its high haystack, climbed to the top and burrowed his way in, falling asleep inside almost immediately.

I could hear a dog barking close by. I peeked out: the barking dog was trying, unsuccessfully, to climb the haystack.

After a little while, a farmer came out of the cottage to investigate the ruckus. He climbed up the stack and found my hiding place. I told him I was a Canadian on the run from the Germans. He said something like, "You are safe here, stay put. I'll be back after dark for you."

True to his word, he came at dusk. As we walked across the field to his house, I told him about choosing between the two cottages on either side of the road.

"You made the right choice," he said. "I have connections with the Underground. If you had chosen my neighbour's haystack, you would have been in the hands of the Gestapo by now. That man is a collaborator. He has turned in Allied men in the past."

Is that a coincidence, or is it one more example of the way good luck seemed to have dogged John's footsteps?

The two and a half weeks I spent at the farm were memorable for me. Mme. Potelle, the farmer's wife, used to make a special soup for me. It was great. I don't know what was in it but it was delicious. I can still remember the smell and taste of it even after forty-five years.

One of the odd things I still remember was that the farmer kept a herd of cows, and it was a daily event that customers would come to buy milk. A pregnant woman customer seemed to grow bigger before our eyes. We had a pool on the date and sex of the child. She delivered a healthy boy on the very day we were liberated, I later learned.

No, Lucky John didn't win the pool, but the coming of American engineers that day made up for it.

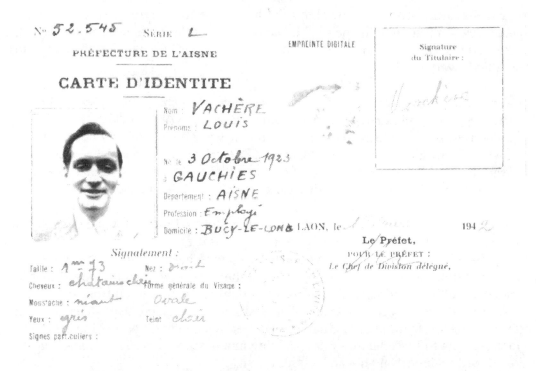

John Neal's 1942 fake identity card, dated March 15, 1942, in the name of Louis Vachère. Note the authentic-looking stamp of the local authority.

I remember that every week or so an elderly German soldier used to come to buy eggs and milk. I got talking to him, and he told me he was from Bavaria. I don't think he knew or cared who I was, because he was so worried about his own farm. He had no sons, only daughters. How were they getting all the chores done, and looking after the farm, while he was on occupation duty in France? This was his main concern.

One day, I was interviewed by members of the Resistance. They were concerned that Germans were infiltrating their ranks. I convinced them of my bona fides, and they arranged for my transfer along the line of safe houses. I got clothes belonging to the Potelles' son, who was in the Resistance, and they took my uniform and dog tags. The local leader and some of his people came a few days later. They took my picture, gave me an identity card with my new name on it and drove me through the woods to the little village of Bithancourt Marizelle.

Here I was put up at the home of a young couple. And to my great surprise and delight, I made contact with Bob Lindsay, the navigator on our Halifax. From the time we were shot down until that day, I had been separated from the crew and had no idea what had become of them. Able to vouch for each other, we were now totally accepted by the Resistance.

A week later, John was moved to the town of Chauny. Here he stayed with M. Daubercies, a justice of the peace. M. Daubercies and his wife displayed a formal, reserved manner that concealed a kindly, generous spirit. He was a stalwart friend of Allied evaders.

I remember just before the last flight, when we were shot down, I stepped on a rusty nail. I hadn't noticed it at the time, but all the walking I did in those first few days in France made the wound fester. It was now painful. My hosts were aware of my uncomfortable limp. Unsure of a local doctor who could be trusted, they looked around for some kind of medicine that might help. They came up with a bottle of Absorbine Jr., and that did the trick: it healed up nicely.

John stayed with the Daubercies' for about a month. Predictably, he once again lost his heart, this time to the girl next door, Josette.

As she tells it, when she was seventeen, living with her mother, father and sister, she went next door to Mme. Daubercie's kitchen and saw a young man sitting in the corner. "Madame said, 'You don't know him, do you? He fell from the sky.'"

When Josette realized he was an Allied airman, she burst into tears — partly from joy, and partly from fear. She had never seen a Canadian before. Joy won out. Josette came to see John every day, helping him pass the time. They played cards, joked and walked hand-in-hand in the town.

She took John to the local barber shop in the town square to have his long, scruffy hair cut. Swathed in a sheet-like bib while in the chair, John felt the barber lean over and whisper in his ear, "See that building across the road? That's Gestapo HQ!"

Josette Ponchaud in 1944.

Was John calm and still as the barber trimmed his hair, in full view of the Gestapo? His response to this question was a skeptical "Are you kidding?"

June 6, 1944, D-Day. Word had come from the Resistance that I was to be ready to leave in two days' time. The truck rounded up five or six of us, including Lindsay and our pilot Jack Kupislak, USAAF. We were taken to the village of Bethancour-en-Vaux, where we stayed with a family named Reyns, this time keeping discreetly indoors. After dark we walked around the farmyard to get a bit of air.

Originally I was supposed to start travelling to Plouha on the French coast to be taken off by submarine and returned to Britain, but of course the D-Day landings cancelled this plan.

As the weeks passed in that summer of 1944, we knew that Allied troops were getting closer and closer to our farmhouse. On September 1, at 10:00 A.M. a troop of American engineers arrived to liberate the area. Celebrations lasted for three days, the highlight for us being a gathering of thirty-three evading and escaped Allied airmen from the surrounding area.

Then began the waiting period while the confusion of advancing armies, hosts of displaced refugees, POWs, deserters, AWOLS and evaders of a dozen or so different nationalities was untangled. By the second week of September, John decided that waiting for the RCAF bureaucracy to get around to him was too much. He'd never seen Paris, so he decided to walk or hitchhike there. His luck almost ran out on this little outing. American Military Police stopped him on the road to check his ID. He had no official papers with him! The MPs threw him in the stockade with seventy-five German POWs until things could be sorted out.

When he was released, he resumed his trip to Paris, via Laon, where his odyssey had begun. From there he did make it to Paris to celebrate his liberation. He was given a tour of the city by a postman, had a series of odd encounters with the local populace, who were ecstatic seeing Allied servicemen in their midst. All too soon, he was transported back to Britain to face the usual debriefings and form-filling, and submit to a battery of medical exams.

The vagaries of wartime communications are often confusing, and sometimes so peculiar that one suspects a mischievous intelligence is fouling up the works.

> The day I was liberated was the day my mother heard from Ottawa that ''nothing has been heard of the aircraft or crew since takeoff . . . Flying Officer Neal's kit and personal effects have been collected and forwarded to the Central Depository . . . May I convey my sincere sympathy to you in your great loss.'' Not very comforting words, but good news was on the way.

John is certain that he is "the most lucky fella." Not without some modesty, he says, "I was lucky all my life." And he can recount an amazing number of instances, both before and after his service career, to prove his point. He even good-humouredly suggests, "Flying with me ensures your safety from accident, collision or other unfortunate events," and claims that this has held true from his earliest days in the air force to the present time.

In September 1943, doing "circuits and bumps" (take-offs and landings, round and round the airfield area) at Wellesbourne, the pilot headed in for the final landing of the exercise.

> Instead of sitting in my usual position beside the pilot, I was braced behind the main spar. Sure enough, the landing gear folded, the plane swung and we headed across the field. I can still hear Chester yelling at me to get out.

Then in December of that same year, over the Welsh highlands, the automatic pilot device began acting strangely.

> We found ourselves heading straight down. We were at 8,000 feet and the hills rose up to 4,000 feet. It looked like we were running out of sky in a hurry. The pilot struggled with the controls for what seemed like an eternity until we leveled off.

He is still not sure how close to the hills they came, but John is certain it was only inches.

A month later, coming back from a raid on Berlin, "even the German nightfighters and the flak couldn't do to us what we almost did to ourselves." Crossing the North Sea at sunrise, a radio message came through that their home base was fogged in — they were diverted to Coltishall which had a 400-foot ceiling. It was suggested that they head through the cloud cover over the sea until below the 400-foot ceiling.

Down, down, down, with me in the nose as extra eyes for the pilot. And with the down, down, down, I saw nothing, nothing, nothing. Until, there they were: white caps about two feet below my nose. 'Pull up, pull up,' I yelled. Eric, our pilot, must have yanked the stick as far back as it would go. I am certain, even today, that we literally bounced off the North Sea on that run!

There were other minor crises in training and on ops that contributed to John's conviction that good fortune walked beside him. Even on the Laon run in April of '44, "with a plane full of fire, a nightfighter on our tail and a load of bombs in the bays below me, I knew I was indestructible in the air."

Lucky John Neal.

CHAPTER SEVENTEEN

OUT THROUGH THE UKRAINE

Jack Nixon would not pretend to be an "evader," yet his experiences had many similarities to those of others who were shot down in enemy territory, avoided capture and got back to home base.

Nixon enlisted in Ottawa in September 1942. Following the usual training for aircrew, Jack was stationed in Quebec City, Toronto, Crumlin, where he earned his navigator's wing, and Halifax. He went overseas to the United Kingdom in March 1944.

RAF 192 Squadron was organized to fly on RCM (radio countermeasures) missions. These included carrying a normal payload of bombs and/or secret electronic devices and "window," strips of foil released over enemy territory to confuse enemy electronic equipment. The idea was to divert German ack-ack and nightfighters away from the main stream of bombers.

At Kinloss, in Scotland, Jack joined a mixed crew: five Canadians (the pilot, two gunners, a bomb aimer and the navigator), a WOP from Australia and the flight engineer, an Englishman. As well, a "special" operator for working the RCM equipment was assigned on each flight. Jack had been commissioned on graduation: by the spring of 1945 he was a flight lieutenant, and squadron navigator.

He began flying Whitleys, popularly known at Kinloss as flying coffins, then his crew was transferred to Yorkshire to convert to four-engined Halifax bombers. By March 1945, Nixon had completed approximately twenty-four operational flights, just half a dozen short of a "tour."

In the winter of 1944/5, plans were developed for a series of heavy bombing raids on German cities aimed at shattering German public morale and the industrial capacity of the Nazi war machine.

When Hitler invaded the Soviet Union on June 22, 1941, he expected the campaign in the east would be over in a matter of months. Indeed, in six weeks, his armies were within 190 miles of Moscow. However, the Russian climate came to the Soviets' aid. The winter of 1941/42 stopped the German advances, inflicting terrible casualties on the invaders. At the same time, the western allies came to the side of the Soviet Union, contributing equipment and other supplies that allowed them to hold out and build up an offensive. By the spring of '44 pressure on Hitler's eastern front had wiped out all the gains made in 1942.

Operation Thunderclap was organized at a time when the Russians in the east and the western allies were poised to invade Germany itself. On the night of February 13/14, 1945, Dresden was almost totally destroyed by firebombing as part of this offensive.

On the night of March 5/6, 1945, 760 aircraft — Lancasters, Halifaxes and Mosquitoes — set a course for Chemnitz, southwest of Dresden, near the border of Czechoslovakia.

In their briefing sessions the crews had been instructed to head for the Russian lines to the east if they had to bail out or make a crash landing. The advancing Soviet army had moved across Poland: by January 1945, they had reached the western sector of Poland invaded by Germany in 1939 — the action that had kicked off a world war.

Nixon's aircraft was to carry out diversionary tactics, using its RCM equipment to confuse enemy defenses. Fourteen Halifaxes, drawn from a great many squadrons, were lost on this raid.

Nixon's aircraft, "S for Sugar," took off from Foulsham in Norfolk. They were attacked by a German Junkers nightfighter while heading for the target.

The rear gunner reported to the pilot that a nightfighter was coming up on our tail. Evasive action was taken: we dived, rolled and climbed again to prevent the Junkers lining us up in his sights. At about 18,000 feet on the upward leg of that maneuver, the perspex nose of our aircraft broke when it clipped the tail of a Lancaster — we could feel a whoosh of very cold air. Everything went flying: all my charts and things were all over the place.

The bomb aimer, who was forward in the aircraft, wasn't wearing his gloves: his hands froze. I gave the pilot a course for the Russian lines and we flew for quite a while until we thought we'd crossed their lines. The pilot gave the bail-out order.

Nixon's diary and letters record his experiences that night:

This is quite an experience. I'd be enjoying it if I could let you all know I'm all right. I keep wondering if they have sent you that darned cable saying "missing on active service over enemy territory." I keep wondering where the rest of the boys are. I think they are all okay. Four of them jumped before I did and Nat was going to try to land old "S for Sugar" after we were all out.

We came down near Cracow, about eighteen kilometres from a small place called Kosy. The field I landed in was covered with snow. I couldn't see a thing. I just unhitched my parachute and started walking across the field where I saw a signpost printed in Russian.

My flying boots were awkward. I slipped and twisted my knee, which was quite painful. Then I saw a barn with a light on inside. From a window I could see a man working. I started towards the door to get in out of the cold, when a Russian uniformed soldier challenged me with a rifle. I couldn't understand the word, but I knew what he wanted and put my hands up fast enough. I flashed my British flag — part of my escape kit — at him. The response was cautious, and he took me into custody.

I've never been frisked so well in all my life. They went through everything I had on and with me. When they were satisfied I was okay, they gave me a nice hard bench to sleep on. In the morning they brought me some bread and butter and tea. The bread was very brown and had an awful acid taste to it. The tea you could see through and was terribly sweet.

At one point I was taken into Cracow, and I remember there was an old Polish lady who brought me some food. She indicated that she didn't like the Russians at all — not that I could understand her words, but with sign language and facial gestures I got the point. She was quite friendly, but then none of the people I came across were unfriendly. The Russians were suspicious, but not unfriendly. Perhaps it was because I was not armed. On a flying mission we never carried sidearms. They were issued to us, but I never carried them. I was treated quite well.

By this time I was having lots of visitors. Everyone came and had a look at me and my clothes and kit, and they would laugh and I would laugh and everyone was happy.

I was alone in a room when a soldier came and tried to talk to me, but I didn't understand him and he didn't understand me. Various ranks would try this out for a while. Some even tried to teach me a few words: *Pokop*, or *Poppo*, he'd say, and I'd repeat it; I think it meant colonel or something. And, of course, *Dasvydanya, Sposibo*, and so on. They got a doctor to look at my knee, so I was treated fairly well.

After bailing out, the crew came down at widely dispersed points. Nixon didn't encounter any of his crew for quite a while, and indeed for a week or so he didn't see any Canadians, Americans or British troops — until he had been moved into the Soviet Union. Their mid-upper gunner, Bill McCulloch of Toronto, had encountered some Russian troops when he came down. They shot him for some reason: perhaps they had shouted and he didn't reply, or some other mix-up. He was shot in both knees.

Jack remembers that as they moved him further into Soviet territory, he saw nothing of Russian defenses or sensitive installations along the way. He wasn't allowed to wander around on his own. Sometimes he was kept in a house or a barrack or at an airport in an isolated room. At one point they took him by jeep to the office of a Russian colonel.

They put on quite a spread on for me. Beautifully served food, and all kinds of liquor. Vodka for toasts, you know. The colonel would take a drink, and I'd take a sip. But that wasn't good enough: I had to put my head back and drink the vodka right down, Russian style. In no time at all I got sick and ruined the whole party. I was just a kid of twenty-two, not used to drinking a great deal, and couldn't take it.

The Russian soldiers are doing their best to make me comfortable and make the time pass quickly. They have tried to teach me a few words of Russian. One chap has been trying to read a newspaper to me. We try to get ideas across and sometimes do, but I'm afraid I must look pretty stupid at times. I have also had three chaps in with a squeeze-box to serenade me this evening. This afternoon I found a rubber ball and have been bouncing that against a wall to pass the time. I think I have just about run out of songs to sing. I try smoking my pipe: they brought me a dirty great package of tobacco. It looks more like green tea and is just as dry.

Jack was in friendly hands, but with very limited contact with people and things that were familiar. Food was very much on his mind. Many of his diary entries talk longingly of missing comforts: frequent baths, ripe tomatoes, mattresses free of bedbugs, and so on.

This place looks as if it was once a seminary. After breakfast I was taken for another bath and had my clothes fumigated. . . . I slept a few hours, then had some lunch. Jock Young, the special equipment man flying with us, arrived. That was really the best thing that has happened to me. Someone to talk to at last.

. . . The food here is terrible, and there isn't a great deal of it. We are hungry most of the time, so naturally the conversation is generally about what we used to eat and where we used to eat and what we'd like to eat.

After breakfast this morning we went into town and really had a gala day. Wherever we went, people flocked around us and a lot of them spoke English. We finally managed to get some money changed and, of course, our stomachs came first. Our guide took us to a restaurant where we had a very good meal. It started with vodka, then came bread with minced meat and white cheese. Then radishes and sauerkraut, potatoes, tenderloin, wine and rolls covered with salt and caraway seeds. We walked around and went to an English movie, *The Sign of the Cross*. It was pretty old, but we enjoyed it.

Nixon remembers seeing quite a few Russian soldiers but never a draft of troops or columns of marching men heading for the front. They were probably suspicious of him until they got to Odessa and confirmed he was not a spy.

On the journey into the Ukraine he was flown in a Russian transport plane via Lwow. He had met up with one of his crew from "S for Sugar" in a camp outside the town, along with about a dozen Americans.

We were assigned to a barrack room, and after we had settled in for a bit one of the Americans said: "Let's go to town, see what's doing." So we headed out and walked into Lwow. It was Easter Sunday. Walking down the main street we met a British major and a Canadian flight lieutenant coming towards us. Were we surprised! We stopped to talk. They were on some kind of mission having to do with supplies and equipment.

"We're staying at a hotel. There's lots of room there. Why don't you fellas move in with us," they suggested. Quick to agree, we rushed back to camp, picked up our gear, briskly marched back to the hotel, moved in and were just nicely getting settled when a couple of Russian trucks come roaring down the road. They stopped outside our hotel, banged up the stairs and took us unceremoniously back to the camp. We weren't exactly prisoners, but we were watched fairly carefully.

They were taken by plane — a DC-4 — to Kiev and then by train to Odessa on the Black Sea. Each given a Russian uniform — a tunic, very blousy pants and a fur hat — they were decked out like Soviet officers, but underneath they wore their own battledress. Then it was off to a reception centre with British and American troops.

Lady Spencer Churchill, Sir Winston's wife, was touring the Soviet Union on behalf of the British Red Cross, and she turned up in Odessa. While there, she came to see the British troops waiting for repatriation to Britain. Nixon, the senior British officer present, acted as her host.

About the first of May, they were loaded onto a Norwegian passenger ship. The food was very good and the crew friendly. The British troops and a number of French civilians left the Soviet Union via the Black Sea, the Dardanelles and the Mediterranean. On VE Day, May 8, they stopped in Naples. The troops were allowed ashore for a week or so, while the French civilians continued on board the Norwegian ship for passage to Marseilles. The vessel returned for them about a week later, then they sailed for Britain via Gibraltar. At Glasgow they disembarked.

By August 1945, Nixon was back home in Canada, to see his family, begin his studies for a medical career, and head westward to Vancouver for a new life.

ITALY

CHAPTER EIGHTEEN

A LONG WALK IN ITALY

Mussolini became Prime Minister of Italy in 1922. Over the next four years he gradually acquired dictatorial power for himself and his Fascist party. His sense of imperial destiny, of creating a modern Roman Empire, led him to invade Ethiopia in 1936, and when he became convinced that Hitler would win the war in Europe, he joined the fight. Initial Italian military success in North Africa was gradually superseded by defeat after defeat.

By 1943 the Allies had retaken all of North Africa, and on July 10, 1943, they invaded Sicily as a first step in their drive up the Italian peninsula. An Armistice was signed on September 8, 1943, by which time the Germans had occupied all of Italy north of a line from Ortona on the Adriatic to the mouth of the Garigliano River on the Tyrrhenian Sea.

At the time of the Armistice, the Italians held about 80,000 Allied prisoners, most of whom had been captured in Africa or had been shot down over the Mediterranean. In the military confusion after the armistice, many camp commanders simply opened their gates and let the prisoners move out.

Some of the prisoners joined local partisan bands that soon sprang up; a few hid to wait out the arrival of the advancing Allied armies, and many were recaptured by the Germans. In at least one prison camp, the Senior British Officer ordered the prisoners to remain in camp, on pain of court-martial, until German guards arrived. There is some evidence to suggest that this officer was acting on orders from Montgomery, the Allied Commander, who didn't want thousands of liberated prisoners wandering around blowing up bridges and creating havoc with the supply lines that he would need to support his advancing armies.

Travelling in Italy as an escaper was difficult. More than one-third of the country is mountainous, with many high ridges and longitudinal valleys. As was the case in northwest Europe, main roads were too dangerous for escapers to use, but in Italy the mountainous terrain made walking arduous even if there were mule tracks to follow. The Germans quickly exerted their control over the northern part of the country, and unlike northwest Europe, escape lines had not developed in which civilians were organized to help escapers and evaders make their way to freedom.

Yet there were thousands of Italians ready to help an escaped prisoner of war. Most of them were the rural poor: shepherds, old women, *contadini*, peasant farmers. They had no doubt what would happen to them if they were caught, but like their counterparts in northwest Europe, they were prepared to help where they could. They were also encouraged by Allied radio broadcasts that promised help after the war to those Italians who assisted Allied former prisoners. On the other hand, the Germans were prepared to hand out cash immediately for any prisoner turned in.

The quicker witted, tougher, luckier and more resolute of the prisoners who were freed got clean away. One of them was John Hall, a pilot from 38 Squadron RAF, Middle East. John's story is different from most of the others in this book. He was in the war from the beginning. He saw service in France during that short period in 1939–40 known as the phoney war. As the Germans drove west in the spring of '40, John's army co-op squadron saw action over France and Dunkirk and helped calibrate the anti-aircraft guns over London during the Battle of Britain. He also flew in operations in North Africa and was a prisoner of war in Italy when that country surrendered in September 1943. He was both an escaper and an evader, having walked out of one camp when Italy surrendered and escaped from another after the Germans had recaptured him near Subiaco, a few miles north of Cassino.

John had joined the Royal Air Force before the war. His squadron had been destined for posting to India, but then the war started. He describes those first few months in rather a laconic way:

> We were posted to France, near Lille, and when we were pushed out of there we flew back to Hawkinge on the southeast coast a few miles west of Dover. The squadron did many reconnaissance sorties over Dunkirk and got shot at by both sides. After that we went to the Cambridge aerodrome and did dawn and dusk patrols from west of Dover to the Humber. The Flying Training School Tiger Moths were fitted with bomb racks taking four twenty-five-pound bombs under each wing and we released them by wire. England was so short of aircraft that even training aircraft were being armed.

Some time after that, John trained to be a bomber pilot, and on completion of that training he took off for Gibraltar.

> We hit an electrical storm over the Bay of Biscay, which screwed up our navigation. Our radio was out and we couldn't take a star fix because of the cloud cover. We set course down the coast of Spain and three hours later the sun came up dead on our tail! So I flew east into the sun for three hours and a bit and the navigator figured we had hit the coast of North Africa, so we flew north along the coast outside the three-mile limit. The terrain was low with no mountains visible, which corresponds to a bit of Portugal south of Porto.
>
> We had been in the air for about eleven hours by this time, so I decided to put down on a beach. After we all got out, we set fire to the aircraft because we didn't know where in the hell we were. We discovered that we were in Portugal when we were picked up by the Portuguese police. The Portuguese Air Force contacted us and said that if we were ever in trouble again we should just fly to the nearest Portuguese airport and they would fill us up again and send us on our way. Our Intelligence thought this information invaluable. We were finally taken off by

a Portuguese boat to the three-mile limit somewhere south of Porto and transferred to a British contraband patrol boat, which took us to Gibraltar.

After being returned to Britain, Hall and his crew flew to Malta on September 3, 1941, to join 38 Squadron.

We were on Malta in the quiet time, thank God. The Germans were not yet operating against us and the Italians used to come over once in a while and drop their bombs in the sea about five miles out. In the three or four weeks we were there, one bomb hit the island.

From Malta, Hall flew to Shalufah, a base at the south end of the Suez Canal. The front line was then around Matruh, or about two hundred miles west of Cairo.

We used to take off from Shalufah and fly up to a desert base called 0-9 and from there to Benghazi, which meant a two-day trip to do one operation. On our third trip, on November 12, 1941, we were in this clapped-out Wellington, "M for Mother." My own aircraft was new, but it was on one of its regular inspections. We lost an engine somewhere near Benghazi and had to do a forced landing in a salt marsh near Gazala. We were captured and taken to Benghazi and then to Italy on an Italian cruiser.

We were placed in a transit camp near Brindisi. Two army officers, Lieutenants Cook and Payne, got out through the wire but were recaptured within five minutes because Payne was about six feet four and they don't have men that tall in southern Italy. The general in charge of the prison camp told Cook and Payne to show him the place where they got out. When they did so, they were shot on the spot; Payne was killed, but Cook survived. That was one Italian general whose name we put on the list.

From the transit camp Hall was taken to a camp at Montalbo, near Bologna, where he spent the next year and a bit. There were no successful escapes from that camp.

Many of the prisoners were British army types and permanent army officers who thought the sun shone out of their "fundamentals." They thought the air force crews were a bunch of dummies, but we used to have bridge and chess tournaments and we usually won the duplicate bridge. I won the chess handicap competition; I had given up two knights but I somehow managed to win.

The facilities at Montalbo were very poor and it was impossible to maintain proper hygiene. Food was also in very short supply, although, according to the Geneva Convention, prisoners were supposed to get the same rations as the guards.

We had a mess meeting one time that I recall took an hour to decide whether our ration of sugar should go on the porridge or in the porridge. There were a lot of Scotsmen in the camp and they didn't take sugar in their porridge. Many others wanted to put their ration of a teaspoon of sugar on their bread because there was nothing like jam or butter. And there were others who wanted to exercise their individual rights as a matter of principle to decide the fate of their sugar ration and do whatever the hell they liked with it. I don't remember what the final decision was, but I think it was for not putting the sugar in the porridge.

In early 1943 the whole camp was moved to Fontenelatto. On September 8 of that year the Italian government surrendered, and Italian guards in the camps were on the Allied side by that time. A hole was cut in the back of the wire fence and the prisoners were all marched out in good order from Fontenelatto.

We spent the first night in a dry irrigation ditch, then got the order to disperse because the Germans were looking for us. Some of us headed for La Spezia, where it was rumoured that the Allies had landed. To get there we had to walk up the Liri valley. We had the first warm bath in two years in that river. It had poured very heavily and September had been quite warm. Muddy water was pouring chest high down the valley. No soap or towel or anything — just water, muddy at that, but it was bloody wonderful. Just like kids, we were.

The escapers always split up into pairs at night to go to different farmhouses for food. No farm family could possibly feed more than one or two people.

Most of the farmers who were out working in their fields carried their daily rations in their pockets. One of them gave us a hunk of bread and a raw egg. We asked him what to do with the eggs and he showed us. He bit the top off one and ate it raw. So I learned to eat raw eggs and I have done it many times since, though not lately! Since then I learned that raw eggs are supposed to be indigestible.

Hall and two others made their way to a place about twenty miles north of Cassino.

There had been four of us at one point, but one army lieutenant had seen a nice-looking girl in one of the small villages and decided to stay, and we never saw him again. We were walking early one morning and asked a farmer for directions in order to avoid Cassino. He pointed to a mountain meadow and indicated that we should go that way. There was a farmhouse about a quarter of a mile away in the meadow, but the silly man didn't tell us that there were Germans there! We walked up to it and knocked on the door to ask for bread and something to drink. A German answered the door. We didn't exactly panic but he must have been suspicious. He pointed to a well and we wandered over to it as casually as we could and then on through the meadow. But we were soon surrounded by German soldiers. We were captured again.

Hall's next and last prison camp was at Fara-Sabina, near Rieti. It had been a prison camp for other ranks and was being changed from a prison camp to a field hospital.

There were no perimeter guards. The people who were doing the work were Italian peasant boys who had been conscripted for a couple of days or more. Three of us were sitting on some steps watching these men work. They were distributing beds from a storage area as part of this conversion to a field hospital. I said I was going to have a look, so I took off my jacket, put it on the step and walked across the road that divided two rows of huts, then went into the nearest hut and right to the other end of it. There was about a ten-foot drop. I jumped down, ran across the grass and clambered into a dry trench. I ran to the corner, climbed out and crawled under the first set of wire but couldn't get through the outer wire because the strands were too close together. So I climbed the steps of the sentry box, which was not occupied, got over the top and ran the quickest mile of my life.

When my adrenalin stopped flowing I asked a man whom I saw whether there were any other people around. He said there was a cave up in the hills with several British prisoners hiding in it. These men, two months after the Armistice, hadn't moved more than five miles from the camp. They were very snug and were getting food to cook in the cave, where the smoke was fairly well dispersed. I asked if any of them wanted to come with me but none did, so I started retracing my steps back towards Carsoli and Arsoli.

Apart from occasional help from a farmer, Hall had been on his own the whole time since he had escaped from Fara-Sabina. But now he was in trouble. A toe on his right foot had become infected, and it had become too painful to walk. He found a railwayman's cottage and this man took him to the village of Riofreddo and the D'Ortenzi family.

I stayed with the D'Ortenzis for about two months until my foot healed. They were peasants and just great people. They had wires coming into their house from a sort of barn with two beds in it. At night a bamboo pole with a hook and wire were used to short-circuit the meter. I shared this place with a Jewish gentleman who was hiding from the Fascists and the Germans. We would have supper brought to us by one of the D'Ortenzi family, while the rest of them entertained one or more Germans in their house. I guess this was the best way of allaying suspicion, but they were running the risk of being caught as collaborators.

A typical day began about 6:00 or 7:00 A.M. I walked across the yard to the water trough and washed my face and hands. Every other day I would take water back for a shave. The latrine trench had at least three holes and there was a canvas screen around it. One morning, while I was having my morning constitutional, the elder daughter of the house came round the screen and sat down beside me with a cheerful "*bongiorno.*"

Breakfast consisted of bread and milk with roasted wheat "coffee." The bread was excellent, the best in the world. It was made from stone-ground wheat into flat, round loaves baked on the ashes in a hemispherical oven. After baking, the ashes were brushed off and we ate the magnificent crust with gusto.

On one memorable day while with the D'Ortenzis we had a feast. They had a pig hidden way up a hill to prevent the Germans from "liberating it." The pig's litter had been weaned and it was very large. With one man on each leg (one of them was me), somebody plunged a long skewer into the pig's heart. The squealing for a few terrible minutes was horrible, but within an hour or so hams were hanging in the outhouse, the rest of the meat chopped fine, the guts cleaned and there were yards and yards of salami hanging from the rafters.

Dinners were often something called *polenta*. Its base was a corn porridge that Mama poured onto a scoured table. Then she ran a spoon around the edge to make a gutter. A vegetable-meat sauce was poured into the centre and little rivulets of it ran down into this gutter. The trick was to cut yourself a wedge down one of the gravy rivulets aiming your fork at a piece of meat at the centre. It all seemed so natural at the time; in retrospect it is hard to believe that it was enjoyable. (The most memorable *polenta* I ever had was served up in the chestnut forests of Tuscany by an ex-Paris model in a mod dress with high-heeled shoes. The chestnut *polenta* had a ghastly sweetish taste and was as indigestible as anything I have ever eaten.)

After eight weeks or so with the D'Ortenzis I was asked to move on because the Germans had started searching the houses for escaped prisoners.

Hall walked on alone. On one occasion he was infested by body lice.

I had been sleeping with some Italian soldiers who were on the run from the Germans. Body lice go for warmth, so at night every hour or so we had to roll over onto the other hip, then feel the lice making the migration from one hip to the other. With no change of clothing and our jackets and pants loaded with eggs, they all had to be burned and our bodies shaved when we finally got back to Naples.

Soon John found himself with an American bomber crew who had parachuted into the mountains after their plane was hit. Four of them were living quite happily in a hut. The exciting news that the Allies had landed at Anzio on January 22, 1944, motivated John and a new partner to get going again. Sonny Fassoulis, from Syracuse, New York, was a member of the bomber crew, and the two of them decided to walk over and try to get south of the beachhead. It took about a week to get across to the south of Anzio, following mule paths for most of the time. These paths were very narrow — about two mules wide — but they were safer than the roads. By the time they reached the coast the Allied beachhead had been fairly well established.

There were three things against us: there were a lot of Germans; there were minefields; and the Allies would shoot at us if they got a chance just as hard as the Germans would. We got south to Norma, which is on the escarpment looking down on what used to be called Littoria and is now called Latina. Quite often the artillery shells would reach high up this escarpment, and we had a grandstand view of the artillery duels, and on some occasions we even had ranging smoke shells land within a few hundred yards of us.

What with the close proximity of the fighting and the presence of several other soldiers and airmen on the loose, any one of whom could have been a German stool pigeon, Hall and Fassoulis decided to move on. They reached the town of Terracina at the south end of the Pontine Marsh and there met a wonderful lady with whom Hall is still in contact.

Amalia Legge had been evacuated from her home in Littoria and was living in a cottage near Terracina. She was the same age as John, 28, and unmarried at the time. The Pontine Marsh had been rather like parts of Holland, with gates and dykes, with the water pumped out to make extremely fertile land for agriculture.

The Germans had opened up the flood-control gates and there was a large flooded area when we arrived. Amalia got her nephew to steal a rowboat for us. It was a sea-going fishing boat they had found a few miles from the dyke. This nephew got five friends, and Sonny and I helped them carry it to the sea. It was an eighteen-foot clinker-built vessel, and, being water-logged, it weighed about a ton.

We carried it through vineyards and over the road on top of the dyke down to the sea about halfway between Monte Circeo and Terracina. It was exhausting, but the prospect of a sea voyage to freedom gave us lots of motivation. I had noticed that there were only two oars with the boat and wondered how all eight of us were going to propel this thing through the water. I soon discovered that the six Italian boys were not coming with us, so Sonny and I were on our own.

We started rowing. He was a navigator and I was a pilot so we figured we could set a proper course. Monte Circeo is a great rock about as big as Gibraltar sticking out of the sea. We lined that up with the North Star and nineteen hours later we got to an island of the Ponsa group — a distance of about thirty-five kilometres. Our asses were so sore we couldn't sit down for about three days. Sonny said it was a new way to earn a Purple Heart.

They had landed on the small island of Zannone. It was controlled by the British and right on the communication line between Naples and Anzio.

There were no Brits actually on the island when Sonny and I arrived. There was only a lighthouse keeper and a few other people and some wild pigs. The people from the main island used to come over and shoot the pigs sometimes. The island had no harbour, and no military value, really.

We gave the boat to the lighthouse keeper, whose gratitude for this undreamt-of gift resulted in a lavish meal complete with a white table cloth — something we hadn't seen in years. And so we had our first night of freedom.

John Hall returned to Britain in June 1944 and finished the war in a variety of postings in the air force. He had intended to go to Leeds University to study engineering but instead thought he should start earning a living. A few years later he brought his wife and three children and twenty dollars to Canada and settled first in Winnipeg.

I wanted to go to Winnipeg because that's where my navigator had come from. He had been killed in the war. His father found a house for us for a month. He picked us up and took us to the house and that was the last we ever saw of him. It was too painful for his wife to see us. He was a very nice fellow, and I'm certain he would have helped us more, but his wife couldn't stand it. Since they were good church people I couldn't understand their attitude. Despite that, Canada has been very kind to us.

John recently retired with his wife Peggy to Vancouver after many years of operating his own business. He is currently one of the few members of the Royal Air Forces Escaping Society, Canadian Branch, living in Vancouver.

Amalia Legge married a doctor after the war, but he died shortly after the birth of their daughter, Rita. John Hall found out that Amalia was destitute and he asked the Royal Air Forces Escaping Society representative in Rome to see that she got some help. The society bought her a sewing machine and, working as a dress-maker, Amalia raised Rita, paid off the mortgage on their house, and kept her home going. Rita and her second husband, Corrado, visited Canada in 1984 as guests of the Royal Air Forces Escaping Society, Canadian Branch.

CHAPTER NINETEEN

OUT OF THE SEA AND OVER THE ALPS

He's short and chunky. He's got a big grin that spreads across his face like the sun emerging from behind a cloud. They called him "Spanky," for Spanky McFarlane of "Our Gang" comedy fame.

He probably hadn't cared much for the nickname in the beginning, but eventually he got used to it. You couldn't look at him without being reminded of a chuckling, mischievous kid. You smiled instinctively when first you met him. You kept on smiling, and later, in solitude, you smiled in pleasant anticipation of a further meeting.

At the outbreak of war there was a rush of young men to join one of the services. Along with many of his age group, Gordon Reneau joined the Royal Canadian Air Force.

Why did he join up? Ask almost any veteran of that war and you are bound to get a variation or combination of the following:

- My buddy / brother / father / cousin was in the navy / army / air force.
- I wanted to get away / see something of Canada / see life / see the world.
- I wanted excitement, adventure / I didn't want to miss the big show.
- I've always wanted to fly / go to sea / fight.
- I hated what the Nazis / Fascists / Japs were doing.
- I was patriotic. I wanted to fight for my country.
- I was out of work and needed cash.

Like most Canadians, Reneau's reasons were a combination of most of the above. He was twenty-two years old when he showed up at the recruitment office in his hometown, Toronto. After pilot training in Canada, he was posted overseas to England in early 1942.

Courses as a torpedo pilot led to a posting to Coastal Command on Beauforts. He flew Beauforts from Bath to Egypt via Gibraltar. Early in 1943 he was posted to 43 Squadron RAF, at Ginaculis, North Africa, a Coastal Command ops squadron that took on anti-shipping sweeps and anti-submarine convoy escorting duties, then transferred to 47 Squadron.

The Beaufort, a four-man aircraft, carried a pilot, navigator, wireless operator and rear-turret gunner. In the late spring of 1943 the 47 Squadron Beauforts were tired, overused and in need of replacement. Operations were often cancelled as

Beaufighter pilot and plane: the intrepid pilot Gordon Reneau poses beside his Beaufighter in the desert in 1943.

aircraft returned to base reporting loss of power or instability of controls. Worn-out engines that failed on take-off caused a series of fatal crashes, costing the squadron at least three splendid crews.

On June 1 came the welcome news of conversion to Torpedo-carrying Beaufighters. After a short familiarization course from a canal-based aerodrome in Egypt, the squadron was dispatched in mid-June to Propville, south of Tunis.

Attacks were made on Axis shipping in the Mediterranean from the base near Tunis. The squadron kept an eye on supply lines between Italy, Sicily, Sardinia and Corsica. In 1943 Allied troops had invaded Sicily, and later the Italian mainland.

The Beaufighters carried one torpedo and four cannons; its two-man crew, pilot and navigator, flew with a fighter escort (a non-torpedo-carrying Beaufighter from their own squadron) on shipping strikes. The art of torpedo-launching required careful, concentrated handling. The fighter escort flew protective cover as the other crew launched the torpedoes. The pilot and navigator kept their minds on the launch and were grateful for the fighter cover.

Torpedoes had to be dropped from a carefully calculated height, as Reneau recalls:

> If the plane's nose was put down a few degrees, the torp would go in and dive. If it was dropped with the nose up, the torpedo would run flat and porpoise or transfer. You had to come up about sixty feet and fly dead straight and level at a controlled speed of about 210 kilometres an hour.

Right from the first operation at this new Tunis base, the squadron was successful. On the first day after settling in, Squadron Leader Lee-Evans took four aircraft out on a strike against a merchant vessel escorted by destroyers and sank the ship. The next day, June 23, I led a flight of three aircraft that successfully blew up a heavily escorted ammunition ship. There were some anxious moments with six enemy aircraft, but we managed to evade damage, although one of the crews was shot down on the run-in to the attack.

Another day I was flying in the second formation behind the squadron leader. They went whacking through a convoy and everybody missed. Stu Cowan, my tent-mate, was flying cover for me. As I came around, I went roaring through and then: "Oh my God, I've got a hangup: the torp's hung up!" So, in a moment of ridiculous bravado, I decided to go around again.

Thank God Cowan came with me. I was fortunate enough to be able to go in, level the plane off so I was flying low and straight. Cowan followed, firing his cannons to keep enemy heads down, and I was coming in like a lame duck. I fired my button and pulled my jettison switch at the same time! The torp went off and we got the ship amidships. By great good luck Tony Crawford, Cowan's navigator, had a hand-held camera and he got a picture of the hit.

For these and other successful sorties during June '43, Reneau was awarded a DFC on July 20.

Patrolling the Mediterranean on August 2, 1943, Reneau and his navigator were shot down. Earlier that day a reconnaissance report had come in detailing a sighting of a 10,000-ton freighter in the harbour at Cagliari, the largest city on the south coast of Sardinia. Lee-Evans led the first formation and Reneau took out the second: two torp planes and two fighters each. As Reneau's formation turned in to Cagliari the ship was smoking. There was a huge fire, billowing black smoke and the ship itself was listing at a precarious angle. They went charging in, then turned around to come out, shooting up anything they saw. Reneau was the last out. Looking out from his port side, he saw one of the squadron planes on fire. Pulling up alongside, he radioed the pilot, Snowy Kemp, to shoot off the ammo and jettison the torpedo to lighten the load. The squadron will get you home somehow.

Just then my navigator, Len Hutton, shouted, "Our starboard's on fire." Looking out the starboard side, I could see the engine covered in flames.

Follow the drill, I told myself: feather the prop, cut off all the fuel going to the starboard engine. But the prop wouldn't feather. I jettison my torp and fire off all the ammo. The fire just won't go out.

As I was heading for the water to ditch, I remembered that I had to jettison my cockpit cover. Len had jettisoned his. We were fortunate: the Beaufighter went into the drink easily. It hit hard, but then it slid in. I was thrown forward into the windscreen in spite of my safety belts. The water came roaring over the top and splashed my face. I scrambled out the top, holding on tightly to the little one-man emergency dinghy. We never had our parachutes on, we sat on them but didn't put the straps on. If any of the torpedo aircraft ditched in the sea, we might not have time to take the 'chutes off.

When I got out, I found that the aircraft dinghy, stored in the nacelle of the port engine, was there in the water, fully inflated, with Len sitting right in the middle of it, blood running down his face. This dinghy is designed to inflate as the aircraft hits the water. When we came down, Len had his feet braced on the ammo trays and his head and arms against the back of the plane, but he didn't have his safety straps on. When we hit, he lunged forward, caught his head on the edge of the bubble, catapulted out of the aircraft, did a somersault through the air and ended up sitting in the dinghy! He didn't even get wet!

I shouted to him, "Lenny, cut the rope." Using the dinghy knife he cut the rope that attaches the dinghy to the airframe. Our Beaufighter sank in fifteen seconds.

Lenny was still conscious but not quite with it: Reneau got out the Red Cross box, bandaged the deep cut in the navigator's forehead and surveyed the scene. He figured that they were about eight to ten miles out of Cagliari. When he looked up, one of the squadron's planes was right overhead, hanging around doing lazy eights but eventually flying home. To keep from drifting too far, too fast, Reneau tossed out the drogue. In the distance he saw an enemy flying boat. Later he found out that the flying boat picked up Kemp and his navigator. Then out came a couple of Italian fighters, who used them for target practice.

Thank God, those Italian pilots couldn't hit a barn door. They weren't even close.

Later in the day four Lightnings from a USAF squadron from North Africa arrived. They did lazy eights overhead for a couple of hours. It looked as if there might be a RAF flying boat coming to pick us up.

When night came, Reneau took a benzedrine pill to keep awake. Comforted by the hope of being picked up, they drifted all night. Len was still dopey. Next day, nothing happened. No rescue launch, no flying boat, no aircraft overhead. They drifted in the hot sun. Reneau had a handkerchief tied over his head to keep the sun away. But all the time they were moving closer and closer to shore. Finally, at last light, he cut the drogue. As midnight approached the dinghy moved right down to the same harbour they had shot up. They touched the slimy sea wall at low tide. Carefully, Reneau poked along it, until he could see a wide gap in the sea wall. He then realized that they had been drifting towards a submarine boom with mines attached to it. Luck had been with them again.

Cautiously, they drifted into shore at first light, and found themselves staring into the eyes of a very young, very nervous Italian soldier — pointing a gun at them.

We were prisoners. We were driven into Cagliari, and for some reason the car stopped in front of a church. A little boy of about ten or eleven spat on me. Without even thinking I just struck out in reaction. I wasn't being brave or anything. Immediately there were six guys after me. Fortunately a priest arrived. Later I learned that the city had been badly bombed by the Americans.

Year		Aircraft		Pilot, or	2nd Pilot, Pupil	Duty
Month	Date	Type	No.	1st Pilot	or Passenger	(Including Results and Remarks)
—		—	—	—	—	— Totals Brought Forward
July	13	Beaufighter	JM289	Self	Sgt Hutton	Strike – 6 A/c against 2MV, 2DR off east coast of ~~Italy~~ Sardinia. Attacked 2000 ton MV. 4 torp. Dil
					(See Back)	Not come off first run in. Made second run & hit MV. 9 miles S.P. All A/c returned J.R.
July	17	Beaufighter	LX780	Self	Sgt Hutton	Air Test and w/t Test.
July	18	Beaufighter	LX780	Self	Sgt Hutton	Testing Cannons – no stoppages
July	19	Beaufighter	JM322	Self		Air Test after main-plane change
July	20	Beaufighter	LX780	Self	Sgt Hutton	Strike – 8 A/c against convoy N. of Elba Is. Nothing sighted diverted to E. coast of Corsica
					(See Back)	and attacked 3 T.L.C.'0 carrying German flag. Blew bow off one with cannon fire. F/o Hunt ditched 5 mi. off W. coast Italy
July	20	Granted Immediate		Award	of	Distinguished
		Flying		Cross.		

OPS TOTAL. 105:05   28:55
COM TOTAL. 16:55

GRAND TOTAL [Cols. (1) to (10)]
539 Hrs   20 Mins.

Totals Carried Forward

Reneau's log book: the July 20, 1944, entry at bottom of the page recorded, in capitals, the true feelings of the moment.

After Reneau was shot down, there was the usual delay in informing his family. An official telegram was sent to his mother, and later the commanding officer of the squadron wrote to his parents to say that he had been shot down, but was seen alive.

We drove up to a little inland town called San Luiri — to a police station where there was a small transit prisoner-of-war camp. There we found the crew from an RAF Wellington torpedo aircraft and also Kemp and Fisher from 47 Squadron, the crew that had gone down just before I was attacked.

We were there about a week and a half, interrogated by both Germans and Italians. The Germans were trying to convince us that we'd be better in a German POW camp, but they were only after information about our aircraft and operations. They kept saying, "You must tell us where the rest of your crew is, and fill out these Red Cross cards."

The captured officers in the transit camp were fed from the local Italian army officers' mess; the other ranks' rations came from the local OR mess. The difference in the quality of food was so obvious that to be fair the rations were combined and shared by all the aircrew.

One fellow prisoner was a very strange chap: he was always plotting impossible escapes. When word came that the three POW officers would be transferred in a flying boat to the mainland, wild plans for escapes escalated. One idea was for us to overcome the crew, grab the Italian air force Marchetti and head for North Africa. Great heroics! When we got to the plane we learned that we would be flying in a flight of six aircraft with fighter cover. The Marchetti was full of German and Italian officers. We were seated with enemy officers separating the prisoners from each other. Those plans went out the window.

While waiting to board the aircraft, an Italian Red Cross worker, speaking quite good English, said to me:

"You are a Canadian, sir?"

"Sure."

"I would suggest you take your Canadian badges off. Leave your rank up if you like."

"Why should I do that?"

"Well, the Canadians in Sicily did not take prisoners; and Canadians are pretty greatly disliked here right now."

I was no hero. I took the badges off.

Arrival at Rome airport was the usual mess-up: there was no one to pick us up. We three officers were put in a small hut, until a *carabinieri* sergeant and driver eventually arrived in a station wagon. They were normal, outgoing, friendly Italians. The sergeant announced that he had been a tour guide before the war, and if we "gentlemen" would give him our word not to take off, he would show us a little bit of the Eternal City, on the way to our transit camp. That seemed fair.

He drove us around the tourist route. The Trevi Fountain, the Colosseum, the Forum, St. Peter's Square, and so on, all the time giving us his usual guide's speech, until we arrived at a villa, high on a hill overlooking the back of the Vatican. It was a centre for interrogating prisoners.

Among many English, Americans, Australians, and other odds and sods at the transit camp, there was one officer, named Richards, who claimed to be the Senior British Officer there. We were very suspicious of him: was he an enemy officer planted in our midst to gain information? We never found out.

We lived mainly on fried eggplant, apples and cheese, and we were constantly being interrogated. After about six or seven days they finally nailed me down.

"We know who you are! You are Flight-Lieutenant Reneau from 47 Squadron and you are flying Beaufighters out of Propville."

I don't know how they did it. Perhaps I was indiscreet, or perhaps they put it all together themselves. They told us we would soon be going off to a permanent prison camp. Accepting the clever thinking of an American paratroop sergeant, we decided to try to escape one night. We cut down all the blinds from the villa's windows, made a long, strong rope out of the cords, went out an upstairs window, down the wall and over the wire fence, heading for the Vatican backyard. We had watched the guards coming on duty late at night. Half the time, they would arrive about one o'clock half-soused, go into their huts and fall asleep. We waited till 2:00 A.M. and went out my window. The American paratrooper was first out. He got down the rope, about five or six feet, and I was just coming out the window when the guard awoke and spotted us. He didn't say halt, or stop, or anything; he just started shooting. We scrambled back up the rope, pulled it into our room underneath the mattress and feigned sleep.

Lieutenant Belli, the Italian officer in command, and the guard came rushing into our room, found us and the rope. We were thrown into solitary for a week. It was just a very foolish, badly planned and juvenile attempt at a jail break — not at all like the movies.

After a time, the three POW officers were sent to board a special train for Bologna, and a permanent prison camp. In the main station in Rome, people were quite kind, offering the prisoners food from their own small supplies. The guards kicked a bunch of people out of a compartment, loaded the prisoners in and off they went to Florence by train. Three or four hours in the station at Florence, then on to Bologna. They arrived late at night and again, as usual, had to wait for transport. After a while they slept on tables in the station dining room, and were woken at 6:00 A.M. No transportation again! Instead of the usual rough and ready trucks, they finally went to camp by taxi!

The prison was originally built as a convalescent hospital. First they were taken to a Royal Navy lieutenant commander, the Intelligence Officer for the camp, then to the Senior British Officer for interrogation.

Everyone wanted to know what conditions were like "out there." Did I notice anything while travelling up by train? What was the morale of the people? I didn't notice anything. I hadn't been that observant! I was a little ashamed I hadn't been keeping my eyes open for all this stuff, and I had few answers.

We picked up soap, a razor and a towel. As I was shaving I heard people coming down the corridor, saying, "It's gotta be him, it's gotta be the crazy little bugger, it has to be him." In walked a bunch of guys from my squadron who had been shot down earlier. They had heard that the little Canadian had come in and were there to welcome me. I was in that camp for about ten days.

On September 8 the Italians capitulated. Everyone was excited, thinking we were about to take off. The Senior British Officer:

"Nobody leaves. We are going to go out of here tomorrow morning, marching by fours to Rimini on the Adriatic coast, where we will be picked up by British destroyers."

I don't know where this story came from, but nobody was allowed to escape. That night, we were told to sleep in our clothes, with a little kit of personal things handy. Later, when the bugle sounded, we came roaring out of the huts and ran into the biggest bloody German *Feldwebell* I had ever seen in my life. And he's got the biggest bloody machine gun in his hand and he's shouting "*'Raus*, get going."

The German patrol put us between double rows of the prison-camp barbed wire. *Oh my God, I'm going to be part of an incident here.* Some wanted to attack, but there was a machine gun every twenty yards. *Holy Jesus!*

Corbin, who was from 47 Squadron and spoke quite good German, went up to the German captain in charge and said, "Why are you doing this?"

"Well, why do you think?"

"You aren't going to do anything ridiculous?"

"Of course not," he replied, "but I would have my reasons. My wife and my son and my daughter were killed in air raids on Essen. My mother and father are dead because your aircraft bombed Berlin. I have reasons. But I'm putting all of you between those barbed wires so I can count you and make sure all of the prisoners are accounted for."

Later we were allowed back to our quarters. Immediately everybody began to make escape plans. There was feverish activity, perhaps to make up for the disappointment of being caught asleep in the early hours of the morning. Men were burrowing into the ground, some into the attics, some into the drains, some were even sewing twigs onto their battledress so they could hide in a bush!

Two days after that, at 6:00 A.M. the order came: *Everybody out to the trucks. Everybody is going off to Germany.*

A couple of hours of frantic packing followed. They were allowed to take one blanket, one tin cup, a tin plate, a knife, fork, spoon and anything from their Red Cross food boxes that could be rolled into one blanket — cigarettes, soap and so on. No kit bags. They were piled into trucks, driven to Modena and loaded into freight cars — thirty or forty per car. Reneau got separated from his friends and was shoved in with a bunch of Aussies and one American. It was very, very cramped.

The car had been last used to transport celery and lettuce. It was very wet: the wooden floor was just rotting away. They folded up their blankets for cushions.

They sat in the railway yard that night. The next day the prison guards let out five men at a time to go to the toilet, then they travelled to Verona, where they were allowed off again.

Soon the townspeople of Verona found out that these prison trains were in the siding. When prisoners were allowed out to relieve themselves, the people brought apples, pears, bottles of water, and so on, to the prisoners.

These Italians were very brave and extraordinarily kind, but it did get a bit embarrassing. There would be a guy sitting there doing his business and someone would come along and give him an apple.

That night our train took off, heading towards the Brenner Pass. The Aussies in our car were quite clever. Using the knives that the Germans had allowed us to bring with us, they would hit one blade against the other to make a small saw. Down in the very corner of the car they cut a hole about two feet wide by eight or ten inches high. They slid the board out just far enough for it to be fitted back in place temporarily. Every time the Germans came around to count us there was someone sitting on the blanket covering up the hole.

That night I fell asleep, waking up about 3:00 A.M. The chaps opposite me who had cut the hole were gone! Their friend who had helped was still asleep. Those who wanted to escape had drawn numbers to determine the order of taking off. I was about number sixteen; those others who had worked on the hole were numbers one to six. I poked the sleeper next to me.

"Hey Mac, your buddies are gone." He was furious.

"Okay Canada, you wanna go?"

I said, "Sure, I'll go, but I've got a terrible number — sixteen."

He looked at me and said, "You are now number six and a half. Get the hell out that hole!"

I grabbed some cigarettes, some soap and some chocolate, put it in my battledress pockets and Mac pushed me out the hole, onto the buffers, then I helped him out, and reached around to the ladder on the side of the car.

"Okay Canada, you go off first, I'll go second. I'll stay still and you run back up the railway track to me."

We were fortunate that our car was the middle one of five. The Germans had set up a flatcar with machine-gun crews after every fifth freight car to watch for any escapers. It was a beautiful moonlit night and I thought, *Oh my God, I'm gonna be seen for sure.* But ours was a middle one, between the guns. We were hanging on the side and the train was going about 30 mph. After about a mile or so, near Trento, we began slowing up. It was time to go. I was about to jump when Mac grabbed me:

"Just a minute, we're going over a bridge." I waited, jumped and scrambled down the bank. Had I been seen? I was sure they couldn't have missed seeing me. Then the Aussie came off and was tripped by a wire strung up to operate a track switcher. The wire catapulted him right into a cornfield. It had cut right through his battle-dress but fortunately only scratched the skin on his chest. I was running up the bank when he whistled to me. We met up in the cornfield.

"Well, Canada," he says, "what'll we do?"

"I don't know about you, but first I'm going to relieve myself," or words to that effect.

The two new friends stayed in the cornfield till early morning. A little way ahead, they could see a small, isolated farmhouse. Mac had been a prisoner for over a year. Reneau had been in for about six weeks, but his Italian was much better than the Aussie's. They went up to the house, foolhardy as could be, and in halting Italian mumbled, *"Ufficiale Inglese, prigioniero di guerra, scappata"* (English officers, prisoners of war, got away"), and asked for help.

The farmers were delighted to trade civilian clothes for their battledress. Once dyed, with insignia and buttons cut off, the uniforms made nice warm clothing. Reneau and Mac were hustled into the basement, a bunch of potato sacks to shield them from prying eyes, while the clothes were exchanged.

Two pairs of tattered trousers, shirts made from several shirttails, along with their own sweaters worn under the shirts, tattered vests and boots completed the trans-formation. The hobnailed army boots were scuffed in mud and horse manure for a scruffy, well-used appearance. The farmer's family were very frightened.

"You must leave now and go down to the river," they said. "Look for a little French-man, he will help you."

Going through the cornfields, the escapers could see airplanes flying up and down. Later they learned that about eighteen men from the train had escaped in the area and were hiding in the cornfields as the planes tracked up and down the rows.

At the riverside, they found the little Frenchman. In halting high-school French, Reneau asked what they should do. The Frenchman told them they could not get out by way of the valley — it was full of German troops. Nor should they try to go south.

"My advice is to go across the river, through the mountains and head for Switzer-land. Wait until the village clock rings six o'cock. All the peasants will come out of the fields, cross the bridge and return to their homes. You follow them. Climb the high hills above the village and make for a small inn a few miles down the road. Go to the back door. The innkeeper will help you."

As we waited by the river for evening, we ran into another Australian escaper, Bob Donnan, who had been on our train. Shortly after the 6:00 P.M. bell, we three followed the workers to the river bridges. The fast-running current had five branches, with a short distance between each bridge.

We were almost to the last bridge when a small German truck came speeding towards us. It was too late to run for it. We could only hope to bluff it out. The truck pulled up across the bridge. A very big non-commissioned officer and an impeccably dressed German *hauptmann* got out.

The captain wore an immaculately pressed uniform, brightly polished boots and soft grey gloves. We were dirty, unshaven, wearing patched clothing and posing as simple farm labourers. Subjected to rapid demanding questions in German, all we could think to reply each time, in halting Italian, was "*Non capito, Kapitan.*"

After two or three exchanges in this unsatisfactory conversation, the captain's temper was becoming frayed. Mac had a brainwave: what to do to appear as simple Italian peasants?

Mac was standing right in front of the German officer. Without any warning and without the aid of a handkerchief, he performed a peasant-like function: placing his thumb against one nostril, he gave a mightly blow — right on to the German captain's polished boot!

There was a moment of breathless silence. The officer gazed first at his boot, then at the "simple Italian peasant," then back at his boot. Then, in utter disgust, he turned away.

I clapped Mac on the shoulder and shouted *Andiamo* (Let's go). Mac answered with a huge grin — "*Si, si, andiamo*", and we slouched leisurely away as the two Germans were left to their own devices.

All that day, we chortled over the daring inspiration of Mac's peasant ploy, and its well-deserved success. The look on the German captain's face has stayed with me from that day to this. I never have to search for an escape from despair. Recalling that incident fills me with a love of the inspired lunacy that can transcend logic and reason and outshine officious pride and pomposity.

So we continued on our way, across the bridge, up through the village, a mad scramble up the mountainous hill to a night huddled together under pine boughs.

In the early morning, we tramped down the road to the little inn that had been recommended by the Frenchman. To our delight we were given polenta and eggs. Then the innkeeper brought out an Italian tourist's hiking map of the whole area, detailing the mountain paths all the way up to Switzerland. He gave us paper to make tracings of the route. Then off we went.

On the second day on our journey, we had stopped by a little mountain path. Sitting there, we heard, "*Cooee, Cooee,*" the summoning cry of Australians in the outback. We got off the path. About twenty minutes later three guys came striding along in formation, almost at a quick march — left, right, left, right.

"Look at those silly buggers, they're marching!" We let them get by us, and then we started to *Cooee* — almost startling them out of their wits. They joined us and now we three have become six. Far too many — we've got a bloody delegation going here.

These three Australian officers told us they had talked to the same innkeeper who had helped us the morning before. They were interested in examining our traced map.

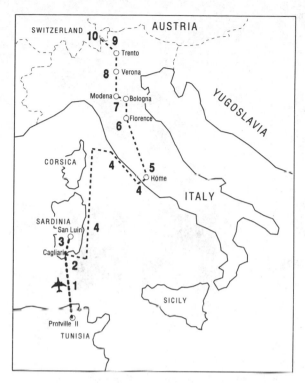

1. Dawn take off from Protville II, south of Tunis Attack MV in Harbour Cagliari - Sardinia
2. A/C damaged over harbour. Ditched B-10Mi to sea in Dinghy. Aug 2 & 3 , drifted back in to harbour. Early Aug. 4 POW of Italians
3. Transit POW camp - San Luiri - Sardinia. Aug. 4 - Aug. 20
4. Aug. 20. Flown in Italian transport to Rome - via Cagliari - Sardinia & Corsica coasts - Elba - W. coast Italy to Rome.
5. Aug. 20 - Sept 2. Interrogation villa in Rome overlooking Vatican back gardens
6. Sept. 2 -3 By rail Rome to Bologna POW camp - in POW camp Bolgona to Sept. 11
7,8. Sept. 11 - Moved by German army by truck to railroad yards at Modena. By goods cars at night via Verona and Trento.
9. Sept. 13. Early a m jumped to escape from POW train near Trento. Walked through mountain trails etc. to Bormio and Italian/Swiss border town Livigno.
10. Sept 20. Over mountain pass to Scanfs in Switzerland (near Samaden)

One of the new group was Flight Lieutenant Fred Eggleston. He had an MA from Melbourne University and could speak Italian and German. He became their leader and shepherd, doing all of the foraging for food and lodging as the six of them travelled through the country. To avoid drawing unwelcome attention to themselves, they had divided into three pairs, each travelling about a mile apart from the others.

The Italian peasants were helpful and generous to the evaders. On about the third day, they had been directed to a place run by a man who had made his money running booze across the Detroit River during the American Prohibition era in the twenties. He had retired back in Italy and built a mountain villa. He was the major-domo of the area, and a delightful rascal, who fed them and sent them on their way.

They headed northwest up the mountains, climbing all the way. At the top, they ran into an old crone and her daughter who were out foraging barbed wire — from the old Austrian-Italian border put up before World War I — to be sold for scrap.

It was now September/October 1943. Reneau wore boots, pants, a sweater, a shirt and a vest — none of the others had much more. Later he found a sack, cut a hole in it and made himself a poncho. That helped a bit. Atop the mountain they looked down the northern slope and saw a glacier dead ahead of them. The others decided to go around it. Macdonald and Reneau opted to cross it, slipping and slid-

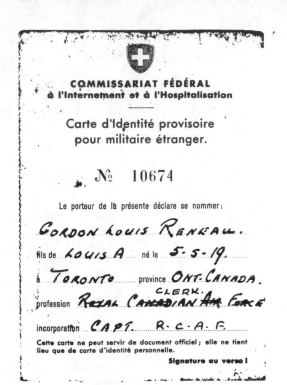

Swiss Identity Card and photograph: Gord Reneau's Swiss Identity Card issued to "interned foreign military personnel." The photograph portrays him in civilian dress, appropriate for his status and for the fact that his uniform had been traded off in Italy, allowing him to pass for a peasant labourer.

ing all the way. Fortunately it had a good deal of summer melt still on it, so there were no cracks or snow bridges to stop them. If they saw crevasses, they just kept away. It took about an hour and a half to get across; the others took four hours going around the safer terrain.

From then on we were passed along from family to family. We slept in their barns, and they would give us a little bit of polenta and maybe a bit of cheese. They were very, very poor, but that didn't stop them being generous. Fred kept a record of their names and locations, and after the war he visited the area, retraced our route and did his best to repay the peasants or their families for earlier generosity.

Two days before we got to Switzerland and came down off the mountain, we came to quite a splendid area called Santa Caterina. We went to an *auberga* there. It was owned by an extraordinarily kind lady and her husband, who was a colonel off in the mountains with the Partisans. She took us in and fed us a nice meal. She told us:

"You will sleep in one of the *auberga*'s beds, but I will get you up at 3:00 A.M. and you must be gone, because the Germans do a bed check every morning at 4:00 A.M. In their very methodical way, they do the bed check not at two, not at three, not at five, but always at four. You must be gone at three."

So at 3:00 A.M. we're up, and off we go. We are walking down this road at six in the morning when we notice people coming our way, cleanly dressed, looking at us strangely. A priest comes by on a bicycle. He stops, gets off and looks at us. We wonder, what's so strange? Suddenly it comes to us. It's Sunday morning. The locals are going to mass. We are dressed like peasants and going the other way. So we rush off the road and head for the shoulder of the mountain, keeping away from the churchgoers.

We continued up and down the mountain trails, walking for about fifteen hours continuously after leaving the *auberga*. Thank God we were young and fit.

Finally, we came to the top of a hill and looked down on Livorno, the last village before the Swiss border. Over the mountain from Livorno is Scanfs, down the line from Samaden and St. Moritz. The six of us were sitting there, about 6:00 P.M. Looking up on the far horizon we can see a couple of huts: that's the Swiss border. Do we try for it tonight or do we do it tomorrow? Rest and start out fresh? Or keep on, now that we are in sight of it? It's decision time.

Suddenly two Italian youths about seventeen come bounding along.

"*Oho, Ufficiali Inglesi.*"

Fred began to talk to them.

"You're English officers; you are escaping," they said. "We read all about you in the papers. The Germans are after you all over the place."

"We want to go to Switzerland."

"Yes. Well, we'll get you smuggled in."

Fred said, "We'll give you a letter to take to the British Legation and they will give you cash for helping us."

"How can we do that, we are smugglers," one of them said. "Have you anything to barter?"

We gave him a fountain pen and four watches — one wasn't even running, because it had been in the water. The two boys said, "Fine, we'll take this into the town. One of us will come back with some money and arrange to have you smuggled in. We'll be back soon."

An hour later, one of the boys came back up the hill. The young lad gave us fifteen hundred lire, which is nothing today, and said:

"At dark, go down to that hut on the edge of town, and about midnight, two men will come. They are smugglers. They will take you over the border. They are terrible men, they are awful men, they are greedy men, they are selfish men. Don't give them any money, ever, until you see the boundary rock that says *Svizzera* on one side and *Italia* on the other. Never give them any money until you see that rock."

We got down to the little hut and holed up in the hayloft. Much later these two scoundrels come in with a big flashing lantern.

"Hey, *Inglesi*, come on down."

Freddy tries to quieten them down.

"Oh no, we take you."

And they do, right through the middle of Livorno, at 1:00 A.M. — these two guys, one with a light, the other with a great big rifle on his shoulder, trailed by six escapers.

We said to them, "What do you want with the rifle?"

"We see *Tedeschi*, and *rat-tat-tat!*"

It was absurd. Right out of a Mack Sennett comedy. We start up the path and it rains, and then starts to snow. We pull into another mountain hut.

"Give us some money," they say. "We are wet, we get changed, we go down to town and get some vino, we get bread."

Fred says no.

They say, "Yes, we go tomorrow."

Fred says, "No, we go tonight or we don't go at all."

After a lot of palaver, the six of us start off again, heading in the general direction of Switzerland. Sure enough, the rascals come out and get ahead of us, leading us up through a narrow, steep shale path. Now the weather is turning nasty: we are in the middle of a real blizzard. Two or three hours later after a struggle to the top of the pass, we come to the rock marker, and it does say *Italia* on one side and *Svizzera* on the other. Right along from that rock is a low mountain hut for stranded climbers. We crawl in exhausted. Fred gives the smugglers the money and they are gone within a minute.

We wait until first light and then head off on the Swiss side of the marker, charging down the mountain into what we later learned was the National Park at Scanfs.

We come around a turn and there is a patrol of soldiers. Oh my God! It's a German patrol! We've somehow come back across the border into Italy.

I didn't realize then what I know now: the Swiss patrol uniform looks the same as the German *Wehrmacht* uniform. The only difference is that the Swiss have a cross on the button.

Fred says, "Leave this to me, leave it to me."

He tells them that we are escaping Italian soldiers that the Germans are going to send to the Eastern Front. The patrol officer nods, saying "Yes, yes, we must take you down to the internment camp."

Fred comes to us and whispers it's okay for the moment. We say, "Fred, for God's sake tell them who we are, or they'll intern us." He turns back to them and says in English, "I want to tell you that we are six British officers."

The patrol officer says, "Yes, yes, we know. Your Italian wasn't very good."

Fred says, "Well, what now?"

"I'm going to take you down into the town and get you something to eat," he replies.

With great relief, they got down into the town where the local people took up a collection, gave them clean clothes, something to eat, and put them up for the night. Then they were put in an internment camp near Samaden. There were Turks, Yugoslavs, Bulgars, Romanians, Italians and a lot of Brits at the camp — 150 evaders, escapers and internees housed in a big old school.

The British Consul from St. Moritz came to the Interrogation Camp and arranged to have them sent to Wil St. Gallin, where they were immediately quarantined with other British officers just in from Italy. They stayed at the Bahnhof hotel right by the railway station for about two weeks, forbidden to leave the town.

Once safely into friendly territory, Spanky cabled this message to his uncle in London, England: *Bursting with health during strenuous times*. Put yourself in the place of the family reading this. There had been no direct word from the boy for three months; then this enigmatic message. What does it mean?

Then the evaders were taken by train to Bern to meet the people at the British Legation, where they were given some money, outfitted in civilian clothes, then sent off to Arosa.

In Arosa all air force evaders and escapers were billeted in a small hotel. The Legation arranged and paid for daily lodging and meals. A portion of their pay and allowances was forwarded to them every two weeks. During the fall and winter their numbers increased as more escapers came in.

Reneau's group was there for six months until April, in the charge of a Swiss ski instructor. The Legation was concerned to ensure that everyone kept fit.

> I learned how to ski and travelled around the country playing hockey. They thought all Canadians were Charlie Conachers or Gordie Drillons, but most times I played on the second team. However, five of us ended up getting our Gold Test in skiing.
>
> We got moved down to Montreux on Lac Leman for the summer and stayed there from April until October.

Then the Swiss began to get really tough. They lost the ski instructor, replaced by an officious semi-retired colonel. He did bed counts!

During this time the Germans were being pushed back from southern France. Some of the RAF evaders began to bail out of Switzerland. Even though they were ordered not to, on threat of court-martial, they took off on their own, crossing into France. Reneau and his buddies found out later they got away with it — some all the way to England via Gibraltar.

Late in October the British Legation decided to send the rest of the evaders out of Switzerland, under strict controls. They were taken by train from Geneva to Annecy, in France, where the railroad line had been blown up. They went on foot into Annecy, where they met up with the Maquis, who took care of them that night. The next morning, they met with an advanced Allied patrol in an American truck, commanded by a British major, who took five of them into Lyon, where they were put up at a big hotel. It had been taken over by the Americans and was run by a top sergeant who in civilian life had managed a New York hotel.

We were treated as if we were heroes — identified, as far as the Americans were concerned, as escapees from prisoner-of-war camps, who had made their way from a German *Stalag* via Switzerland to France. The Americans were sure we were all Battle of Britain pilots. They were extraordinarily generous to us. The top sergeant gave us the bridal suite, booze, cigarettes and even money if we wanted to go out on the town.

Next morning five of us decide to head for the airport. Perhaps we could get a lift back to Britain!

There were never-ending flights of USAF transport aircraft landing and taking off. Pilots in Transport Command had an immense freedom to pick up and carry army loads all over the place, without much supervision. We came across a lieutenant who had been flying out of Algeria. His home base was Croydon, just outside of London.

"Well, why don't we go to London?"

Eventually we convinced him to take us but he didn't have any maps.

"Never mind, we're all familiar with the route; we'll navigate you there." It was just bravado, but it convinced him.

So off we went. He detoured around Paris: the weather was clear so there were no problems seeing our way. From the channel crossing, he knew his way to Croydon. When we got there we were immediately taken to be debriefed by RAF Intelligence.

We weren't allowed to fly ops again. The RCAF admin officer said, "You will go back to Canada immediately," but I said, "Wait a minute, I've got a medal to pick up."

"Fine, you'll get it from the Governor General or in the mail." I wanted none of that.

"I'd sure like to get it from the King."

"You can't do that. It takes four to six weeks for an investiture."

"I'll wait."

So I went on leave again. I'd been on the loose for over a year in Switzerland, and here I had to go on leave again.

Finally I got the royal command to appear before the King. I was allowed to bring two guests. I took my stepfather's brother and his wife from Hounslow with me. They were immensely proud to be in Buckingham Palace, in the presence of the King, to watch the ceremony.

All medal recipients were ushered into an ante-room. We were arranged by status — that is the most prestigious awards first and then the rest in order of precedence. Within each award grouping, we were arranged alphabetically, the traditional service way. The VCs came first; then the George Crosses, George Medals, the DSOs and so on. An Admiral of the Fleet with gold braid up to his elbow called your name. You go up a ramp to meet His Majesty. You had previously been warned *not* to shake his hand.

My moment arrived; Flight Lieutenant Gordon Reneau, Royal Canadian Air Force. When I stepped up, an aide handed my medal to the King. His Majesty turned it over and read the inscription — 1943. (This is November 1944.)

"My, my," he said. "You've been a while coming to us."

"I say, "Yes, sir."

"Strenuous times," he says. "Delighted to have you with us."

I go down the ramp and into an ante-room. A hand comes out, whips off the medal, slaps it into a satin-lined box, and all of a sudden I'm outside, clutching on to the box with my medal in it. They'd pushed me out a side door. And that was it.

It was great stuff.

Reneau doesn't make any claims of derring-do or great heroism concerning his wartime experiences. The overall impression one has when meeting him is of a happy, friendly man, contented with what life served up to him, and with a personal estimate of his own achievements that are neither modest nor immodest. Of his wartime experiences, he says only: "Guess I was just a guy who had more than his share of luck."

CHAPTER TWENTY

THE PATRICK BOYS

There were five of them, and they all joined the RCAF!

The Patrick family had moved from Saint John, New Brunswick, to Connecticut, USA, in 1927. The nervous maritime economy since the earliest colonial times had motivated emigration from Canada to New England. The outbreak of war in 1939 brought a temporary reverse to the traditional flow as thousands of United States residents swarmed to Canada to join up. The Patrick boys, one by one, made the trip, joined up, trained for aircrew, got their wings, and received His Majesty's commission as officers in the Royal Canadian Air Force.

As one of the Patrick boys' wives recalled nearly fifty years later: *"Mother Patrick was so proud of her boys."*

Robinson, the oldest, retired from the air force in 1958, with the rank of squadron leader. Roland had signed up before the war began, in August of 1939. He was Commanding Officer at No. 5 Radar School in Clinton, Ontario, with the rank of group captain. His work entailed frequent trips to the United Kingdom to meet and work with Sir Robert Watson Watt, the inventor of radar. For his contributions to the war effort, he was awarded the OBE by King George VI, and the Legion of Merit by the US government. Murray joined 117 Squadron of the RCAF on September 14, 1939. He was commissioned as a wireless air gunner and served as an instructor.

Edmond and Keith have the distinction of being the only brother escaper/evaders of any Allied air force during World War II. Their stories run parallel in that they both came down in enemy-held territory in trying circumstances, were discovered by the enemy, were taken prisoner and were helped by patriots when they escaped. But their experiences differed sufficiently to make each story fascinating in its own right. The fact that they had somewhat similar experiences is only incidental. It may be, however, that both survived because of something they shared either in upbringing or inheritance; something that allowed them to hang on in tough times, and never give up.

Mother Patrick — like all mothers of serving Canadians — felt pride, hope and fear every moment she thought of "her boys."

Edmond Patrick

I joined the air force in Moncton, on October 10, 1940, went from Manning Pool to guard duty in Brantford. I had been advised I was probably too old, at twenty-eight, for aircrew, so I expected a posting to a stores or equipment department. But service life was full of the unexplainable: my first posting was for pilot training.

I was sent to Windsor Mills, Quebec. The others in my courses were just kids out of high school. I found it very difficult to keep up but managed somehow to survive. I received my wings on July 1, 1941. I was too old to go overseas, so they explained I would become an instructor. Three days later I got married, and was immediately told to report to Halifax for an overseas posting. I guess they were having such heavy losses that they needed pilots — even of my age.

We embarked on the *Ascania* — an armed merchant ship that had eight-inch guns mounted on the deck, part of a very large convoy. Almost at the British coast a Sunderland flying boat came out, soon followed by units of the Royal Navy. We were disappointed to see our ship turn around and apparently head back towards Canada, but eventually we dropped anchor off Iceland.

We were put up in an RAF transit camp, where conditions were quite primitive: we washed and shaved in the river; the food was terrible; we slept on the floor and generally felt miserable. Luckily the US Marines had a station there and provided us with fresh-baked bread, jam and so on. The only thing I did like about Iceland was going up to Alefoss to swim in the hot springs. Reykjavik was out of bounds. The reason? Apparently Canadians who went over just before us didn't know how to behave when they saw mixed nude bathing there!

In February 1942, Ed was posted to a Ferry Command squadron flying Wellingtons to the Middle East for the buildup to the Battle of El Alamein. On March 4, he landed a brand-new Wellington in Malta, in the middle of an air raid. German bombers attacked, knocking out newly landed planes, including the one Ed had piloted, and badly damaged the runways. This was not an unusual event: the Germans attacked the Lucca airport daily. Yet daily, runway craters were filled in. Between enemy attacks, Lucca was operational on an *ad hoc* basis. Ed Patrick was grounded in Malta until the twenty-eighth, taking on all sorts of tasks as a duty pilot and crater filler, until he got out on a flight to Egypt.

Two days later, we were flown in a C47 by the USAAF to Lagos, Nigeria, stopping off at Khartoum and all the places in Africa I read about as a boy. Then, on April 23, 1942, we embarked on the SS *Cuba* arriving in the UK about a month later. On June 4, 1942, 99 Squadron was transferred to India, I had received my commission and flew as second dickey, first to Gibraltar. We had a bad landing: coming in too close to the rock, we were flipped over on our wingtip. Everything went flying in the aircraft, but we were all okay.

We moved on, flying nonstop to Cairo. It took us nineteen hours in the air: we stayed awake with the help of caffeine tablets. I was very sick in the air and on landing was taken to the RAF hospital in Cairo. I had a busted appendix and was operated on while my crew was sent on to India. I convalesced in Jerusalem and Port Said.

On August 6, 1942, Ed was posted to Aguir, Palestine, where training in desert flying continued. Here he received his certification as first pilot. In October Ed

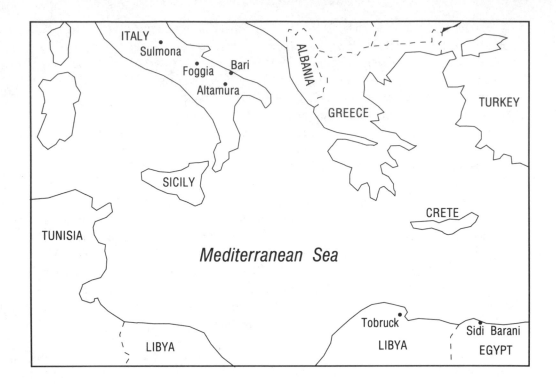

managed to get transferred to 108 Squadron in Egypt, where his brother Keith was serving. Air force policy frowned on brothers flying together on the same squadron, but in this instance it was overlooked.

He was crewed up, and sent out in the desert on his very first flight. Keith, flying as WAG, happened to be working a flight at the same time and picked up a distress call from Ed's plane. The message was passed on to Keith's pilot, the squadron CO.

"Well Patrick," the CO said, "what do you want to do — search for your brother or do what we were supposed to do?" Now, there's a moral dilemma!

Ed's Interrogation Report, filed when he got back to Britain, describes the events that followed:

> We left landing ground #236 outside CAIRO, at 2130 hrs. on 19 Oct. 1942, in a Wellington aircraft. Our target was TOBRUK. At 2350 hrs. the starboard motor seized up completely, there appeared to be an oil leak. Bombs were released, and flares, etc. jettisoned. We crash-landed successfully, no one being hurt, although the back of the aircraft was broken. It was then 0030 hrs. 20 Oct., and our position was about 75 miles S. of SIDI BARANI . . .
>
> We stayed by the aircraft until 1700 hours. Then, after having painted a direction arrow on the wings, we set out, marching East [toward a large water well].

We carried a 5 gallon water tank and five water bottles. We walked until dusk on 26 Oct. by which time our water had given out. I had been very ill after the first day. I had only very recently recovered from two operations and also had had a bout of dysentery. I advised the other five to go and leave me.

I eventually made my way to the road, which was, I think, about I mile away. There I 'passed out' behind a pile of stones. This was near the QUATTARA DEPRESSION.

This matter-of-fact description narrated a year after the event hardly gives a clue to the seriousness of his plight. Pilot Officer Edmond Rupert Patrick, RCAF, 108 Squadron MEF, RAF, as the Interrogation Report styles him, had crashed, walked for six hot days and slept for six cold nights in the desert. Out of water, unable to keep up with the rest of the younger crew, he urged them to leave him there. The crew recognized the plight they were in and had little option but to go, leaving Edmond.

Before the crew set out on its easterly walk to Allied lines, it prepared the aircraft according to pre-planned instructions. The IFF (Identification Friend or Foe) device was blown up, but the rest of the plane was left intact. Using a gallon of yellow paint and a paint brush provided for the purpose, they painted a huge yellow arrow on the wing pointing in the direction they were walking for any search aircraft flying overhead. It was usual for downed aicraft to be left intact, so that LRDG (Long Range Detection Group) could salvage oil, gas and parts while operating behind enemy lines.

Moving at his own pace, Ed made it to the shade of a rock in a desert depression, passed out, came to, and waited till his strength returned or the enemy or nature decided his fate.

"We had noted the location of a lake on our maps and were heading in that direction. Later we learned that it had been salted by the retreating British."

Meanwhile, trekking through the sand, the other members of the crew were picked up by a patrol of Italian guards driving a truck. The crew persuaded them to go back to get Patrick. They found him and he, too, was taken prisoner rather than left to die in the desert. He remembers nothing of that trip in the Italian truck: he woke up in the medical tent of the Italian encampment, with two doctors working on him. In that particular theatre of operations, all aircrew wore big sidearms, while Italian sidearms were the little Berettas. The doctors, amused at his huge gun, called him "Buffalo Bill." After a few days of very good care, he was sent back to join the rest of the crew in the POW tent.

We were then taken to Mersa Matruh and turned over to Rommel's Afrika Corps. I was interrogated by a German officer who spoke better English than I did. He had gone to Cambridge and respected the fact that I was an officer. After asking questions beyond the ''name, rank and serial number,'' he accepted my refusal to answer, then said, ''I am going to punish you.''

"You can't do that. It's against the Geneva Convention."

"You don't understand," he said smiling. "I'm going to punish you by not sending you back to the Fatherland." At this, we both smiled.

"Sir, that suits me fine. I don't think I could get out of Germany, but I will get out of Italy."

He smiled and said, "Well, I hope you do. For you the war is over."

On November 4 they were flown to Lecci on a three-engined Savoie aircraft of the Italian Air Force, with a large group of Allied POWs. Ed was the only pilot in the group. Some of the Australians asked him if he could fly the Savoie. His reply was that he'd fly it if they could overpower the Italians, but the odds were against them. Italian guards separated each row of seats, and the plane's crew were locked away inside their own cabin.

I'll never forget marching from the train that took us to the disinfection camp at Bari. The young people on the streets were spitting at us and the old people were crying. I thought to myself, well, that balances the ledger.

Ed came down with jaundice and on New Year's Eve 1942, he was sent in a cattle car to a hospital in Altamura. All the way Ed was battling with an Italian soldier threatening to shoot him if he didn't give up his shoes. After a month at the hospital, he was sent back to Bari, then on March 4, 1943, he was sent to the prison camp at Sulmona, where he came across other Canadians, including evader Ray Sherk.

Food was the big problem at Sulmona. They would not have survived without the Red Cross parcels that reached the camp. Italy was just about at the end of its tether at this point in the war: they could barely feed their own troops and people, so the POWs were on short rations.

The next hurdle for a POW was trying to hold on to his sanity. Patrick had some drawing skills: he copied out a book on navigation, illustrated with his own diagrams. He drew caricatures of all sorts of people, including many of the guards and fellow inmates. He made a desk out of Red Cross packing cases. Keeping busy was the best cure for boredom.

On September 12, 1943, a massive break from the camp was made. Once out, Ed was sent to Font D'Amore to free POWs in the town jail. They moved them to the bottom of a hill, left them with instructions to stay there while a group reconnoitered the area, returned to where the newly freed prisoners had been left, and they were gone. To this day, he doesn't know what happened to them.

It was inevitable that German troops would come after the escapers. They shot up the undergrowth, searched the area thoroughly, shouted coaxing messages — "Come back, you will be treated well." Escapers gathered, then broke up into pairs to avoid appearing conspicuous. Ed teamed up with Flight Lieutenant Middlemass (now of Edmonton) and decided to head south. Looking for help from local farmers, especially a little food, and a roof over their heads, they were careful to avoid raising suspicions.

A group of Canadian POWs in Sulmona, Italy, in 1943. Ed is the dapper pilot, rear row, second from the right.

At one point we met up with a British agent, who called himself ''Peter,'' operating behind the German lines. I didn't trust him. You don't trust anybody in that situation. He told us where our troops would be and which direction to head. He had a little cage with pigeons in it. I didn't think they could be using them in World War II.

Later, Ed discovered that indeed Peter *was* a British agent, in fact one of the best in the area.

We were often put up in haylofts. One time we were so tired, we literally fell asleep when we hit the hay. I was always a very light sleeper. I awoke to hear the barn door being locked. A few minutes later I could hear a donkey moving away from the farmyard. I put two and two together, deciding we were going to be turned in. I woke Middlemass, we checked the door, found it was locked as I had suspected, so we broke open the barn door and beat a hasty retreat. I often wonder what happened. If that fellow brought back some Germans and we were gone, what would have happened to him?

Patrick's Interrogation Report, records:

We headed over the mountains, and met F/Lt. Chappel at a shepherd's hut, where we purchased a sheep. We all had a good meal. I stayed in the mountains nine days, obtaining food from woodcutters, etc. The Germans were in the valley searching for evaders, but the local peasants tipped us off when to hide.

We split up into parties; myself, five officers, and one O.R., were guided down to SANVITTORINO in the vicinity of CARAMANICA on 21 Sept. 1943. We stayed there 18 days, as none of us were in very good shape. We were well looked after in this village — in direct contravention of German orders.

Once outside the prison camp, heading south, the men on the run found that many Italian civilians were willing to offer help. In San Vittorino, Ed found shelter with Aguilino Orsini and his family. The whole village worked to protect the evaders, knowing how serious the risks were if their activities were discovered. They made a hiding place in a woodpile — fortunately the Germans never did find them.

They had a central bake oven, where each week a different family baked bread for all the village. The Orsinis shared what little they had with Ed. After the war the family eventually emigrated to Melbourne, Australia. Ed has kept in touch ever since.

On October 9 they set out from San Vittorino heading towards the columns of Allied troops pushing northwards. They found it heavy going in areas where German troops were blocking Allied advances every step of the way.

Patrick's group kept changing as they picked up evaders here and there. Fearful of the group's becoming too big and too noticeable, they kept splitting up, then the group would grow again, over the tense days of October.

The Orsinis were the only helpers whose names I knew. Mick and I had a helper who took a group across at the end, but I never knew his name.

On the night of October 21, together with two American evaders, Sergeant Robert Williams of the US Army, and Sergeant Albert S. Romera, a wireless operator downed in a USAAF Liberator, we were guided across the Tringo River and around Salciata across the main road, avoiding a sentry post. We put up during the day about three kilometres from St. Angelo. That night we cautiously headed south and ran into three Italians who had escaped from France and one old man who was crossing the river to get some salt.

We had already crossed two rivers and two German lines. At 3:30 on the morning of October 22, 1943, we crossed the Bifferno River by bridge, with no one in sight. At 5:00 P.M. we came across two soldiers who we figured were British. They turned out to be "vandoos" from the Royal Canadian 22nd Regiment. We were told afterwards that their motto was *Shoot first and talk later.*

Out came their automatics. I thought to myself, "My God, not after all this." Fortunately, they didn't shoot. We were marched back to HQ. An officer took charge. When I saw pictures later, I thought it was Colonel Triquet, who was awarded the VC, but I never did find out if this was the case. First we were given a meal: canned meat and vegetables and real tea. It was a banquet!

I had taken notes of where we were going on our trip south. We were in between two batteries of eighty-eight-millimetre cannons. When I mentioned this to the Intelligence officer, he said, "Oh my God! They've been playing hell with us. You'll get the MC for this." I said, "I don't want the MC. I just want to go home."

He *did* get home. They went by train to the southern tip of Italy, passing near RAF Foggia, recently taken over from the Italians. Conversation between Patrick and Middlemass covered the bureaucratic peculiarities of service life. Here they were, headed for Algiers by train, while the RAF was right there in front of them. Needless to say, they got to the adjutant, told their story, then repeated it to the commanding officer who had a celebration in the mess that night for them.

The next day I went to the adjutant and said, "Sir, I want to go home. I left my bride of two weeks back in Canada two years ago. But first I'd like to go back to Cairo to pick up my kit."

It was all arranged. The CO gave me first priority on an aircraft from Foggia to Cairo, then to the UK. We left Foggia on October 28, in a DC-3 of 267 Squadron, stopping at Catania in Sicily. On October 30 I boarded a Liberator from Cairo to Gibraltar then on to Portreath, UK. I cabled home, letting them know I was well. I was granted a month's leave and came back on the *Queen Mary* to New York. On December 2, 1943, I arrived in Toronto, where I was met by my wife, Mary.

Now suffering from tuberculosis, he spent most of 1944 in hospital in Muskoka. But he did get home. No, he didn't get the MC, but Edmond Rupert Patrick *was* mentioned in dispatches, of which he is very proud.

Keith Patrick

As a Canadian living in the States I was always a royalist. I was working for the American News Company in the distribution department when war broke out. The manager happened to be a real nasty type, a great twister of the British lion's tail. As news from Britain was getting worse and worse, he took great pleasure in waving the headlines in front of my face, knowing I was a Canadian.

In January 1940, when things had sunk to a low ebb, the manager made a nasty remark about the RAF. I was fed up. I told him what he could do with his paper and quit. I said, "I'm going to go over there and join those boys."

That night I was on the bus to Saint John, New Brunswick, to join up.

Keith was one of many young men — he was twenty-one years old at the time — crossing the border in those days to join the RCAF. Moved by the plight of his countrymen, he was determined to demonstrate the strength of his convictions through personal action. From Saint John he trudged out to Millidgeville airport, filled out the forms, then on to Moncton for more forms. Disappointingly, they told him to go home to await his call up. On July 1 he was ordered to Manning Depot in Toronto, then to guard duty at 119th Bomber Squadron in Yarmouth. It was there that he had his first experience in an aircraft.

Doing guard duty meant you had to be ready to be inspected by an officer at any moment. I had worked my head off shining my boots and buttons. The Commanding Officer walked down, looked me over and said: "They're clean, but they're not polished." I could have killed him.

A few days later I was on duty at the main gate. I had never drawn that duty before. I was told how to recognize the CO's car by the little pennant on it. Boy, I thought, I'm going to show that guy how to give a commanding officer a salute. Sure enough, I saw his car coming toward me. I gave him a fantastic salute, he opened the window to return it and starts laughing like hell at me.

"Real smart," he said, "but how the hell am I going to get through the gate?" Was I embarrassed! I'd forgotten to raise the barrier. Quickly, I opened it, and gave him another smart salute.

I wasn't at Yarmouth too long when they decided to give one airman on the base a plane trip out on a submarine patrol in the Atlantic. The CO selected me — I guess I was the only one he recognized.

Keith was soon on his way to the various training schools from which he graduated as a WAG — a wireless air gunner. He was sent overseas in June 1941 on the *Indrapoera*, an old Dutch East Indies merchant ship. The convoy was big, with six troopships. The *Indrapoera* was the smallest (carrying only about a hundred men), and the slowest. As well, there were seventeen destroyers and two battle cruisers.

I remember being down in the hold in the barbershop getting trimmed up, when a depth charge went off: *Whannggh!* It was just like you were in a pipe hit with a sledgehammer. What a racket! And nobody batted an eyelash. They just kept on with their work.

He received training in advanced signals at RAF College, Cranwell, Lincolnshire, then got posted to 22 OTU at Wellesbourne, Warwickshire. Two experiences there he will never forget: On November 6, 1941, when on a "crosscountry" trip, they ran short of petrol and had to land at Boscombe Downs. As soon as they touched down on the runway, the engines stopped: they were out of fuel entirely, and had to be towed off the runway. On February 25, 1942, he survived a crash when they overshot the runway and tore up a stretch of the London-to-Birmingham railway track!

He was posted to Ferry Command at Harwell, Berkshire, where he crewed up in March 1942 and transferred to Overseas Air Delivery Unit at Portreath, Cornwall. This was the staging area for delivery of Wellingtons to Egypt.

On April 16, 1942, Keith took off for Gibraltar, Malta and Egypt. Like Ed, they landed at Lucca in Malta, probably missing each other by a few weeks. Also like brother Ed, Keith was delayed in Malta by the German bombing of the airport — the brand-new Wellington being transported to the Middle East was blown up on the ground the night they arrived.

I did learn one lesson on Malta. Never go down into a well to hide from bombs. I squeezed into a shallow well: there were rats down there. I was sure that every bomb coming down was aimed at me. It was a terrifying experience. I found I was better off squatting down beside a wall.

His lanyard with whistle, pistol and case for dark glasses at the ready, the smiling Keith Patrick in Egypt, 1942.

> The whole of Malta was a honeycomb of tunnels dating back to medieval times when the Knights of Malta were defending the island against attack from all sides. I was billeted in a leper colony on the island. The patients there were all dressed in white; they were lovely people.

Keith flew on to Egypt on May 3 not as a crew member but as a passenger in someone else's plane. He joined 108 Squadron, RAF Bomber Command, backing up the Eighth Army. Working with the navy in support, they bombed Tobruk when the commandos were raiding the town. They also attacked tanks, columns of troops, railroads and other strategic targets.

On November 12, 1942, after forty-five trips, Keith was shipped out. Flying via Helwan and Luxor, Egypt, Khartoum, Sudan, Madugaria, then Lagos, Nigeria, to No. 1 BOR's transit camp. After about four weeks they shipped from Freetown on the Ivory Coast and then transferred at sea to the *Indrapoera*, the ship he had sailed out on the year before. Then across the Atlantic to the South American coast, northward up the eastern seaboard of the United States and back across the Atlantic to Liverpool. The roundabout route, which took six weeks, was to avoid submarine packs that were active in the shipping lanes. Conditions on board the *Indrapoera* had deteriorated a good deal. The officers who were quartered in the deck cabins weren't too badly off, but being crammed in below decks for six weeks was no treat.

February 1943, and back in Britain, Keith was allowed a little leave. He called some civilian friends he had made in Bournemouth and said, "This is Flight Sergeant Keith Patrick." The reply came, "Oh no you're not. You are Pilot Officer Keith Patrick." His commission had come through while he was in the desert. All that time he was cruising the Atlantic in below-deck quarters, he could have been using an officer's stateroom above decks.

Keith took up new duties as a signals instructor at RAF 29 OTU, North Luffenham, Rutland, and at Bruntinethorpe, Leicestershire, and during this period he served for three months as signals liaison officer with the Eighth USAAF B26 (Marauder) 456 Bombardment Squadron, teaching American wireless operators the Bomber Command Signals Organization and improving their skills at signalling using the Morse system.

In November 1943, it was decided to send home fifty aircrew who had completed a tour on a month's leave. This was an experiment. Keith Patrick was given leave (while brother Ed was evading his way south through Italy, trying to find the Allied lines). He sailed on the troopship RMS *Mauritania*, returning from carrying troops eastward to Britain. It was almost empty this time.

> That was class! And as an officer I had my own stateroom, with linen sheets on the bed. White tablecloths and pure white granulated sugar on the table and bowls of fruit. Waiters waiting on us. We sailed into New York harbour and they put us all on buses and drove us up Broadway. Wow! Then to Grand Central Station and a ticket to Ottawa, where we received a civic reception. Then on to Saint John, New Brunswick, to be with my family.

I was home in New Brunswick for a month. Mother and I went to see my brother in the sanitorium in Connecticut. I called Phyllis Taylor whom I had known in 1939 in Marblehead, Massachusetts. She remembered me and invited me to visit. A couple of days later I proposed and she accepted. She was taken with my uniform. You can't say no to that air force blue uniform; it's still the best one. I was then shipped back overseas. What a month!

When he got back to Britain he was sent to Battle School, where there was commando training and exercises on "How to Escape." Then training on Halifax bombers. Finally, on May 27, 1944, Keith was posted to 427 "Lion" Squadron RCAF at Leeming, in Yorkshire. Here Keith acquired a mostly Canadian crew. While he had completed one tour of forty-five flights, the other men were on their thirty-first operational flight.

On June 6, 1944, they had their first trip together over enemy territory in their new Halifax Mark 3. The "Lion" Squadron had been adopted by MGM, the Hollywood movie studio, whose logo included Leo the Lion. When they had completed their sixth trip, aircrew were given (probably by MGM) a silver badge in the shape of a lion as a memento of their service with the unit.

On June 12, almost a week after D-Day, they took off on their sixth op headed for the rail centre at Arras in order to bomb the marshalling yards. Intelligence had learned that a large number of troop trains would be coming through Arras to bolster the defenses at Normandy after the Allied landings a week earlier.

On the way, something went awry and we were late at the target. On our approach, there was a little bit of ack-ack; then it all stopped. We knew we were in trouble. It was very dark. We were still flying in on the target, v-e-r-y steady. The bomb doors were open. Still no ack-ack. Suddenly it became bright as day; chandelier flares were dropping all around us. We knew we were in plenty of trouble.

On the intercom, gunners had reported fighters circling around. We dropped our bombload on the target, then one fighter at a time would swing in to attack us. Our gunners kept after them as the pilot headed for the coast. Almost immediately, the rear gunner was hit and probably died in his turret. The mid-upper gunner and the flight engineer were hit but able to function. The plane's controls had been damaged and no longer functioned. The pilot ordered the crew to bail out.

Records indicate that on that night, seventeen Halifaxes and six Lancasters were lost on raids targeting Arras and Cambrai. One of those planes was the Lancaster in which Andy Mynarsky was posthumously awarded the Victoria Cross (see Chapter 3).

The crew had started their sixth flight that night, but they didn't complete it. They never got a silver lion. Recalling the events of that night nearly half a century later, Keith can reel off the unhappy fate of the Halifax's seven-man crew.

The rear gunner never got out of the plane. The navigator bailed out, but his parachute didn't open, the mid-upper gunner and the flight engineer bailed out, floated

Date	Hour	Aircraft Type and No.	Pilot	Duty	Remarks (Including results of bombing, gunnery, exercices, etc.)	Day	Night

#427 (R.C.A.F.) SQUADRON. — LEEMING, YORKSHIRE. — Time carried forward:— 302:30 — HALIFAX III

June 2, 1944	1455	LV986-V	F/O Fulton.	W/Operator	Local Flying.	1:25	
June 3, 1944	0930	LV-986-V	F/O Fulton.	W/Operator	Fighter Affilliation.	-:30	
June 3, 1944	433	LV-946-Q	F/O Fulton.	W/Operator	Cross Country, Base, Sywell, Newmarket, Base.	2:10	
June 4, 1944	2330	LV821-X	F/O Fulton.	W/Operator	Condé-Sur-Noireau Road & Rail Junction. Op' 46.		5:50.
June 7, 1944	2309	LV-995-Y	F/O Fulton.	W/Operator	Archères, Landed at Eastmoor. Op 47		5:35
June 8, 1944	0810	LV-995-Y	F/O Fulton.	W/Operator	Eastmoor, to Base.	-:15	
June 10, 1944	2215	LV-995-Y	F/O Fulton	W/Operator.	Ops-Versailles. Op'48		5:30
June 12, 1944	1235	LV-995-Y	F/O Fulton.	W/Operator.	— Missing — over Arras Op'49		3:30

Summary for *June, 1944.*
Unit *427 Sqn.*   Aircraft   1. HALIFAX III
Date *14-6-44*   Types   2. ....
Signature. ....   3. ....
                                          4. ....

Total for June 25:05 4:40

20:25

A.W. Murray S/L
O.C. 'B' Flight

Total Time.... 184:39 322:55

A page from Keith Patrick's log book. Note the final entry: June 12, 1944: "Missing — over Arras 'op' 49. 3:30 a.m."

down on their 'chutes and landed in a tangle in the trees: they bled to death from their wounds. The pilot jumped and landed, and the bomb aimer was the last man out and escaped with barely a scratch.

I prepared to bail out, getting down into the escape hatch with my legs dangling out of the plane. Making sure my harness was tight, I grabbed on to the hatch above me as I started to slide out. My gauntlet and my watch strap got caught on the hatch floor.

I felt as if I was dangling there for hours, but it must only have been a split second before glove and watch strap snapped off and I fell through the hatch. At some point in those last few seconds I was hit by something — it might have been the Radom holding the radar equipment under our plane's fuselage. It must have knocked me out completely. I have no recollection of pulling the ring of my parachute, yet somehow I must have done so.

When I came to, I was in a cornfield near our downed plane, and close by was a German ack-ack emplacement. Fire was raging, and ammunition exploding. Lots of excitement! All around the plane I could see the silhouette of German soldiers watching it. I could make out the sound of the German soldiers' voices — of course, I couldn't understand a word. I felt terrible. I was nauseous and cold. I wrapped my 'chute around me and fell unconscious again.

Consciousness came and went all night, until very early, soon after dawn. I came to and looked around: the plane was still smoking and there were soldiers searching the area. I tried to stand up, but couldn't, so I crawled through a field or two, away from the wreckage. It was a slow, painful process. Nearby I saw a roadway, I heard engines, so I lay low against a stone wall. German troops were going by in trucks. I waited until it was quiet. A farmhouse was on the other side of the road. I crawled across, got as far as the steps and banged feebly with my fist on the lowest door panel.

No response. I repeated the rapping again, and again.

The door opened. A man looked out at me, slammed the door quick. Oh boy, what now? Next thing I knew another man came out the door with a bicycle and went scooting off. I picked the wrong house. He was off to get the Jerries.

The door opened once more. Two men picked me up, carried me inside and laid me down on the kitchen table, and later on a bed.

The whole family — grandparents, parents, sons, daughters and all the little grandchildren — gathered around, looking and talking at me. But I didn't know a word of French, and they knew no English. Later I found out that I was in the village of Verchoq.

Keith was not very confident at this point. His future looked dim: he was down, in occupied territory, in no condition to walk. He expected that the people in the farm kitchen were waiting for the Germans to take him into custody. His injured back, broken shoulder and fractured skull were painful in the extreme.

In addition, he had to go to the bathroom! He attempted sign language — not a hint of comprehension. He tried body language — blank looks. *"Toilette?" "Latrine"* — nothing. In desperation, he pointed to his genitals and assumed an excruciating look of pain — success! *"Ah, la cabinette. Oui,"*

Then a scurrying about as people smiled and nodded. One of the little girls was sent out, returning momentarily with a chamber pot. The family didn't move, smiling encouragement at the embarrassed Canadian. How to convey this message? He pointed to the little girls in the room: comprehension dawned on the circle. The little girls were sent out of the room, while the rest remained expectantly. Abashed, mortified and ashamed, Patrick had no option. He performed!

As it turned out, the Hochart family, whose kitchen sheltered Keith, had not sent for the Germans, but rather for a priest. In a letter written early in 1990, Mme. Monique Fillerin described the events of that day in June 1944.

The buzzing of the planes awakened us, then we perceived the failure of a motor — it was stopping — followed by the fracas of an explosion. In the anguish of the moment I said to my sister, "If they are lucky, tomorrow we will have work to do.

Since the beginning of the occupation we had lived under the rhythm of raids of the RAF. We did our best to give aid to the unlucky flyers. It was necessary for us to be quicker than the Germans in order to succeed.

Early the next morning, at daybreak, I was visited by the *curé* of the neighbouring community. He had had an emergency call from a parishioner to the side of a man gravely injured. To his great surprise the unconscious and injured individual (lying on the table of a back kitchen) was wearing an English uniform.

The very Christian family Hochart, concerned at the extent of the unconscious man's injuries, had called on the services of the priest to prepare him for eternity.

As German soldiers were being quartered at the farm, the *curé* found it urgent to move the flyer from such an unhealthy location. Not knowing what to do, he came and asked me if I had a solution. The Germans often became nervous and executed the injured. We decided that I would take the Englishman.

At 10:00 A.M. Charles Hochart, driving his horse, brought Keith Patrick lying on a bed of straw in the bottom of the cart. We placed him in bed, his face smoke-filled, blood coming from his nostrils as well as his ears. Most spectacular were the two black blood clots under his eyes. (Five months later the blood clots had hardly improved.)

The injured flyer was totally unconscious during the day and stayed there for some days. Dr. Delpierre, who habitually took care of flyers, came and saw him near 4:00 P.M. He told me, "There is nothing one can do. It is a fracture at the base of the cranium. You can do nothing for him. We have nothing to help him. He has little chance of coming out of it, and if you put him outside on this cold night, he will be dead by tomorrow night. If you keep him in bed, keeping him warm without help, he will last three days. If you feed him hot meals, take care of him, he may come out of it, but you will have an invalid. If he survives three days we will try to take care of him. But the first thing to do, if you keep him, is to know where to bury him. If he does not die, let me know."

I was seventeen years old. I chose to take care of the Canadian. With my younger brother, I dug out a grave.

I took care of the injured man night and day. When we were assured that he might possibly live, he was given very simple treatment — heating pads, from the head to the coccyx, every three hours, morning and night to begin with, followed by massage with lotions to revive the damaged tissue. Keith Patrick lost the skin on his back, and I lost the skin off my hands, but he recovered and retained the use of his legs.

He had to take certain precautions in order to lift himself and walk; however, the stiffness of the neck remained, as well as of the back — he could not make it pivot on his hips. He also had to bear terrible migraines and dizziness. He had crises of despair, and could not be consoled.

Dr. Delpierre's diagnosis and directions for care, with only the barest of equipment and medicines, was obviously realistic. The sacrifices of Monique and her brother Gabriel — caring for Keith, and sharing their cottage, their food and their friendship — made the difference. The doctor's advice — to prepare his burial place first — was necessary but thankfully not needed in the long run.

Patrick has offered some additions and corrections to Mme. Fillerin's version of the events of that summer of 1944. He remembers that after he had relieved himself that first morning of his evasion, he once again lost consciousness and was in and out of it for some time. Meanwhile Mme. Hochart had got "about a dozen eggs and made a huge omelet and offered it to me. I must have turned green, it was the last thing I wanted. Then I got nauseous."

When the *curé* came with the fellow who had gone off on the bicycle, Patrick was impressed by the tall, bearded fellow carrying a rifle.

> I swear it was an old, old rifle, like the ones people used to have in the mountains of Kentucky. And there was a blonde girl, Gabriel Gruel, who spoke perfect English. She began asking me questions, which I couldn't answer. Finally, she said, "Okay Pat," and she handed me a piece of paper. It was a piece ripped from a Sweet Caporal cigarette box, and Don Fulton (our pilot) had signed his name on it. She said, "I have him in my house."

He recalls that he was taken to the village of Renty, near St. Omer, the site of a big German air base in the Pas de Calais area about twenty kilometres from Dunkirk. At Renty, Gabriel turned him over to the Filleron family — Genevieve, aged eighteen, Monique, sixteen, their brother Gabriel, fifteen, and their old grandmother, who was in her nineties.

Their mother and father worked for the Pat O'Leary Line and were captured, after having passed about fifty airmen through their property, sent to a concentration camp and horribly tortured. They survived, got back home after the war, but of course were never the same again.

> We were raided a few times by the Gestapo. Of course, I had to be helped. We were taken to a little wood, a few fields above us, right across a narrow-gauge railway regularly patrolled by the Germans. We would wait until they had passed by, nip across and hide in the ferns and undergrowth.
>
> They gave us each a rifle when we were hiding, and one night I hid in a stack of corn. The next day the oldest daughter walked by and just slipped a bottle of water and a hard-boiled egg into the shock of corn and kept on walking by. We stayed there until night and then slipped back into the house. That was unusual. Normally, I was hidden in the woods.
>
> Once they raided the house before I could get out. I only had time to stand flat against the wall. They came into the room, but didn't look around. The searcher went out of the room, had a drink and just left.

Less than a mile from the village of Renty was a tiny hamlet strung out along one street. The Germans had surrounded the place with V1 rocket sites. Each of

Keith's helpers: Back: Claire Cadet, Genevieve Fillerin, Monique Fillerin, Madame Fillerin, M. Fillerin and Madame Cadet. Gabriel Fillerin kneels in front.

these sites was equipped to launch the pilotless V1 "doodlebug" missiles against southern England.

The RAF targeted the hamlet and its rocket sites for a raid on a particular night. Word was passed to the French Underground, who quietly evacuated the immediate area. Everyone had left — everyone, that is, except one ancient lady who refused to leave her cottage. When the planes came, the pounding of the bombs was extraordinary, as Keith recalls:

> Just up over the hill from us was the tiny hamlet. It was late summer of '44. I would never want to live through anything like that bombing again. It was worse than being shot down. They flew in at chimney height and just obliterated everything in the place, including the V1 sites of course.
>
> I thought it was the end of the world. Monique's place shook and rattled. In the kitchen there was a huge fireplace, the kind you could stand in. There was a stove in the centre of it where the cooking was done. During the raid, I dove for the fireplace. But Gabriel had a vicious dog and he dove for the same place. It was a battle between the two of us, though he didn't bite me and I didn't bite him. We both huddled in there shaking through the raid. It was quite an experience.

When people went back to what was left of the village, the old lady's house was half gone. But she was still in her bed, and alive.

Twice I made an attempt to leave the farm, and was captured by "them." No way were you going anywhere. Our instructions after D-Day were not to try to get away. For one thing, there were so many troop movements in the area, with artillery and air bombardments, that it was dangerous. Then, of course, you could easily endanger the lives of the helpers. I didn't get more than two fields away. One of them came up behind me: "Where do you think you're going?"

Between Septmeber 12 and 13, 1944, Captain Tursky, a Polish officer, and some Canadian and British soldiers liberated us.

A month later I was back in Canada.

The Patricks — all five of them — served with distinction in the RCAF. Neither Ed nor Keith think of themselves as heroes. Like most evaders, they look back on their experiences with a certain amount of wonder and with gratitude that strangers thousands of miles from New Brunswick would risk their own lives to help Canadians in distress.

The remarkable feature of the Patricks' story is in the singularity of two brothers carrying out evading activities from different areas of operation during roughly the same period of time. There is no other case on record of brothers who have shared similar experiences.

How remarkable, too, is the family history. Although there are several cases of many family members serving in the Second World War, the Patricks stand out as particularly distinctive. Mrs. Patrick, the mother of the boys and a woman of British background, was honoured by the RCAF with a presentation made to her upon the inauguration of the Air Force Tartan.

BURMA

THE BURMA THEATRE

Evading in Burma was a very different experience from those of evaders in northwest Europe. Canadians were more likely to be familiar with European languages than Asian. In most Nazi-controlled areas, at least English-speaking natives could be found. Many Canadians had some acquaintance with French, and some whose parents or grandparents had recently emigrated to Canada were familiar with German or Italian. Southeast Asian tongues, however, were a closed book to most Canadians. Those serving in Asia might pick up a few words, but sign or body language was the normal, if highly unsatisfactory way of asking for help or information.

Also Holland, Belgium and most European countries were densely populated. Distances between towns are often a few miles only. Highways, roads and paths connected communities in almost every direction. The countryside was cultivated, often in very small farm holdings, but the wooded areas giving cover to the evader were sparse compared to the jungles of Burma.

Farms, especially in the Low Countries, could provide food for those on the run. A chicken coop, vineyard, field or orchard could be, and often was, raided in the dark of night.

The unfamiliar jungles and farmlands of Asia could offer cover, and food and drink, but there were no labelled warnings to alert the unfamiliar, and no recipes to make palatable the strange, ugly or peculiar for desperate foreigners.

Asian politics created situations that westerners found hard to interpret. In the 1940s many Burmese wanted independence from Britain: many aided the Japanese in joining the Burma Traitor Army. Thousands of Indians were also recruited by the Japanese for similar reasons.

Invading Japanese troops treated natives suspected of siding with the Allies very harshly. Civilians were terrorized into shunning Allied troops who strayed into their territory. Failing to do so could endanger the population of an entire village. The Japanese were determined to use every means available to control occupied territory.

Every army has been accused of mistreating natives and prisoners of war, but the reputation of the Japanese is probably the most unsavory. Dave Bockus claims,

> They took no prisoners of war, and would not waste bullets on those captured. They preferred using their bayonets and swords, brutally executing uniformed men without regard to the Geneva Convention, or any so-called rules of war. They strung up prisoners and used them for bayonet practice.

Disease was as deadly an enemy as the Japs. Western troops could contract malaria within ten days of arriving in the jungle, unless they had anti-malaria pills. Many westerners who served in tropical climates feel the effects of tropical diseases to this day. Dysentry and denghue fever were common, typhus ticks were especially virulent. A group of a hundred men, returning to Assam, bedded down for the night in a tick area: fifteen died and between sixty and seventy became very ill.

The experiences of airmen like Bockus and Johnson were unique in the global context of World War II evasion. Intelligence planners had little advice for servicemen caught behind enemy lines in Asia. Eventually, the experiences of those few who had made it back were passed around from camp to camp and talked about in briefing rooms and messes all over that theatre of operations.

In the long run, the inventiveness of men like Johnson, who created his own "escape kit," and Bockus, who was determined to get back, created evasion techniques to suit the unique terrain and conditions in Asia.

Dave Bockus states unequivocally, "There were no helpers, no underground, no Comet Lines. When I was up in China, my civilians were Chinese guerrillas." The conditions were just different from those facing European evaders.

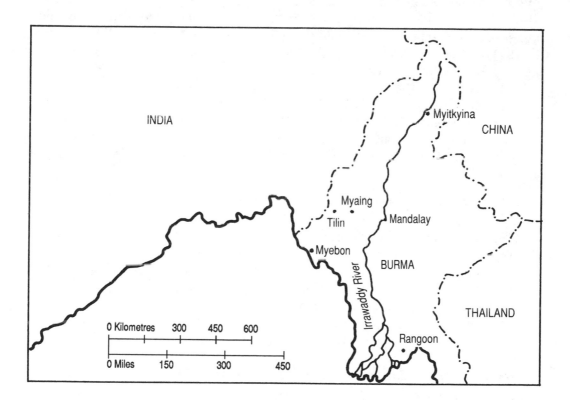

CHAPTER TWENTY-ONE

I WOULD NEVER ADMIT THAT ANY ENEMY SHOT ME DOWN

He is a wiry man, five feet, ten inches tall, with an easy smile and an infectious laugh. In the 1930s he was a scrappy teenager playing varsity football for Parkdale Collegiate in Toronto. His classmates included Johnny Weston, a junior Ontario gymnastic champion and football star.

When war broke out, young Dave Bockus, and Johnny, like so many of their generation, couldn't wait to get into the thick of things. Bockus joined the air force in 1941 and got his pilot's wings the following year. He was posted to England, joining 616 Fighter Squadron.

On his posting to the Middle East, thousands of miles from home, he looked up Johnny Weston. They were eager for the adventure and action promised in the recruiting posters with the punchline, "World Traveler at 21." Like many fellow Canadians, they were contemptuous of the niceties of service protocol, the spit and polish of service life. The uncertainty of tomorrow demanded that you get all you can out of life today.

> Johnny, who was in Algiers, heard I was in Tunis, so he whipped over and we jumped a plane and flew to Sicily to see if we could bypass the bureaucracy and get on a Fighter Squadron. We got to a wing over there and they said, "Sure we need pilots, go back to Tunis and we'll send a telegram for you to return." We got to Tunis and they grabbed us. We went before the adjutant, the AOC in Carthage, who called us "undisciplined colonials." This created a real rhubarb! They put Johnny on a plane to Gibraltar and I was sent east.
>
> I went on out to Tripoli, Benghazi, set up with a couple of cronies in Cairo, and ran out of money there. They put us on another plane east, via the Dead Sea, Iran, Karachi, Delhi, and we ended up in Chittagong, India, with 67 RAF Squadron. We were flying Hurricanes but were scheduled to be switched on to Spits.

In late 1943 Bockus was interviewed by Special Operations Forces, a British organization for field service requiring daring and initiative. Colonel Scott, a field commander with Special Operations, had a high opinion of Canadians. Bockus joined the group and trained for jungle fighting in early 1944.

> Early in '44 I had broken my ankle. The bone wasn't healing properly. Eventually, the plaster cast was cut off, but I wouldn't let them put a new one on. The British

Bockus and Spitfire in England in 1943 with 616 Squadron.

medics insisted I was not fit to fly, but Dr. Faulkner, a Belleville, Ontario, medical officer didn't agree. I went back on training, while the doctors argued.

British control of Burma was challenged when the Japanese began their drive for domination of East Asia. Japanese forces had advanced into Burma, seizing the southern terminus of the Burma road. Supplies to the Chinese were cut off.

General Wingate planned a guerrilla operation to harass the enemy deep inside the Burmese hinterland. The Mandalay railroad near the Irrawaddy River was the main target. The plan was to blow up bridges and conduct hit-and-run attacks to sabotage the Japanese.

On the night of March 5, a force was set to take off for ''Broadway,'' the code name given to one of the clearings in the jungle about 200 miles behind enemy lines. ''Broadway,'' ''Piccadilly,'' ''White City'' and ''Aberdeen'' were designed as jungle airstrips for supplying the guerrilla units raiding enemy troops, transport and supplies.

The airstrip locations were to be kept secret as long as possible. A silent approach, with gliders towed behind Dakotas, was organized. About fifty gliders, lightweight frames covered with fabric, flying without the aid of engines, were detailed for the fly-in. Once off the ground, they could soar on air currents, rising and falling by manually manipulating rudders and flaps. Troop- and equipment-carrying gliders had been used in North Africa, Sicily and, later, in the Normandy landings.

In the Burma campaign, the glider pilots had not seen the drop area in advance of the landing, and had to rely on photographs. That kind of operation would be like landing on an open spot in northern Ontario at night, with no landing lights, no ground lights and no ground signals to assist a safe setdown. Night landings on an unfamiliar, unlit field were never easy at the best of times. The clearing inside occupied territory made it especially difficult: was it a trap? Had the clearing been booby-trapped? Were the Japs waiting just beyond the perimeter of the clearing to attack when all the equipment had been landed? Until the landing had been completed the risks were uppermost in everyone's thoughts.

There was moonlight the night when the takeoffs were scheduled. Each Dakota had twin tows, pulling two Waco gliders. Once aloft, the gliders were towed so as to come in as close to the strip as possible, when the tow rope would be severed for a landing and the glider was on its own.

I had been grounded. At the take-off strip I watched the first gliders leave. After a bit of conversation with one of the pilots, a Texan, Lt. Dick Kuonsler, he looked at me speculatively and said:

"Boy, I could use some help. My co-pilot is under the weather. Pulling on a twin tow, at night, with no landing field: it's going to be quite a handful."

I said casually, "Why don't I go with you?"

He grinned, "Okay!"

So I went with him as his co-pilot, in one of the first gliders to take off.

The kind of *ad hoc* situation Bockus found himself in with Special Forces was very different from the highly controlled and scheduled and careful accounting that characterized air operations in the United Kingdom and Europe. The offhanded conversation between Tex and Bockus — "Why don't I go with you?" "Okay!" — would have been unthinkable in any but the fluid conditions of Southeast Asia.

Once aloft, the pilot asked, "How are we doing with the other glider?" I said, "We don't have to worry about it, it's gone." There was its tow rope dangling right there in front of us. Our tow rope held.

When we got to Broadway, it was very dark, we could see very little. Now we had to land: a glider comes equipped with a spoiler to help lose both height and speed. It works in reverse to a plane's flaps, by cutting off the flow of air over the wing, thus cutting off the lift. Tex decided he would fly the airspeed and I would call out the heights and also look after the spoilers. This was going to be tricky: you cut loose and glide; if you pull the spoiler up a little too early, the glider will stall and you'll go straight in.

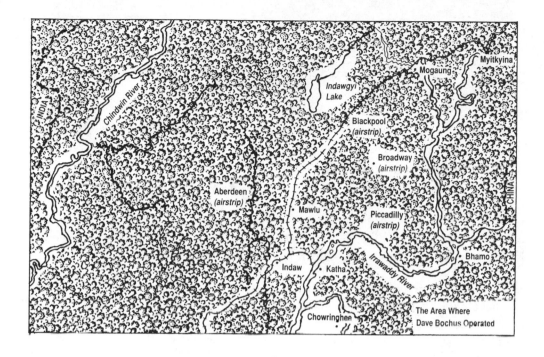

The Area Where Dave Bochus Operated

In so many cases with gliders, the pilots want to come in and get out in a hurry. They often came in too fast, too high. We went around once to get a little bit lower and slower. I said to Tex, "We're too fast and too high." He said, "To hell with it, we'll go around again."

We came back in a little lower. "We haven't got much room. When we come in, hold on," I warned.

The glider was loaded with all kinds of things — mules, radio equipment, RAF sergeants — it would be quite a bump when the spoilers were forced up. Right at the last second, I said:

"Tex, here we go," and when I pulled on the spoilers, we hit: and when we hit, we hit. We had no room to roll to a halt. The landing tore the wheels and the wings off. We stopped about twenty feet from a large log. During a forced landing or crash in a flimsy glider with everything being torn away, you wonder if it will ever stop. But no one was hurt, we all managed to get out with only a bruise or two.

I found Colonel Scott, my CO, who was in charge of the first group in. In an exasperated voice he said, "What the hell are you doing here?"

"I think you need help."

''I can use all the help I can get, but you are out of here in twenty-four hours. The first plane out of here, you're on it.'' By this time, his manner was only slightly irritated.

But it was almost three months later that I caught that ''first plane out.''

And then, I flew it.

The scene that night at Broadway was a mess. About fifty-seven gliders were scheduled to fly in, but only about thirty made it to the strip. Gliders smashed in to those on the ground and piled up in the clearing. To those who looked on in horror the only reaction possible was to shake your head and repeat, "It's one hell of a mess."

Neil Turnbull, of Oakville, Ontario, a corporal radar mechanic, had been brought into Broadway with eight or nine men to set up a surveillance and control unit. His recollection of those early days confirm Bockus's account.

Broadway was a kind of crazy business all right. It was just a clearing in the jungle where gliders had all piled into each other. When we landed, our brakes failed and the thing wouldn't stop — we ran into barbed wire that surrounded the stronghold to stop the aircraft. We were immediately surrounded by soldiers telling us not to get out, the area where we were was all mined. We had to get up on the back of the aircraft and walk down off the tail.

The CO brusquely shouted at us: ''Who are you?''

''We're radar, sir.''

''Oh.'' He replied. We later learned he was furious because I was only a corporal and a colonial at that. He absolutely refused to call me corporal and ever after that he called me Radar, just Radar.

The atmosphere at Broadway was one of confusion amidst massive destruction. There was genuine fear for the safety of the operation if an alert Japanese unit were close to the strip. The dead and dying were all over the place. Crashed gliders that couldn't get off the strip added to the confusion. Attempts to control more landings with flares were useless. The gliders that had already come in were front-row centre, blocking the way for any new arrivals.

"Soyalink," the codeword for "stop the operation" was ordered sent back to base. It was not clear for several hours whether the signal had been received. Meanwhile Wingate thought the Broadway operation had been a disaster, that the Japs had lain in wait for the landing, and had wiped out the entire force. It was only after a dawn reconnaissance that the situation was clarified.

Scott got his machine gunners and patrols organized. The one small American bulldozer used to make the strip was put into action to clear away the debris. Patrols were sent out to secure the strip from the Japs. Before first light the organization of the landing strip was well in hand. Manhandling the gliders out of the way and getting the injured attended to was proceeding rapidly.

Casualties were high, with about thirty killed and sixty missing. There had been no Jap interference at that time. If there had been, Wingate's worst fears would have been realized: Broadway probably would have been wiped out. After the war it was learned that the gliders and two planes had been seen and reported to Japanese Lieutenant-General Mataguchi. He, however, judged it a minor nuisance and failed to take immediate action.

The strip was made ready for the first night of operations. The code word "Porksausage" was sent, indicating that Broadway was ready for the first of the DC-3s to start supplying the strip and taking out the wounded.

> We had the strip ready, with a flare path. The DC-3s were loaded with barbed wire, Gurkhas, some twenty-millimetre guns, machine guns and landmines. By evening, we had most of the injured out. Very few of the gliders ever flew again. I think the operational life of a Waco glider was about six hours.

The Dakotas hauled in the Chindits: within minutes, they were out on patrol. There was no delay. Flight Lieutenant Bockus, RCAF, was in there, on the ground, doing whatever was needed. He helped with the codes and communications for the outpost and, at times, as an air controller bringing in the planes.

Life on the ground required special skills not usually included in training manuals. Barbed wire was everywhere. Gurkhas were detailed to maintain and patrol the barbed-wire fence. Most were unfamiliar with English. Each man was given a code number allowing him back inside the barbed-wire perimeter. The code was a measure to prevent Japs from getting inside. Unfortunately, the Gurkhas could never remember their code numbers. Instead, they would say, "*Tek Hi, Johnny.*" Of course, the Japanese caught on and tried the '*Tek Hi, Johnny*" too, but Gurkhas, the fiercest of fighters, would chop the heads off any enemy they sighted.

Neil Turnbull describes the Chindit columns in graphic terms:

> They would go out and then come back in for a rest. I have never seen anything like it. They were like zombies when they came in. Their eyes were dead, they were filthy and they reeked. Living off the land, they had crawled through the wet, the jungle undergrowth, the slime. I saw one column coming down the clearing in single file: suddenly, the man in front walked into a barbed wire barricade. It stopped him! But the others piled into him like an accordion and just stood there. I went over, saying "Can I help?" No response. I took the leader's hand and led him around the barricade and the rest of them followed. They were out on their feet.

It was decided to bring Spitfires in. The Americans were opposed to this plan. They argued that just as soon as these fighter planes came in we'd get hit.

> The Japanese had an odd relationship between their army and the air force. The air force seemed to think that it was the army's job down there and their job up here. We'd had one raid, but once we brought Spits in they really hit us. In a Japanese attack, Bob Day, of Vancouver, shot down two enemy aircraft. But in the

long run, only two of the original five Spitfires were left. They wiped out Turn-bull's radar station in the first sortie.

A couple of days later they brought in six more Spits: four were wiped out right off the bat. That was the end of the Spits; we never had any more.

Wingate's view was that the Chindits should be used to put a stranglehold on the rail lines or main highways, forcing the Japs to attack. The base at Broadway was made secure. To attack, the Japanese would have to cross the strip and the barbed wire and minefields. The rear was mined, wired and positioned for good crossfire.

At one point, Scotty said, "We have to meet up with this other column down near the Irriwaddy and operate as a roving patrol, so when Broadway is attacked, we can trap them by attacking from the rear.

I went with them. I was looking after the codes and wireless and I would pick a spot for the air drops, and co-ordinate any air strikes. We spent five solid weeks with the column, wandering around, blowing up anything we thought was important.

At this stage, there weren't any light planes available to pick up casualties, a job the L5s were designed to do. Eric Loken, a fellow Canadian from Kelowna, B.C., had been flown in to replace Bob Lasser, of Vancouver, killed the first night. When Dave got back to Broadway, he decided to try to get two beat-up L5s and one L1 to fly. The Japs had put a few bayonet slashes and a few holes in them. The Americans had left them there during the ground attack. Could they be salvaged?

I talked to Scotty about it. "We could do a better job of it if we could get them going."

"Great," Scotty said, "get at it."

We got two of them going. We painted out all the American markings. In effect, we stole them, just kept them. The L1, we couldn't get going. We gave that back to the Yanks.

I was always sorry we didn't have a Canadian flag. We were always called Yanks or Englishmen. If only we'd had a Canadian flag. We painted out the markings and let everyone know we were Canadians, but we didn't have anything to paint on the plane.

We dropped supplies: ammo, food, medical supplies. Each wing had a release harness that held the boxes and 'chutes, or bombs. We always carried hand grenades too. Nothing was official. Technically I don't think we existed. I had no rank showing. Eric had his times signed by Colonel Rome at Broadway. I didn't. There was nothing, just a diary.

About 1980 I wrote to Ottawa to see if they had any information to help me fill in the details of those weeks. The archives sent me a letter showing 106 trips with the L5 in occupied territory. This figure is low. Possibly no record of flights after Broadway were filed.

Dave Bockus and Eric Loken with their home-made Stinson at "Broadway." The cover of the 1944 Christmas edition of "Wings Abroad," the RCAF newspaper, has been pasted on the fuselage. The 31 stencilled parachutes and the single bomb indicate the number and type of ops flown. (DND PHOTOGRAPH PL27467)

The L5, a marvellous light plane built by an American manufacturer, picked up casualties on request. A radio message to Broadway asked for a pickup or a drop-off in a particular spot. The L5 landed, then a quick turnaround and the job was done. Eric did 122 sorties, about 130 hours. He and Bockus must have accounted for at least 260 trips between them. Pickups were just another trip, but drops of ammo, food and medicine outnumbered pickups.

Some pickups were interesting, some real tricky. I remember we took out one Chindit. His column was in a bad spot: one of the Chindits was dying. They had no choice but to leave him behind in a village. I knew the man. We asked if they could find a spot where we could pick him up. They said they could hold out for forty minutes at most. Exposure time was limited. If they took too long they would be surrounded and all hell would break loose.

To save time, we didn't circle to find him; we just went in. They dumped him in the back seat, tied him in, then ran into the jungle for cover. We turned around and advanced out the narrows. Just as we headed down the paddy, the Nips showed up and started firing. The L5 was hit in two or three places. We skimmed over the heads of the last four or five Nips as we left the ground.

Our Chindit passenger was in real bad shape. He seemed to be out of it for the most part. His face was pale, once or twice his eyelids fluttered but remained shut. His breathing was shallow. He looked barely alive.

Then, in a faint voice, I heard him say: "Is that you Dave?"

"Yeah," I replied.

Then, with an effort, he said, "I knew you'd come and get me."

There was a long silence. I couldn't say anything, a choking feeling came over me. He had said something that was best left unsaid. We did what we had to do and never spoke about it. The Chindit's words have echoed in my mind down the years for close to half a century. I can hear them still, and I still get all choked up.

And I think he lived!

The L5s were also useful for picking up mail. They had long poles with a light rope oval in the centre. We would fly in between them carrying a weight and a hook on it to pick up the bag. Mail drops and pickups were real morale builders.

One day, the Americans came in with two L1s to pick up 3 people in China. I had been there three days before, so I knew the area. They weren't familiar with the place. They weren't too sure that if they got in they could get out. Would I go up with them? I said sure.

We landed in Yunnan province, China. The whole area is surrounded by hills. There was sporadic firing when we touched down. The first L1 made one pickup and took off all right. My pickup, a Lieutenant Critch, was loaded aboard, but something went wrong on takeoff, and we crashed. Critch and I were okay, but we heard the enemy and guerrillas trading fire all around us. The other L1s took both his and my passenger in his plane, but there was no room for me. Sorry Dave, that's it!

Now the firing was getting closer and closer. I hid in the underbrush and watched attacking Japs set fire to my plane. I hid out that night, figuring that if I just stayed in the area, as close to the spot as possible, I would have a better chance of getting out. It's rough country, and I was too deep inside enemy territory to make it back without help. I had my camera, a .38, two grenades and that was it.

The next morning I joined the Chinese in the poppy field, actually marking and gathering the opium. Then Eric showed up in our other L5, circling around looking for me. It was too risky to try signalling him. He was flying low and encountering a lot of rifle fire. I'm not sure he realized how bad it was. A rescue attempt would likely backfire on both of us. He circled around for a bit and then left.

Later that day, there were fewer patrols. So I thought, what the hell, I'd go back to my L5. I took a picture of the burned plane and some of the Chinese guerrillas, and slipped away into the bush.

While hiding out, I encountered some Chinese who led me to another English army officer also on the run. I think his name was Kennedy. So we joined up. We spent part of the night in an opium basha with six to eight Chinese, all of whom had passed out except for one tall, skinny man who didn't seem particularly friendly. Kennedy and I took turns staying awake. When the lanky Chinese decided to leave, we were suspicious. Are we going to be betrayed?

It took only a few seconds to decide to leave. Later that night, we heard someone calling to us. Were they friendly Chinese? Japs? Our lanky friend ready to turn us over to the enemy? We decided to get the hell out of that area.

We had heard that a little north and west of where we met, an American — Pete Joost, trained by the OSS — had been dropped to organize Chinese guerrilla units.

There were twenty-five Japanese divisions in China. Chiang Kai-shek had wanted to pull out of the war and the Americans were trying to keep him in. As long as Chiang was fighting, the Jap divisions would be tied down.

The next day we dodged most of the Jap patrols. We had one tough experience crossing a canyon. We spent a lot of time carefully crawling down, and across that canyon and climbing up the other side. We decided to stay the night. We caught something — we didn't know what it was, and to this day, I still don't know, but we ate it, raw, and it tasted really good. We hadn't eaten for some time. And as we ate we could feel the energy coming back. It was a very strange and warm feeling.

In the narrow canyon we found a spot where we could sleep. Shortly after we bedded down, the rain began. These canyons are treacherous when it rains — we had to get out. In the dark, we moved up to higher ground. By morning you could hear the roar of the water plunging deep into the canyon. It was a fearful noise.

We started across the top of the ridge, so damned happy we had made it. Then we hit a real Jap outfit. It was a dandy, not just a patrol; there were a lot of Japs. We were hiding, perhaps forty feet from them, watching and waiting. We estimated that there were two hundred in the first group. As the company moved on, the last four men stopped. There was some jabbering and two of the four went off in one direction, a third moved in the other and the fourth stopped right in front of us.

He pulled out his rice and started to prepare his meal. Sometimes the Japs would fill a section of bamboo with water, rice and other pieces of food. The end would be plugged and the unit placed in an open fire. In a few minutes, the bamboo would crack open, leaving a stick of cooked rice.

As he began eating his loose rice, the other fellow called to him. He got up and went back to see what was up. As soon as he moved, Kennedy and I nipped out, stole his rice in one quick grab and made it back into the bush. We could hear the jabber of the irritated Jap as we moved into the jungle. I think we actually laughed.

We ran into a few more patrols, but survived. After a while, you acquire a sixth sense that warns you of impending danger. I'd had some training with the Chindits that made me feel more confident.

We gradually made our way until finally we came across some of Joost's guerrillas and then made it to his hideout. Here he talked about his adventures. He
had been an American cavalry officer working with General Stilwell's command
in the field. His experiences seemed endless: encounters with Chinese, Indian, British
and American guerrillas, and stragglers like us, were only the bare bones of the
exciting life he led in those days.

Pete was a fantastic person — easygoing, familiar with the area and friendly with
the local people. We got along famously. He'd say, "I want to go down into that
little village. They say that's where the spies hang out? Do you want to come with
me?"

Villages out there are not like ours. They are very small, just one or two houses
in an insignificant clearing. This one was typical. A little creek ran down near the
clearing. We decided to have a bath. Pete sat on the shore with a machine gun
while I had a bath, then I sat on the shore while he had a bath.

Pete and I had a couple of skirmishes with the Japanese. When one of our guerrillas was shot in the upper leg, Pete said we had to take the bullet out. We had
nothing to give him to deaden the pain. He never said a thing. We cut in, probed
around then cut the bullet out, cauterized the wound and filled it up with sulfa
powder. He never said a word, nor showed any sign of the pain he must have been
suffering.

We wandered around the hills, sometimes feasting on wild goat, keeping in touch
with the Chinese guerrilla groups. I was itching to get back, but Pete tried to per-
suade me to stay. He said, "This is a great life."

And really, he's right. You are up in the hills, and it's fairly secure if you are
careful. You don't have the bumph and the flies to put up with. And the water
was good to drink, far better than down below. As he said, "What better war
could you have? The guerrillas are great; they hit and run; you don't have to charge
up a hill. You shoot somebody and just run."

I finally convinced Pete that I had better get back. He called for a plane and the
L1s came in to pick me up. On May 4, 1944, I was back in Broadway, nine days
after I'd left.

Eric and I flew back to Semipa on three occasions, landing twice with supplies
and picking up wounded. The third trip looked like a trap, so we didn't land.

Some evaders have documents recording times of takeoff and return, full details
of the operations, equipment, personnel. For Bockus there were almost no documents. He was never even declared missing. He had already been in Burma for
seven weeks, behind the lines. When they flew him back to Broadway he was still
behind the lines. How could he be declared missing? Patrols would be sent out for
two days and come back ten days later. They were just delayed.

Later, at Broadway, the Americans loaned him another L5. He had promised Pete
and the guerrillas that he would return if needed. They were to send a message
and could rely on his help.

On one occasion an American light plane went in to pick up a flier who had cracked up. He came down and couldn't get out. So they sent another L5 in and *he* cracked up too. The Americans then changed their rules: if you crack up you have to get out yourself. They were ordered not to risk any more planes or pilots.

One day some Americans came into Broadway and said to us: "You guys don't seem to have any officers; no one seems to give you any orders. Do you think you could go in and pick up a couple of our guys?"

We did. We went in and picked up three pilots in three trips. After that we had no trouble getting L5s or parts. They couldn't do enough for us. They gave us the jungle hammocks with the rubber tops and they came back up to China and picked me up. One favour deserves another.

White City was about thirty-five miles southwest of Broadway, more than two hundred miles behind the lines. It was named for the hundreds of supply parachutes that were caught in the trees. White City became the centre of a cruel and costly battle between the Chindits and General Yamaguchi's 20,000 troops. The approaching monsoon season contributed to the difficulties. Chindit casualties were heavy, but it was estimated that they accounted for 12,000 Japanese killed in the operation. Eric and Dave's L5 crews picked up Chindit casualties at White City, Aberdeen, Clydeside and Blackpool.

As the Japanese put the squeeze on the strips it became very difficult. Eventually the small planes could not get in to pick up anybody. Three Daks tried it at Blackpool, but they were blown out of the sky before they could get their wheels down. The casualties were terrible. When bases had to be evacuated, some troops were left behind. It was decided to withdraw from Broadway about May 13. There was no way the strip could be held. Most of the Chindits were in very poor condition. Calvert's 77 Group, which made the first landing at Broadway, had more than eight hundred casualties by late May.

The little diary I kept showed we were moving troops out of Broadway and other strips that the monsoons had made unusable. Eric was so sick on the fourteenth, we attempted to fly him out but couldn't make it. Terrible weather and high hills. We had to return. We eventually got him out. We took off and headed north towards Ledo. We hadn't seen Jap fighters for days.

Flying north, we saw two Japanese Oscars. We were about four hundred miles from our own territory, so we decided to head into the hills. One Jap took a look at us and decided not to attack. I guess they were heading back from some raid and were not too anxious to remain in the area. We headed northwest, landing at Ledo. I never told anyone about the Oscars. Eric was semi-conscious.

Years later, in 1970, we were visiting Eric and his wife in Kelowna, B.C. At dinner, Eric said, "I thought we'd had it when we saw those two Oscars." I said, "What are you talking about. You weren't even conscious."

"I was just conscious enough to see them." That was twenty-six years later. All that time and neither of us had ever mentioned the incident.

In those days, everybody got sick. Chindits on the ground were in terrible shape — tired, sick with high fevers, dysentery, everything under the sun. My memory of this time is quite blurred. I remember very little about the landing at Ledo and putting Eric into the hospital.

The Americans approached Dave to see if he would help them with some casualties. He doesn't remember too much about it. His diary notes mention "casualties, casualties, casualties" and "a sweat-it-out strip," but nothing is clear in his memory, nothing detailed. His last flight was around May 22. One medical report said he was treated for malaria and denghue. "They poured so much liquid quinine into me I lost my hearing." He ended up in the hospital in Calcutta and remembers people talking about D-Day. Next he was sent to India to recuperate, and then back to fly with 67 Squadron.

They had Spits now, and were based in India at a place called Camilla. It's July '44, and I'm back in the air force. No one ever said, "Where the hell have you been?" One guy said, "How stupid can you be?" And sometimes I agree with him.

Anyway I went back to 67 Squadron. We flew ops in the Arawak scrambles, strafing, low-level bombing with Spits through the rest of '44. We were told that as soon as the army took a strip we would go in and land. On January 1, as I remember it, the AOC took a light plane and landed on the strip at Akyab Island. And then took off and said there aren't any Japs there. The military still hadn't reached the Akyab strip when we landed and held on to it. The Japs attacked us by air most nights.

Then, on January 11, we were scrambled early in the morning. We were escorting a flight of B25s on a bombing raid on Myebon, a Jap coastal base. I lost my engine at Myebon and headed for the sea, hoping for a soft landing. My number two sent a mayday call for me. I had left it too long, however. I tried to flip over to bail out, but she went into a spin. I remember saying to myself, "Boy, the odds are getting too high on this one."

I tried to slip out the door, and my R/T or oxygen cord jerked my head back. In a moment or two the cord pulled loose, I slid off the wing, and pulled my rip cord. It was a great feeling when the 'chute snapped open. I'm a life member of the Caterpillar (bail-out) and Gold Fish (life saved by using a dinghy) clubs.

You have lots of things spinning through your head as you float down over the water: these are not friendly waters, they're Jap waters, and shark waters — crocodiles too?

The little dinghy was small and tricky to use. The compressed air bottle was in the way, but I managed to sort things out and awkwardly heaved myself into the darned thing. I kept my helmet because of the sun, but I wasn't too happy. A few days earlier in the same area, the Japs had shot down an air-sea rescue plane.

I was close to shore and kept thinking I was a sitting duck. I saw planes flying along the shoreline but couldn't identify them. Then two of the first air cover of 67 Spits showed up. They circled around the dinghy: it was a great sight. The squadron flew cover for several hours. I felt good; I was protected and would be picked up in no time. I didn't want to spend the night out there. The coastal air-sea rescue was American, but for some reason they had to bring an RAF plane in from Chittagong. When it landed, the pilot, Bob Day, CO of 67 Squadron, stuck his head out and shouted at me: "What the hell are you doing sitting in that goddamn thing? Don't you know we've got ops to fly?"

Dave's activities in Burma are so extraordinary that one is overwhelmed by the detail and the gusto with which he tells his story. His voice, his choice of language and his wealth of supporting detail confirm the authenticity of his descriptions. Added to this is the humour and vividness with which he tells his story. When asked, "How many aircraft did you have shot out from under you? From your account there were at least three. Is that correct or were there more?" his face changes for a moment. With a sternness that contrasts with his previous cheerfulness, he looks you straight in the eye, raises the volume of his voice slightly and responds:

I claim nobody shot any airplane out from under me. No Jap shot a plane out from under me. We lost an L5, we lost a Waco, we damaged a couple of spits. But I'm still here. That last Spitfire at Myebon was just an engine failure.

I would never admit that any Jap shot me down. I would never admit that.

Then, after a brief pause, the grin returned, his eyes sparkle as he continues,

You asked me earlier how I got the DFC. Somebody asked me about that before, so I said: Well, I lost more of our planes than I shot down of theirs so I think it was a donated DFC — donated by the Japs.

CHAPTER TWENTY-TWO

TWENTY-THREE DAYS IN THE BURMESE JUNGLE

Bob Johnson lives in Charlottetown, P.E.I. He has retired from his career as an insurance claims manager, but he still has an interest in the Air Force Reserve, the Air Cadet League, the Air Force Association, the Canadian Legion and, of course, the Royal Air Forces Escaping Society, Canadian Branch.

Polite and soft-spoken, Johnson is not given to boasting of his exploits, nor would he likely mention his Military Cross, yet he is one of the very few airmen to earn this decoration usually reserved for army officers exhibiting bravery on the battlefield. The citation reads:

> Flight Lieutenant Johnson carried out a model, well-considered escape from enemy-occupied territory following a parachute descent on January 14, 1945.
>
> He walked for twenty-two days with a ration of six Horlicks Malted Milk tablets a day only to live on. For the first seven days he had not a drop of water.
>
> Flight Lieutenant Johnson's determination to return to his unit and the exemplary manner in which he carried out his journey, overcoming all difficulties for over three weeks, give a great example and encouragement to other aircrew members faced with the same problem. . . .
> *London Gazette* — June 5, 1945

Johnson grew up in Winnipeg, finishing high school in 1932 at the age of 14. The Depression left thousands unemployed in the West. He tried his luck working on farms, in bush camps and driving a truck. At a government forestry reserve he earned five dollars a month with food and clothing.

> I helped harvesting in southwest Manitoba for two dollars a day. Work started before daylight, and didn't finish until after dark. It was rough. When the war broke out, I was driving a truck, and was lucky to be doing that.
>
> My buddy and I were going by the Minto Street armouries in Winnipeg one day, and saw a bunch of people out parading. We knew some of them, kids we had known in school.
>
> Then, just like that, just three days after the war was declared, we decided to enlist. We walked into the armoury and saw two rows of men, one down each side of the armoury floor. We knew kids in both lines, so we joined one of them. The guys in the other line were drafted into the Winnipeg Grenadiers, who went to Hong Kong and were shortly either killed or interned in POW camps. The line we were in was the Tenth Armoured Regiment. I joined the tenth and was with them until New Year's Eve, 1940.

At Camp Borden, I met a friend from home, Jimmy McIntosh, who was in the air force. He showed me over the Borden air force facilities one night, through all the shops and hangars. Those great big airplanes! I thought, my God, if Jimmy can fly these things, I can too. A few months later, Jimmy was killed in an air crash. The following weekend I went to Toronto, walked into the air force recruiting office on Bay Street and began the enlistment process.

I had to go back the next weekend with my birth certificate and proof of education. On the third weekend, I had an aircrew medical. On my last weekend, while waiting my turn to be sworn in, I asked the sergeant what I should do about my army unit after I got into the air force.

He said, "What army unit?"

"I'm in the army." I was wearing my army uniform, surely he could see that.

"You mean you are in the active army?"

"Yes."

He paraded me before the CO, who thought it was a real joke. "Well," he said, "I'll have to write to Ottawa to get this sorted out."

Back I went to my regiment at Camp Borden. It took about six weeks to sort it out. After I came back from Christmas leave, my army discharge came through. I was paraded before the colonel of the regiment. He tore strips off me for being "disloyal to the regiment." I told him I was just fed up not getting overseas. My brother had joined up after I did and he had gone overseas, and I wanted to see some action before the war ended.

The colonel wouldn't hand me my discharge. He sent me to Toronto with an intelligence officer and a motorcycle escort to deliver me to the air force Manning Pool. It was New Year's Eve. The only one there was a very new Pilot Officer who didn't know whether he was coming or going. He couldn't swear me in or do anything.

The intelligence officer said, "He's not to receive his discharge until he's actually sworn into the air force." I was confined to barracks for the weekend. Later I was sworn in and everything was fine

That's how I joined the air force.

After his unusual enlistment, Bob Johnson went through the usual routine of "hurry up and wait" familiar to servicemen everywhere. The vast machine for training airmen worked like an assembly line. You had to wait your turn to get onto each line, one line for Initial Training School (ITS) another for Elementary Flying Training School (EFT) and so on all the way down the pilots' assembly line to OTU — Operational Training Unit for preparation to posting to a squadron. Then you were ready to get a crack at the enemy! Some airmen whizzed through the system in record time without having to wait between stations on the line. Others spent agonizing weeks and months waiting, waiting, being sent off on "busy work" guarding stores or canals. Some were bypassed on to crash commando courses, or whatever else happened to be going that particular week. Eventually, most made it, and were ready for the "big show." Certainly Bob Johnson was.

In the tropics aircrew wore *beden* suits: a lightweight coverall with lots of pockets. They contained items useful in an emergency. It was the pilot's escape kit. The standard escape issue was packed into one tin about the size of a 1930s 100-cigarette tin. It included some fishing line, a float, a couple of different kinds of compasses (one that could be hidden in a belt loop, another a magnetized needle), a mirror, some chewing gum and a box of benzedrine pills.

A notice on the pill box read, "Only to be taken under the instruction and supervision of a senior officer." How dumb can you get? You're down, on the run. Are you going to wait for a senior officer!

But the most important thing in the tin was one little package of Horlicks tablets. They were not very thick, less than one eighth of an inch. One pocket was for maps — not the silk handkerchief type that were issued in the European area, but the usual heavy paper ones of Southeast Asia.

I felt that this wasn't enough if a person was going to come down in Burma. We were flying with long-range tanks away beyond the Irriwaddy and were out for up to three and a half hours per trip. If you came down at the extreme range it was a long way to walk with only a little package of Horlicks. I knew you'd need more than a few tablets, but I didn't know how many more, or how they would sustain you. I also thought, I'd like to have a flashlight and a lot of quarter-inch maps of a good part of Burma.

On most squadrons, useful information for emergency situations was passed around. Johnson had talked to one man, Flight Lieutenant Huxtable, who had been in a crash and gave a lecture on secret codes to be used when sending Red Cross letters from a POW camp. It seemed to Johnson almost ludicrous, since the Japanese did not admit Red Cross workers to the camps, and in any case took very few prisoners.

After talking with Huxtable, Johnson decided it would be wise to make his own escape kit.

So I cut up a pair of old khaki trousers to make a bag the shape of my parachute cushion, using it as a pattern. I cut a slit up the centre for my parachute harness, a button-down flap and two straps to sling it on my back, and it was done. Of course I had to sew it all up, but the airman's-issue "Housewife" had a needle, thread and thimble, for sewing buttons on shirts. It was just right for this task. I packed the fish hooks and line and three packs of Horlicks, a bar of hard, bitter chocolate I'd saved from the ship coming out from India — why I took it I don't know, but it was bound to come in handy.

I also packed a flashlight and about seven different types of compass. One little round one we used to call an arsehole compass, as that's where you hid it if you were captured. The main compass was an American marching compass, a little larger

Bob and friend resting in front of his tent early in January 1945 before that fateful crash.

than the ones we were given. It had a lid that came down locking the needle tight, and when opened, the ring rotated free, and the pointer was luminous for night-time use. The inside of the cover had a mirror and there was a slit in it to take bearings to find your way. It was an excellent compass.

I usually carried a kukri on my belt but I couldn't find it the morning I took off. I did have a standard-issue knife with a seven- or eight-inch blade. I still have it — I use it for opening lobsters. It's a good knife, but it wasn't very sharp at the time.

Johnson served in Burma with RAF 28 Squadron on Fighter Reconnaissance sorties, attempting to pinpoint the Japanese lines of communications and supply. On January 14, 1945, he was flying low over treetops and paddy fields. While inspecting roads and bridges over the Irriwaddy River, he detected movement on the ground. He swung to port to investigate and sighted a riverboat being loaded with oil drums.

Johnson's low-flying aircraft was attacked, there was an explosion and in no time the plane was just a ball of fire. He was able to bail out and pull the ripcord just as the tailplane cleared his head. The plane roared into a gully. Just before he jumped he saw two little villages below him. He landed just beyond those. Fearful of being chased, he just pulled the snaps loose, grabbed the kit and started hoofing it. Seconds after hitting the ground he was on the move without stopping to bury his parachute. The sound of people yelling alerted him to the pursuers he could see some five hundred yards away on ridges either side of him. He slid down a steep slope and dug into a shallow depression in the hillside where dense, low bushes offered cover.

Pulling the loose foliage over him, he listened as the voices came closer. Cautiously taking his knife out, avoiding any noise or movement that might give him away, he waited, fearfully, silently. Closer and closer came his pursuers — so close that he was sure they would hear the sound of his heart beating furiously as he crouched in the underbrush.

The sound of barking dogs running to and fro added to his panic those first hours of January 14, 1945.

> I decided to hide in the scrub until after dark, alert and listening to barking dogs, and villagers searching for me. About twelve hours later, I took off, heading in a westerly direction towards British-held territory.

After walking until the first glimmer of morning, he holed up under the root of a dead tree. Before going to sleep, he broke out his escape kit and counted everything. He had to have a plan to avoid wasting time and energy. He couldn't afford to blunder his way back by trial and error.

> I had my maps out: the most direct route would take me over occupied territory and lots of villages and open country. I decided that I would avoid any contact because of McVicar's experiences. He had come down and the Burmese had seen him. They professed to be friendly and took him into a village. They gave him some food and drink, as he sat on the steps of a basha in the village. Within half an hour Japanese troops suddenly came running into the village. McVicar rolled backwards into the basha and jumped out of an opening in the rear, then ran into the jungle and eventually found his way back.

The next two days failed to produce an escape from this tropical trap. The jungle provided a degree of safety, but survival was not going to be easy.

> After a while my mouth was so dry! Oh my God! I think that's why I started to get delirious. I was getting weaker, I couldn't walk as far, and I had to rest more often. My fingers were raw and sore from digging for water. By the fourth day, I was delirious, and could barely keep track of the days. It seemed hopeless. I decided not to dig for water any more. Perhaps I could make faster time walking. I was hungry, thirsty, tired and fearful all at the same time.
> After a bit, I sat down to rest and fell asleep. When I awoke and started off again, I stumbled along, and shortly came to the terrifying realization that the escape kit was not on my back.

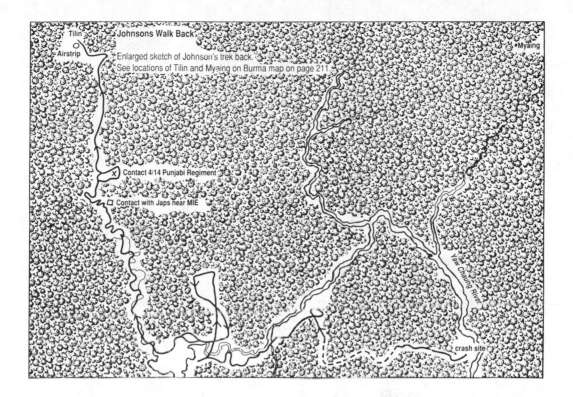

I was in a state of panic and alternately cursed and cried. I was desperate. No matter where I looked on the ground around me it was clear that the pack was gone. I knew I had over a hundred miles still to go. Was there any chance of recovering it?

Eventually I calmed down, forced myself to concentrate and try to think things out. A plan for retracing my steps was the only solution if I was to survive. I devised a systematic search for the lost kit. I began walking back the way I had come in a straight line, then after so many steps made a series of increasingly large right-hand turns. I covered a wide area of the track behind me, and was, in effect, using my air force training to carry out a "square search."

And I found it!

Johnson claims that finding the pack was just luck. Perhaps his rational search plan combined with luck explains his success. Thinking it over later, Johnson decided that he would always keep one tin of Horlicks in his pocket, so that in case of another lost pack at least he'd have one tin to rely on.

I don't remember much of the next three days and nights. My tongue was swollen, my throat parched and I seemed to have a continuous high temperature.

Once, while dozing in the underbrush, he came instantly wide awake. He could feel something slithering across his legs. Gingerly he lifted his head and could see a cobra making its way along the ground, over his outstretched legs and on through the bush. I never moved! I didn't dare. I'd be a goner if I'd frightened that snake.

Throughout all this, Johnson had not been able to refill his water chargall. It was not until the seventh night that he stumbled on to muddy tracks. Suffering from thirst, fever and exhaustion, he found himself walking in wet mud. In an orgy of relief, he sank down on his knees, and desperately gulped down the sludge until he made himself sick.

When his head cleared, he realized that he was sitting in a wallow hole. The Burmese peasants find water oozing up in a gulley; the bullocks are driven down to drink and wallow in it, covering their hides to keep the flies off. These are the bullock waterholes.

Once the nausea had passed, he felt better. After seven parched days, he was able to refill his water bottle. He strained some of the muddy water through his handkerchief and the canvas chargall bag, holding about a pint, was ready to be tied around his waist. The more he used it, the better it tasted. Faced with no viable alternative — he knew he was still a long way from safety — his watchword was: keep moving westwards towards the mountains. It would be a long haul.

As part of his pattern of evasion, Bob walked by night, and slept in the daytime. One day, however, he decided to take a chance, make up time by walking in the daytime. He was feeling reasonably chipper that early morning on the ninth day. A little after daybreak, as he headed into the higher scrub, he noticed an opening in the bush. Running towards it, he almost burst through, when he saw an old lady coming along the path. Fearful of scaring her, he jumped back and crouched down. He pretended he was a dog. "*Arf arf!*" he barked, not even taking the time to feel like a complete idiot, and her face broke out in a big grin. She looked into the bush, probably thinking it was a villager playing a trick on her. She stopped for a moment and her face split into a wider grin, enjoying the moment.

Encouraged by her reaction, he stood up, walked out into the clearing, and immediately the grin was gone. She stood stock still. He pointed to the basket on her head attempting to communicate his hunger. She knew what he meant, shook her head and hurried away. Suddenly, from the gap in the bush where she had retreated, men came running brandishing their split-bamboo weapons. Johnson took off, running a short way then hiding in the bushes. None of the men followed him into the jungle.

When the commotion died down, Bob moved off and kept going for an hour or so until his heart stopped pounding and he could find a quiet place to rest.

For three days he had been walking through dense growth. The insect population had increased: large webs with great hairy spiders patiently waiting for their prey were everywhere. Were any of these creepy things poisonous? The webs could be avoided while walking in the daytime, but at night more than once he abruptly found his face enveloped in a web, clinging to his beard. Clawing and frantically brushing it away still left him with the feeling that something was crawling on his neck.

At one point, he was walking parallel to a river about a half mile or so from its banks when he heard a queer sort of noise. At first, he thought it was dogs barking, but then it seemed oddly different — it couldn't be dogs. Was it some other animal? The unknown is more fearful because it *is* unknown.

Then it grew silent. It was a puzzle. Standing on a hillside, almost at daylight, he heard the barking again. Standing perfectly still he heard another bark. Then, out of the bush came a deer, a tiny deer, white showing on the little stubby tail. It bounded off into the scrub. Then another bark, and crashing through the trees came another and then another, and more of them. They were the barking deer called Muntjac, common to Southeast Asia.

On the night of the eleventh day, there was a moon. Johnson was again walking parallel to a river. Often shallow depressions run down to the river. A bamboo forest near the river forced him down into a gully. As the riverbank narrowed, near the bottom the trees were alive, absolutely alive, with monkeys.

I don't know how many there were there, but I would guess more than a hundred. Those monkeys are strong. They have skinny little arms, but they are strong. They are also dirty creatures. They could tear you apart, scratch you to death. I was definitely frightened. There were a number of young ones and the adults were obviously antagonistic. I backtracked up the same hill. It must have added two miles going around that gorge.

Later I had gone down to a stream with a wide sandbar in the middle of the water. I wanted to wash and fill my chargall. It was night and I decided to walk along the sandbar. I hadn't gone very far when a native called out. I ran up into the bush and hid. Then there was some shouting back and forth, so I took off.

The next day, I was elated at having found the juncture of the two streams. It was the first pinpoint I had — I knew exactly where I was, which gave me a great sense of relief.

Johnson believed the natives could not be trusted. There was no way of knowing if they were friendly or unfriendly, except that it was common knowledge that the Japanese had a price tag on airmen. Moreover, the Japanese had been in Burma since 1941 and had had full control of the country for two years or more. If the Burmese didn't do what was demanded of them, they were goners.

From his reconnaissance flights over the area, Johnson was familiar with the geography of western Burma. His general plan for getting back was to find a stream and follow it north. The mountains in Burma were at times 8,000 feet high and ran south in ridges from the Himalayas. They separated, more or less, India and Burma, the border in the north being the Chindwin River.

He knew Allied troops were just getting into the Gangaw Valley. He planned to head for the valley by following the streams. The difficulty would be to avoid the roads being used by the Japanese troops he had seen on his reconnaissance flights. A road would lead ultimately to the Gangaw Valley.

A day later he felt lost. Landmarks from the air appear quite different when viewed from the ground. Johnson understandably found himself confused, and on more than one occasion it was difficult to avoid panic. He climbed the highest hill looking for a clue to his whereabouts.

> At the horizon I could see the morning sun glinting on water. I calculated that was the junction of two large streams as noted on my map. It was quite clear. I used that as one bearing. Then I looked for a spot-height marked on my map — a prominent peak, easy to get a bearing on. So I had two bearings. I didn't get a third, which would have given me a little cocked hat and would have been more accurate, but that was close enough. It told me I was way off track.

The days were sliding by. Slowly, he moved westward, searching the landscape for familiar sights.

By night, he followed a cart track not far from open ground, and by day he hid out in the bush. One night, towards morning, he heard the drone of an aircraft and headed for a clearing where he could see and be seen. It was a Dakota with the doors open, which generally meant they were going to make a drop, supplying friendly people in the area. He tried signalling with his mirror but they didn't see him. (When he got back he checked the records, but could find no report of a downed airman's signal for help.)

A few nights later, on the nineteenth day of his trek, another aircraft flew overhead. He tried using his mirrors to blink his last initial in Morse code — . _ _ _, . _ _ _, J, J. He thought he saw the plane dip its wings and felt sure he had been seen, but he later found no report of that encounter either.

When he was closer to the Gangaw Valley he heard voices in the bush. The language was not like any he had heard before. He had some slight familiarity with Burmese and knew a bit more Hindi. Could it be Japanese?

> I had my knife in my left hand and was crouched down behind a thick thorn bush. There was no sound. I didn't move. It seemed like an eternity but could only have been a minute or so. Then there was a rattle of stones and a single Jap infantryman came around a small bush with his rifle at the ready. He was perhaps as scared as I was. I had to do something so I just dived and clipped him about his knees and he went arse over teakettle. I lunged at him with my knife and with my other hand grabbed a rock. I banged the rock on his face and he slowly rolled over — almost in slow motion. I didn't wait to see what happened; I just took off.

Within half an hour I saw more of them marching — no, they were slouching — along the bullock cart track near the stream. I'd hidden in case anyone was coming after me. I went off to one side of the track, but nothing happened. Nobody came along. Was it safe? I came out of the bush and back to the track, and had gone about three or four hundred yards when I came into a clearing on a rise of ground.

Just as I came over that rise there before me was a Japanese soldier, with full pack and equipment. There was nowhere to go, no moon, just the light from the stars, and I was in the open, so I just kept going and went around him — just like that. He was going one way, and I another.

Over the rise, I could see a whole troop, maybe twenty or thirty, coming up. I just kept going, walked right through them — if I had put out my hand I could have touched them. I had my Canada badges on, with the flag on my helmet.

They must have thought I was one of their own. They wouldn't just pass by an enemy. They must have thought I was a runner, an orderly or something. I don't know what it was, but they were obviously very tired too. They were just slouching along, not going all that fast. They must have been walking for hours. They had heavy packs, but there were carts carrying their equipment.

After they went by I scrambled up into the hills. It was too dicey walking along that track. I covered myself with some leaves and tried to sleep. Just before daybreak, I went back down to the track and saw more Japanese coming. I hurried back into cover. Looking out from a rise, I could see fires. I didn't go any further that night.

The days were passing. Bob had now been down in enemy territory far too long. He was tired, dirty, hungry, lonely — lonely as much for conversation as anything else. He had not heard a word of English since he'd come down in the jungle. To keep up his spirits he talked aloud to himself, even hummed familiar songs — "The Road to Mandalay" and "Roll Out the Barrel" — through the hills and forests of Burma.

Nearly at the end of his tether, he felt about in his shirt pockets for a Horlicks tablet, and found . . . there were none there. He was sure there had been at least one in his pocket: it must have fallen out away back. There was no possibility of going back to search for the tiny pill. He had been successful once when he recovered the whole escape kit. Chances of finding the Horlicks were too slim to invest time and energy in a search.

It was now three weeks since he had come down, twenty-one days since he'd grabbed his escape kit and run. Going through his meagre belongings, Bob came upon the benzedrine. This was surely the time to try one. The instructions were to swallow one an hour or so before you wanted to feel awake and energetic. He would use them as a pick-me-up for walking. Back on the cart track he began to feel light-headed, to the point where he didn't give a damn if there were Japanese around or not. He was aware of wearing army boots that made a lot of noise on stones, so he took them off.

He walked right through a village, without a care in the world. Most villages have dogs, who eagerly announce the arrival of strangers, but in this village there were no signs of dogs or people. Had the Japanese cleared them out? Without much thought he continued walking. The benzedrine had given him energy, but his awareness of danger was dulled. At the same time, he had forgotten his hunger.

At daybreak Johnson was getting close to the point where Allied and Japanese troops were engaged in action. He climbed halfway up an incline, under good cover, to bed down for the day.

I hadn't been there very long when I heard chinking and jangling. I knew it was mule harness — I'd heard it before. I had heard small arms and mortar fire, but was it ours or theirs? I kept hidden. I felt good that day because I had seen Dakotas making drops down this valley. There were three little knolls at the far end of it, and drops were made somewhere around those knolls. I judged they were about three miles away. The next night I took some more benzedrine and headed off, and by daybreak I was at those knolls. I walked into the valley, where I saw Burmese people, and they saw me, but I just kept going, heading for the drop sites. I thought this would be a great place to stay: if the Daks came back I'd be able to see where the drops went.

At that point I made a decision. I took my pack off my back, laid it against a tree and refilled my water chargall. Then I saw them. Three guys came up over the knoll. They were Indian troops, with British-type flat hats on, not the Japanese. By God, safe at last!

They were slouching along. And as soon as I saw them, I started to raise my hands and *BRRRRR*, the machine guns started up, chattering at a great rate. I dived behind a hefty tree and there was another couple of bursts, mud flying, and I was shaking. Then, everything was quiet. I yelled at them, "Don't shoot, you silly bastards!" There was no answer. So I shouted in Hindi "*Puch nay fire hi.*" Again, no answer. I got my hanky out and waved it about. Nothing happened. I thought the buggers were coming around the hill behind me. I got up and ran back to the ridge and hid under some trees.

That day, I had no Horlicks left and I figured I had to make contact. Our troops were there somewhere.

In March 1991, Johnson heard from a British officer who had been with that Indian regiment. He told Bob that the three men shot at him because his helmet made them think he was a Japanese flyer.

At this point Johnson was sure he could not make it without food. He waited until late afternoon, when the sun was starting to go down, reasoning that if he were chased, he might be able to evade for a couple of hours until darkness came.

He knew that new tactics had better be worked out: if those same guys were encountered again, he had better be sure to be recognized. He stripped to the waist exposing an expanse of white skin. If they were Indians, they would be less likely to shoot: if, Japanese, then it was hard luck.

Within a few hours, Johnson came in sight of some more Burmese villagers. Cautiously, he crept around some bushes in a dried-out gully. They were cooking down there. And, oh, it smelled so good. There was a bunch of men, women and kids. He decided to try direct contact. As he walked down the gulley, the women and kids disappeared. The men stayed. It was very quiet. The men stood in a semicircle on either side of an old man. Johnson walked up to him and sat down. They all sat too. The old man nodded at him.

Johnson desperately tried to communicate with hand gestures. He pointed to his mouth, patted his belly and looked mournful to show he was hungry. It worked. Attempts at speech were mildly successful. He said "English" — they said "*Unglay.*" He tried "Japanese" — they responded excitedly with "*Japoni.*" Again he tried "Unglay" — the old man said "*Unglay, Unglay*" and pointed off in a southwesterly direction. Then he said "*Unglay,*" and pointed at himself. The old man nodded his head, then in sign language, *First we are going to sleep and when the sun comes up off we go.* Remembering McVicar's close call, he just couldn't let the time go by. Putting on a stern forceful look, he said, "Now." The old man indicated okay.

> So he got up and I got up. Then I thought I'd better play this carefully, so I looked around, saw a little kid standing off to one side, and I clutched him by the arm, and openly placed my other hand on my knife. I don't know if the old man got my message or not but I had to do something. So I took the little kid by the arm, and he came along. The old man started off and several more men followed behind us.

Off they went, this little parade: the serene old man, a desperate Canadian, the trusting boy, and some dozen or so paces back, a watchful guard of younger men. They walked for a few miles, and came across some Indian soldiers splashing in the stream. One Indian stood guard with a rifle, on the far bank. Careful not to startle them, Bob walked right up and said, "Commanding Officer, *Kidar Hai?*"

The little parade, now led by Indian guards, continued on, walking into a little gully where a group of regimental officers were having their evening meal. Johnson introduced himself to the colonel.

> He got me some food. I ate too much again, and threw up minutes later. I told him of the Japanese who had just come through and showed him on the maps where they were.

Grateful for the help that the Burmese villagers had given him, Johnson shook hands with the old man, patted the young boy on the head and smiled broadly at the guards. He gave them some Indian rupees from his money belt. The colonel and his adjutant had a quiet discussion to decide whether they would be able to use the paper money. They exchanged it for some coins, and generously added to the pile in the old man's hands. We all smiled, shook hands and they returned the way they had come to their little clearing in the jungle.

"I never saw the old man again."

The colonel, eager to chase after the retreating Japanese, decided to break camp at first light. He apologized for the seeming lack of hospitality, but promised to send him by jeep to a landing strip, where he could get a plane out to India.

On the morning of his twenty-third day away from base, they gave him a bandoleer of ammunition and a rifle with half the stock broken off. Tersely, the colonel explained it had belonged to a cook, no longer with them. Apparently the previous night a Japanese had sneaked into the camp, lobbed a grenade that took off the cook and part of the stock of his rifle. The colonel warned that the area had not been mopped up yet.

"Take care, there could be Japanese stragglers out there."

"I wanted some sort of souvenir from him, so he wrote his name on a piece of Jap currency: 'Lt. Col. Miller, 4th/14 Punjabi Regiment.' I still have it."

The jeep he'd been promised had an Indian driver, a Chin hill man on a stretcher and an Indian medic. The Chin had been wounded through the groin and in the elbow. He was in pretty bad shape, but conscious. He'd been tied to the stretcher, which was slung from the windshield to the rear tarpaulin frames. The Indian medic got in the back seat with Johnson, and off they went.

The jeep set off along rutted and stony tracks. It was very rough and uneven country, the ride very bumpy. The wounded Chin kept rolling out of the stretcher. Finally, it was clear they couldn't continue this way. The wounded man was tied in a sitting position in the front seat. Despite the excruciating pain he was in, he never showed any sign of it, his face remaining expressionless. Stoically, he endured.

Going down one path they came upon a bunch of little brown men. For a moment they were right there, in front of them, then they just disappeared. The driver, the medic and Bob dived head-first out of the jeep. The wounded Chin couldn't do anything. Crouching behind a big rock, the three were amazed to see coming down the path a British officer, nattily dressed, clean and neat as if he were walking down Piccadilly in jolly old London. He had khaki shorts and knee-high socks, with nice little red gaiter tabs in the socks. "It's all right chaps," he said. "We are a Chin battalion."

We talked with him for ten minutes or so. He warned us about going down the track.

"About ten miles down the track you'll come to two little hills. Don't try to go through these hills without contacting my friend or he'll shoot you."

I found out that he and another officer had been behind the lines for about two years organizing the Chins. Both had been in Burma before the war and spoke the lingo. They were supplied by air and worked at harassing the Japanese. The first officer told us that if he had known I had gone through Pasok we might have made contact, as they had been down that way a week or more ago. He could have picked me up.

We came to the two hills, carefully followed his instructions and whistled the pre-arranged signal. From the bush, a big red-headed Irishman came out to greet us. We had lunch with him: hard tack and cheese.

A couple of hours down the track, near the village of Tilin, we came to a landing strip where Dakotas were landing supplies.

The landing strip was just a few hundred yards of cleared grass, long enough for a Dakota to land, unload and take off again without wasting time.

The first plane in was flown by a correct, stolid English pilot. He wouldn't take me. I don't know why, because I must have looked like death, but he said he had orders — no passengers.

An Aussie pilot flew the next plane in. He didn't see that there was any difficulty: he was going back to Imfal main strip. Group HQ was near there.

"Could you put me down there?"

The Aussie thought for a moment, then said, "That's off limits. No one is supposed to land there without permission." There was a long pause, then, "Well, if you'll run right up to the tower and tell them not to send a signal, I'll drop you off."

And so they went. It was a one-way strip. The Aussie pilot coasted, slowed down and took off in a matter of minutes.

He dropped me off and I hustled up to the tower and got the promise not to tell Imphal control. They had a land line there, so I phoned Group HQ. I knew the Air Officer Commanding. He knew every CO and flight commander in his group, and probably most of the pilots too. He was a regular man. When I got through on the land line, his aide-de-camp said "It's Johnson." I could hear the AOC shout, "Johnson! Where in the hell is he?"

He told me to stay right where I was. "I'll have my staff car come and get you."

When I got to Group HQ, a General Stratomeyer, an American in charge of all the air forces in SEA Command, and some other big wheels I didn't know, happened to be visiting. The AOC loaned me some of his clothes, and I got cleaned up. I told them what I had been up to.

General Stratomeyer kept me talking for a good half hour, asking all about my experiences behind the lines, my escape, my brushes with the Burmese, and especially the retreating Japanese. He asked me, "What would you like most?" I thought for a moment and then said, "Well, a bottle of American beer would go down good."

The officer who came from Calcutta to debrief me was Flight Lieutenant Huxtable of Air Force Intelligence, who had lectured us on Red Cross letter codes. I had to go to Calcutta for a medical exam. They wanted to see if there was any vitamin loss. I was more interested in the fact that I had lost about forty pounds.

Bob Johnson in Burma, about a week after he had made it back from his trek through the jungle.

I stayed at an aircrew rest house in Calcutta. One day, out of the blue, an American officer on a motorcycle rode up with a letter for me from General Stratomeyer: an invitation to lunch. The American major who brought the invitation also had a case of American beer for me.

A couple of days later, I had lunch with Stratomeyer and a group of officers. He introduced me: "This is the boy that got back."

CODA

CHAPTER TWENTY-THREE

TOUCHING THE RIM OF THEIR EXPERIENCE

Denis Budd and Donald Smith evaded successfully across the Baltic to Sweden. Ray De Pape, John Dix and others went the other way, across the Pyrenees, through Spain to Gibraltar in 1943. Ken Woodhouse, in 1944, went from Paris to Plouha in Brittany and thence across the Channel by MGB. Lou Greenburgh was one of hundreds of downed airmen who were collected and hidden in the forests of France and Belgium to await liberation. Others, like Jim Moffat and Bill Poohkay, found themselves with an Underground unit and lived and fought with them until liberated by the advancing Allied armies. John Hall and Sonny Fassoullis had rowed to the freedom of an Italian island and Dave Bockus and Bob Johnson made their own way out of Burma.

Joe Healey, like Jim Moffat, joined the Maquis after he crash-landed near Herantels, Belgium, on the night of October 18/19, 1943. For eleven months he evaded capture with the help of many civilians, some of them ordinary folk, like Henri and Maria Maca, other distinguished Belgians like Commander de Pret Rouse de Carslberg, aide to Prince Albert. When Joe was liberated in mid-September 1944, he was serving with the Maquis Falenprise and staying with Mr. and Mrs. Armand Ligot. The American army arrived one day in September 1944, and there was a great celebration:

> There was no fighting. They just took the main highways and rolled through the Germans, who were dispersed in the woods. The Germans disappeared and the village was free. We all gathered in the town hall to celebrate. The people who had hidden us were very proud to show us off to the Americans and were glad of the white bread, chocolate bars and cigarettes the Yanks gave them.
>
> I had been evading for eleven months, probably one of the longest times for any evader. Now that I was liberated I decided to take the train to Tournai to see a girl I knew. She was Ligot's daughter and was training to be a nurse in a hospital there. I got on the train but at a station somewhere a call came over the speaker on the train that asked me to identify myself. The next thing I knew these two British agents grabbed me:
>
> "Are you Joe Healey?" they demanded.
>
> "Yes."
>
> "You're coming to Brussels with us."
>
> "Right now?"
>
> "Yes, right now!"

> I was going to take a couple of weeks off, eh? And have a good time, but they were having none of it. Those buggers knew where I was and they came after me and took me to Brussels, put me in an army uniform, got me on a DC-3 and I was gone to England! Don't ask me why the rush, I didn't see any reason for it. After all, there was lots of time. What did it matter where I was? They insisted that I go back immediately, but I couldn't see why.

And he adds, wistfully, that almost forty-five years later he still can't see what all the rush was about.

John Millar and two of his crew, Geoff Gage and Al Donnell, were hidden by the Jonette family for several weeks in the summer of '44. The recently declassified Interrogation Report, dated September 13, 1944, of mid-upper gunner F.D. Rooks is unusually interesting for the specific names and dates that it contains, the understated account of the dangerous activities of the helpers, and not least for the laconic reference to his broken leg.

> We took off from Croft at 2230 hrs. on 27 Apr. 44 and at approx. 0100 hrs. on 28 Apr. we were forced to bale [sic] out. On touching down I broke my leg. I hid my equipment and with difficulty made off in a S.E. direction. After getting as far as I could, I hid under a thick hedge until 0900 hrs when I knocked at the door of a house and asked for help. I learned that I was in the village of GELIN-DEN (N.W. EUROPE, 1:250,000,Sheet 3,K24). In the afternoon I was taken by an officer of the White Army to his house at Goyer where I spent a day, then moved on to a large house owned by a Countess near WAREMME (K23). I remained there until 2 May 44, during which time my leg was treated by a doctor.
>
> On 2 May the doctor moved me in his car to another house in WAREMME. My leg was still in a plaster cast. Three weeks later I moved back to the Countess and remained with her until I was able to walk again.
>
> About 5 June I went by tram to Brey where I remained 5 days with a tram conductor. From there I went by bicycle to CRISNEE (K33) where I met four members of my crew, F/Lt. Hill, P/O Donnell, P/O Gage and Sgt. Millar.

They were liberated on September 8. The day before, a unit of the German army had pulled into a field right across from the house. Millar recalls the events that followed:

> They set up six 88s and covered them all with branches. About 4:30 P.M. they opened fire for about fifteen minutes and then pulled out. We didn't know what was going on, but we knew the war was coming our way. We were only about eight kilometres from the Dutch frontier at the time.
>
> On September 8 we got up real early. Suddenly there were Germans at the front door looking for a place to sleep, so we ducked out the back and hid in the chicken house all day while the Germans slept in our beds.

About three o'clock in the afternoon they took off and, all of a sudden, there was this one American in a jeep. We ran out and shouted that we were Canadians. He stopped and gave us a long hard look, while all the time hanging on to his Tommy gun. He said he had to press on but there were American troops just over the hill. So up we went and there was this American officer with two six-guns strapped to his side. It wasn't Patton, but it was somebody who acted like him.

We told him about the 88s and that they had pulled out. We told him that it was hard to tell how many vehicles there were because there were trucks pulling guns and trucks pulling other trucks and some pulling motorcycles — maybe as many as twenty all tied on a rope one behind the other to save gas.

John Millar served in the air force after the war, and for a time was stationed in Zweibrucken, Germany. He describes an incident that reflected how some people in Luxembourg still felt about the Germans:

I had a German car with German plates on it. I also had a Canada plate in the back window, but it had fallen down. I stopped at a service station in Luxembourg to ask directions and he pointed to the way I should go. As I was getting back into the car one of our kids pushed the *Canada* sign back up in the window. The attendant noticed this and asked:

"Vous êtes Canadien? Pas d'Allemagne?"

"Oui, Canadien."

And then he said that he was sorry, but that he would never give a German the right directions. That same thing also happened to us in Belgium and other places until we identified ourselves as Canadian.

John now lives in Victoria, B.C. As he looks back on his war experience as a young man, he says it has given him a lot more faith in people than he ever had before:

I had always been callous and believed that I could get by on my own, but when I needed help, those people took me in. They didn't know me from Adam but they helped me anyway. I have found more good people after that experience, and I try to help others because I got help when I needed it.

When a person is an evader, everywhere you walk you are always looking in a store window to see whether anyone is following you. That habit stuck with me, and it took me years to get out of it. I would be walking down a busy street in Winnipeg and would automatically examine every store window for reflections of people behind me. Even now I catch myself doing it the odd time.

Fred Richards and his fellow evaders had been picked up by a Resistance group led by a man named De Vries. They went by bike as close as they could get to the front lines. Cramped in a cellar in the centre of a small town, they found themselves between the two armies, the Germans on one side and the Allies on the other, with a lot of shells falling between them. For about thirty-six hours they stayed there until De Vries decided it was time to go on.

We scurried from house to house, trying to keep out of the line of fire. At one point two of us bumped into six Germans huddled behind a crumbling wall. They were only six to eight feet away as we took shelter, but they ignored us. As soon as there was a bit of a break we moved on. We got into a house close to a railroad track. We ran under a trestle bridge. A little guy popped up from behind a bush and said two glorious English words: "Hands up."

We were taken to an officer and then to local headquarters. We hadn't eaten for some time so we broke open some cupboards to get some food. They had white bread, something we hadn't seen in months. We stuffed our guts until we were both sick. This little soldier thought it a great joke.

They were taken by truck a long way back to headquarters for interrogation, then, on April 19, 1945, back to England by Stirling aircraft with the wounded. Richards phoned his wife and found that he had a son, born while he was missing in Holland.

Forty-five years after landing and evading in Holland, Fred's wife reflects on his life after the war:

He was a bunch of nerves for at least six months after he got back. He jumped; he flinched; he was in terrible, terrible shape. He only weighed 112 pounds. For years he suffered, and still does, with back pains. They later discovered that when he came down in that orchard, he suffered a broken back.

Bob Bodie remembers vividly the day he was liberated. He and some others had been hidden in the home of Mme. Serant, who lived in a small chateau.

The Germans were in retreat and one night they stormed Madame's place. It had a huge cast-iron gate, you know, and they smashed that down and came trooping into the house, looking for a place to sleep. Well, we had the best bed in the house, I guess, so Mme. Serant quickly got us out of there and shooed us into a cupboard in the bathroom. She had a teacher friend, Collette, with her and she put Collette in our bed. When the Germans came up the stairs, they naturally wanted to get into our bedroom but Madame Serant exclaimed:

"Non, non. Consumption, consumption!" And she pointed to the bedroom door, indicating that this poor schoolteacher was dying of a dreadful disease. That's how she got rid of the Germans and saved our hides. Collette used to run messages for the Underground by bicycle as well. When the retreating Germans got too close, she moved us to a little house on the edge of the village. It was a bit shaky for a while as the Germans retreated right by where we were hiding. Then Mme. Serant's farmer drove us to Paris and we were on our way.

Unlike most returning evaders, Bob Bodie rejoined his now famous squadron. The squadron's last operation, on April 25, 1945, involved fifteen of its planes in an attack on the fortified island of Wangerooge, one of the islands that guarded the approaches to the harbours of Bremen and Wilhelmshaven. The last to return, Bodie's plane, with Flight Lieutenant Wickham as pilot, got back at precisely 2015 hours, thus winding up the wartime operational activities of the squadron in Europe. On several occasions since the war he and his wife have made the journey back to see old friends like Mme. Serant.

Clayton Leigh, the Typhoon pilot, must surely be the most notable evader for the number or records he seems to hold. As noted earlier, one of his sorties from foxhole to target and back to the foxhole lasted about eighteen minutes. His evasion took one week or less. He took off from Strip B6 on August 19, 1944, at 11.30 A.M., and was down half an hour later near Orbec, France. According to his recently declassified Interrogation Report, he was interrogated by British Intelligence in England on August 26.

In those seven days he had been taken prisoner, was marched away with some other prisoners, organized a successful escape and was liberated and returned to his squadron, where he was not permitted to resume operations. Along the way, one night he slept in a convent, where a sister told him that the previous occupant of that room had been a dying German field marshall. All in all, quite a week.

The frontline German troops that had captured him turned Leigh over to some military police. As he was marched along, he was joined by other prisoners, until there were twenty-three of them, all told. The group was then turned over to a guard group of elderly German NCOs. Some of the prisoners felt so sorry for their guards that they voluntarily carried their packs for them.

Each night these NCOs would look for a building in which to secure the prisoners so their guards could get some sleep. On the fourth night they were shoved into a convent, apparently very recently occupied by the field marshall.

Leigh's Interrogation Report refers to that of Flying Officer Christianson, USAAF, which contains an interesting paragraph:

> At about 1300 hrs (20 AUG 44) we were joined by more P/Ws. Three were pilots and four soldiers. One of these pilots was called F/O Leigh of 182 Sqn. During this time we had been receiving scant but adequate food, consisting of one stew per day, bread, butter and cheese. Otherwise we were given an odd cup of ersatz coffee. French farmers, however, used to supplement this light diet with an occasional cup of milk.

Leigh, Christianson and a little English tank driver by the name of Wilkinson decided that it was time to take off. Wilkinson approached Leigh and said:

"Sir, are you going to escape or are you going to be like these other guys and sit out the war in a prison camp?"

"No, I'll escape," Leigh replied.

"Let's go then, sir!"

"Hold everything, soldier! Let's do it when we have some chance of escape," Leigh cautioned.

Rain, which was the curse of prisoners held in the open, gave Leigh, Christianson and the scrappy little tank driver the opportunity they were looking for.

> The guards had herded us together and formed a ring around us while one of the NCOs went off to find a building to stick us in. It was very dark and the rain was heavy enough that visibility was very poor. I whispered to the other two guys to back up very slowly and ease our way back through the circle of guards until we could drop into a ditch. Hopefully they wouldn't know we were gone until morning.

The three stole away in the darkness undetected and were soon making time on gravel roads. However, Wilkinson had big hobnailed boots and the sparks that flew off his boots were like rockets:

> I said this was no good, that we would have to split up. But when I looked at Wilkinson he seemed so forlorn that I told him to forget it and we went across country instead.

They found a barn, pulled and shoved each other through a trap door leading to the loft and scraped together enough hay to make a bed, not particularly concerned about the noise they made. Finally, the trio fell asleep.

> When we woke up the next morning we discovered to our great surprise that German soldiers had been sleeping down below, and they were now making breakfast! Why they didn't hear us scratching around I'll never know. They finished breakfast and moved out. We waited a few hours, then I jumped down and hailed a French farmer who had come out to feed his stock. He did a real double take when he saw me, but he brought us some potato soup. Shortly after that, a British recce patrol arrived and we were free.

Leigh returned to Canada shortly thereafter and after serving at Camp Borden was discharged from Trenton. His introduction to post-war civilian life proved to be disillusioning:

> I remember getting on the train to go back to Orillia. There I was, at twenty-five years old, with no education — I hadn't even finished high school. And I was going back to my little town having just left an exciting life as a flight lieutenant. I had been an officer and a gentleman and had lived the lovely life. While I was in England I had my own polo pony stationed on the airfield, and when we moved the squadron, one of the airmen would ride my horse to the next station. The thought of going back to my little hometown with no education, nothing to aim for, was really frightening. I would have jumped off the train at the least excuse, though I don't know where I would have gone.

Clayton Leigh did go back to Orillia. With his $800 mustering-out pay he bought carpentry tools, and began building houses, as his father had done. The first house he built was for a fine Italian family. It was a lovely house, he was happy and the Italian family was happy. His problems began with the next project, a house for a Toronto man.

The trouble was that I had been living with fellows on the squadron who I had trusted with my life and I was a very trusting soul at that time.

   I couldn't get any money from him. I kept going back to him, and finally I said I just had to have some money or I couldn't carry on to finish the house. He said he wasn't going to give me any money — just like that. He told me I could whistle for my money. There was a lawsuit and I got a little bit of money back, but not nearly what I had spent. This guy brought to the trial so-called expert witnesses from Toronto to testify that there were defects in the construction. He had to bring in outsiders because nobody in Orillia would have supported him. That was my introduction to business, after being an officer and a gentleman trusting everybody with my life and being faithful in return.

Fred Reain's journey to liberation took him south, across the Pyrenees to Spain and eventual freedom in Gibraltar. Along the way, he encountered decidedly exotic food as well as dangerous moments. His Interrogation Report contains this excerpt for January 22, after his two days in the hay barn while the Germans searched for him:

The next day my helpers, who were very poor, gave me some civilian clothes and got in touch with someone who could help me. It turned out that the woman who I was taken to could do nothing for me, but she, in turn, took me to another man who could speak perfect English. This man suggested that I should put on my RAF uniform and go into Charlons-sur-Marne and give myself up to the Germans. I left his house. My helpers told me later that he got in touch with the Gestapo immediately.

That same night a fifteen-year-old boy brought him some pickled pork. It was delicious, Reain recalls:

He gave me quite a bit, so I saved some for the next day, and when I looked at in daylight it was crawling with maggots. I suppose I had eaten quite a few of those big fat maggots the night before but it didn't bother me all that much. I scraped them off and ate all the meat.

With the Belloyel family in Marston-sur-Marne, Fred had another unique experience:

To occupy my time, they asked me to clean a bushel of lentils. I was in this small attic room, where I had to stay all day because Germans used to come to the house quite frequently. These lentils were quite small and there were weed seeds and mouse shit amongst them. The only way to clean them was by hand, one lentil at a time. I sorted almost a whole bushel of lentils that way.

Crossing the Pyrenees was no picnic for Fred and his fellow evaders:

We walked endlessly up into the hills. We never slept in a place with heat and our food was always cold. While we were hiding in a barn a farmer would come up with the food. He never said a word to us. He would just leave the food over where he hitched up his oxen and we would go and get it. However, one night while we were there one of the young fellows helping us caught a wild boar and we had a real feast — wine, potatoes and the meat, done to perfection. Another time, Bill Fell, from Hamilton, and I caught a snake, which we cooked in a stew and ate.

When we got close to the Spanish frontier we met a shepherd with a large flock of sheep. He milked these sheep to make cheese. I knew how to milk so we milked these sheep and had enough sheep's milk to feed seven or eight people.

When we were ready to move we drove these sheep up the mountain to hide the scent that we would leave, and in that way we fooled the German guards with their tracking dogs. But there was snow up there and it was getting colder. I had wooden shoes at the time and you have to travel a long way to get anywhere going up a hill!

Eventually Fred Reain, Bill Fell and the others crossed into Spain and were interned by the Spanish police. Later the British Consul from Madrid made contact.

One evening soon afterwards a Spanish guard came to us.

"You, you and you," he said, pointing to three of us. "Be at the side door of this building tomorrow morning at seven o'clock."

The next morning we were there sharp at seven. Right on the dot of seven the Spanish guard on the door wheeled around, shouldered his rifle, and marched up the hall and around the corner out of sight. Then someone opened the door from the outside and this handlebar moustache and long face appeared and said in a distinctly English voice:

"All right, chaps, come along with me."

He took us by train all the way to Pamplona, where we went to a bullfight. The next day the moustache appeared again, this time in a station wagon, and off we went to Saragossa. The moustache arrived on the third morning with the same vehicle and, about six flat tires later, we were in Madrid. There we got new civilian clothes, which shrank as soon as it rained, and we were off to Gibraltar and then by DC-3 to London and M.I. 9 for two days.

After being liberated again, this time from M.I. 9, Fred took some leave, then returned to 408 Squadron for a few more operations. Looking back on his adventures today, Fred notes that, at twenty-five, he was the old man of his crew. All in all, it was an experience he is glad to have behind him, though he doesn't believe it redirected his life in any way.

Brock Christie and his fellow evaders had left the Oosterbrooks and were crossing the Rhine in March 1945, when they saw two German deserters:

We tried to turn them over to the Canadian authorities to save them from being taken by Belgian civilians. Those Belgians had had a taste of German occupation and they weren't very friendly to the Germans. We saw one deserter who had this little suitcase with him. The Belgians took his suitcase, tore it apart and held everything up to scorn. I had some sympathy for those German deserters.

At two o'clock on the morning of March 16, the Canadian army met us. The feeling of being free after six months of having to hide in a chicken house or in trenches is hard to describe, but the minute we were free the four of us just yelled our heads off. We were no longer afraid of being discovered. We could talk, yell, laugh, cry — anything we wanted. The Canadian major who met us gave us cigarettes and we smoked our heads off. For them it was just another day, but for us it was very special. We felt that the red carpet had been rolled out for us and we thought we should yell and wake somebody up and let them know we were there. Then we had a damned good bath. They took away our filthy old clothes and issued us with army battledress with no insignia up.

Liberation for Bert Oosterbrook and his family came about a month after Brock Christie was free.

I remember when, in April of '45, the Canadian army came by our farm. Just the day before we had seen the German army retreating. There were a lot of old men in that German army; maybe the real fighting forces had already gone. These were men as old as sixty-five and there were also some boys amongst them. They were on old trucks or bikes, and some of them were walking. I remember one boy with a baby carriage with all his belongings in it.

A day or two after that somebody at our neighbour's farm said that the Canadians were coming. I had to see that. And man, oh man, they had this mammoth tank; I had never seen anything like it. It stopped right beside the shed where we kept the sheep. We couldn't believe it. We got a chocolate bar. They wanted to know which way the Germans had gone and we told them. They took a couple of German prisoners and we couldn't believe that either. Germans taken prisoner? But the Canadians smashed their rifles and said to them: "You see these tracks?" And they pointed to the tracks made by their tank. "Just follow them and someone will take you." And they did.

We knew the Germans had parked one of their trucks on the road ahead. We told the two soldiers in the tank. They put up their field glasses, sighted where we pointed and then carefully moved the tank's gun a little to the right and up a little. Then there was a helluva bang and that was the end of the truck.

After that, we had the Canadian army staying on our farm. Luckily for us, their kitchen truck stayed on our farm, too! One thing the troops were interested in was the freshly laid eggs our ten chickens produced. They had been used to powdered eggs. Our eggs were there for everybody to see, but nobody touched them. They asked if they could have one. We said yes and they gave us cigarettes in return. But nobody ever took an egg without first asking and then paying for it.

Joe Petsche of 434 Squadron was liberated eighty-nine days after he went down, a week after D-Day — three days short, as it turned out, of the time required to qualify for a pension. He draws a monthly disability pension of $50 for being wounded in the leg, and he still has a piece of shrapnel in one thigh. It doesn't bother him but it still shows up in X-rays.

Yet there were some compensations, he says:

I had a good time in France, and I ate better than I did in England. I lived on a farm and worked in the fields. I lived with the Tripet family in the small village of Louvencourt. I had a nice room there with a back window for escape in case anything happened.

Once a Typhoon pilot was shot down in the area and I had to sleep out in the fields for three days while the Germans did a house search. Another time a retreating German officer stayed at the house with two soldiers. I was supposed to be a Polish worker. Being of Austrian descent, the hardest part was pretending not to understand them when they spoke German, because I could understand it.

When I was liberated we all got drunk on champagne and I found that I couldn't speak English! The next day I went into Arras and turned myself in.

As with most evaders, Joe maintained close contact with his helpers, the Tripets, and has visited them since the war. And, also as with most evaders, he becomes emotional when he talks about it:

We went back in 1979. It was like coming home. Mme. Tripet had one daughter who now has three children, and they all knew about me. They had set aside a room for me and all my things that I had left were there. I had written that we were coming and there were men there waiting for our arrival. When I got out of the car, Nester Tripet rushed up and threw his arms around me and we hugged.

Joe struggles to say this and pauses a moment or two before continuing:

I'm very grateful to the Tripets. They were far braver than we were. We flew for the excitement and had the guns to defend ourselves, but these people put their lives on the line without anything to defend themselves with. They could have been shot if they had been caught.

My experience, I believe, has given me a greater insight into life. I don't worry so much anymore about dying. I was the only Catholic in our crew and I went to church before every trip. The rest of the crew made sure that I did!

Like Joe Petsche, Gordon Stacey "stayed put" and waited for the Allies to come his way. He had hoped to get out through Spain, but after D-Day that was unrealistic. As soon as the railway lines were repaired and word came that it was time to move on, the lines would be bombed again, so he and his mates stayed with Fifi.

We never saw her in the daytime. She was always out running around for food, clothing or anything that we needed or wanted. For a while there were four of

I.S. 9.(W.E.A.)

WARNING AGAINST GIVING INFORMATION ABOUT YOUR ESCAPE OR HOW YOU EVADED CAPTURE

This applies to Members of all Services and continues even after discharge therefrom.

1. It is the **duty** of all persons to safeguard information which might, either directly or indirectly, be useful to the enemy.

2. The Defence Regulations make it an **offence**, punishable with imprisonment, to **publish** or to **communicate** to any unauthorised person any information or anything which purports to be information on any matter which would or might be directly or indirectly useful to the enemy.

3. This document is brought to your personal notice so that you may clearly understand information about your escape or how you evaded capture is information **which would be useful to the enemy,** and that therefore to communicate any information about your escape or how you evaded capture **is an offence under the Defence Regulations**.

4. You must not disclose the **names** of those who helped you, the **method** or **methods** by which you escaped, the **route** you followed or how you reached this country, nor must you even give information of such a general nature as the **names of the countries** through which you travelled. All such information may be of assistance to the enemy and a danger to your friends. **Be specially on your guard with persons who may be newspaper representatives.**

5. **Publishing or communicating** information includes :—

    (a) publication of accounts of your experiences in books, **newspapers** or periodicals (including Regimental Journals), **wireless** broadcasts or lectures :

and   (b) giving information to friends and acquaintances either male or female, in private letters, in casual conversations or discussions, even if these friends or acquaintances are in H.M.'s or Allied Forces and however " safe " you may consider them to be.

6. F.O. (557-44)
   A.C.I. (1896-43)   } prohibit lecturing by escapers or evaders to any unit without
   A.M.C.O. A89-44   prior permission of the Admiralty, War Office, Air Ministry.

TO BE COMPLETED IN THE PERSON'S OWN HANDWRITING.

I have read this document and understand that if I disclose information about my escape, evasion of capture I am liable to disciplinary action.

Signed *V. Brock Christie*   Date: *17.3.45*

Full Name (Block letters) *CHRISTIE, VALENTINE BROCK*

Rank and Number *P/o   J878 5-3*

Unit *48 SQDN*

                       Witnessed by ....

Christie signed this waiver on return from evading in March 1945.

WHAT YOU MAY SAY.

By signing the attached document you have undertaken to maintain a strict secrecy about your experiences. It is realised, however, that your family and friends are certain to ask you questions. *Below you will find suggestions for the best way of answering them :—*

ROYAL NAVY.

(In similar terms to those for Army and R.A.F., altered to suit particular circumstances.)

ARMY (Escapers).

I was captured by the Germans (Italians) and sent to a prison camp in **Germany (Italy).** I managed to escape and get back to this country, but I cannot tell you how I did that without spoiling the chances of others who are trying to get away. *I am sure you will understand that I cannot tell you anything till after the war, and I have orders not to say more than I have already told you.*

or

ARMY (Evaders).

I managed to evade capture and get back to this country. As many others are trying to do the same, you will understand I cannot tell you anything till after the war. In any case, I have orders not to say more than I have already told you.

R.A.F. (Escapers).

I was shot down by flak during a bombing raid. I baled out, and was captured and sent to **Germany.** I managed to escape from a prison camp and get back to this country. As many others are trying to do the same, you will understand it is not possible for me to tell you anything till the war is over. In any case, I have orders not to say more than I have already told you.

or

R.A.F. (Evaders).

I was shot down by flak and baled out. I managed to evade capture and get back to this country. As many others are trying to do the same, you will understand it is not possible for me to tell you anything till after the war. In any case, I have orders not to say more than I have already told you.

Full Name (Block letters) *Brock Christie*

Rank and Number *P/o J87053*   Signed *CHRISTIE V.B.*

Unit *48 SQDN*   Date *17.3.45*

Witnessed by *........................*

F/O Brock Christie (centre); F/O Bernard Raciot (right); F/O Roger Marc-Aurele (left) at RCAF Depot Centre, May 6, 1945.

us staying with her — an RAF navigator, two Americans and me, and she had to feed us all. Most of the food was from the black market. We had some money, which we turned over to her, and I think she got some financial help from friends who were prepared to put their money but not their necks on the line. She found out that I was a model builder, so somehow she got a kit for a model of a Halifax bomber and I built that. Where she got it from I don't know.

We got to know a fellow who was an engineer in a tube factory. He was commandeered to go out on work gangs to repair the rail lines. During every air raid we would go up into the attic and plot where the bombs fell on a city map we had. Then this guy would come back and tell us where they actually fell. It was a sort of game and it made life a little more interesting.

Every day that this fellow came we knew his factory hadn't been hit, but one day he came in and he was as high as a kite; his factory had been wiped out and he was as happy as could be.

We knew the Americans were coming because we kept a map and got our news from the BBC. One evening we heard small-arms fire from the main square in Liège. It was really foolhardy, but we were too excited to stay put, so we went down to the square and met some American soldiers. They were happy to talk to someone who could speak English, but they couldn't understand how we got there. They were mostly interested in having a hot shower, so Fifi arranged that too!

Stacey still can't understand why people like Fifi got involved the way they did. It would have been so easy for them to turn and go the other way, but then he says:

I guess there are people in this world who do not think of themselves first, who do value freedom and who are prepared to put their necks on the line. What really gets me at this time of year [it's November as we talk together] is Remembrance Day. Yet for me, every day is Remembrance Day.

Here in Guelph, Victor Davis, the swimmer, has just been killed; this is his hometown. There have been lots of eulogies to him and rightly so — about him being cut down in the prime of his life. Victor Davis was twenty-five; if he had been in our crew he would have been the old man. I was the second oldest, at twenty-two; our rear gunner was nineteen. Death happened every day on both sides of the war. Four of our seven men crew, all Canadians, were killed. Our flight engineer, Alex Fuller from the RAF, was captured the second day and spent the rest of the war as a POW. Johnny Arscott, our bomb aimer, also of the RAF, was sheltered by the Dutch Underground until Liberation, but I didn't know all this till after I got back.

We had to get rid of Hitler, of course, but how much better it would have been if all those people had been allowed to reach their potential and have children who would carry on.

Fifi survived the war. She lost a lot of friends in the conflict, some of whom were betrayed by their own countrymen. She is bitter about that. She moved to another locality, where she cares for a niece who is mentally handicapped. She never married.

There is a Dutch saying that only dead fish float downstream; live ones swim against it. Certainly Emmy van Taack and her friends swam against the stream as they resisted the German occupation of their country. As we read in Chapter 5, Emmy was involved in the Resistance movement from the age of fourteen. She helped to save Allied airmen like Jimmy Branford and several paratroopers who had survived the attack on Arnhem.

On January 13, 1945, she was arrested. One of the teen-age boys in the Organization dated a girl who also went out with Germans. Apparently this boy bragged to the girl about his prowess with a revolver, obtained as a member of the Resistance. The girl relayed this information to her German boyfriend. The boy was arrested and he informed on the rest of the group. Emmy and her friend Mimy were taken to a military camp.

We hadn't been frisked yet, so our immediate goal was to get rid of the papers we were carrying. We also had some butter that we were to have delivered. We had to get rid of this big manila envelope and we couldn't burn it because of the smell it would make, so we tore it all in little pieces, coated each piece with butter and ate them!

After three weeks or so, Emmy became feverish. It looked as though she had scarlet fever, a further hardship, but one which may have saved her life. Because she was in a German military camp and her disease was highly contagious, the Germans wanted her out of there as soon as possible.

She was moved to a Dutch hospital with a guard, a nurse and a doctor who was responsible for her. After about a week there, she got a message from friends in the Organization that she must escape. She knew too much that, if revealed under interrogation, would be very dangerous for others. However, she had to plan her escape so that it would not incriminate the doctor.

I took a big chance and consulted a nurse's aide. I was in a separate building with a door that was locked. The building had low windows that were covered on the inside with black paper on wooden frames. I put my cards on the table and asked her to do two things for me, then I would forget about her forever and she about me. First, I wanted her to show me where the key to the outside door was kept. Second, I wanted her to take my plan to Annie, who was to assist in my escape. I was going to unlock the outside door at night, let Annie in, lock the door and put the key back, take down the blackout blinds and both of us would go out the window. In that way it would look like I had done it completely on my own with no help from inside. My little helper made contact with Annie and came back with verbal instructions about date and time.

When the night came it was hard to stay awake, but I had to be alert to hear the short tap on the window that would announce Annie's arrival. Finally it came. I got the key in the dark — I had practised during the day to find its location easily and not drop it. Annie brought a flashlight, a dark raincoat and a blue veil for me to wear, and she herself was in a nurse's uniform. It took a tense fifteen minutes to dress and get the blind down. Annie told me that if the nurse came down she would knock her out and that put me a little more at ease. We finally climbed through the window to freedom just as first light started to appear. Her bicycle was hidden in the bushes nearby and she jumped on the front and I on the carrier and soon we joined the stream of people moving north on their daily search for food.

On April 17, 1945, the German army left the area where Emmy was hiding, the Canadian army moved in and she was able to rejoin her parents and begin picking up the pieces of her life. But it wasn't easy:

In that time when I was growing up, between fourteen and nineteen years old, I missed all the normal things for that age. In a way it was worse than if it had been when I was younger. There are lots of things that should be experienced as a teenager. Instead, I had all this misery.

You learn to be so tight-lipped during a war that afterwards it is very hard to have normal communication with people. I think that I'm an optimist but there is a lot of suspicion in me. I would not easily trust anyone else. And I will never, never throw food away — even now, almost fifty years later. I went back to school after the war but I couldn't stand it. I didn't know how to wear a dress anymore because I had been going around in slacks or overalls for so long. We all needed time to adjust.

Emmy van Taack became a physiotherapist and not the doctor of her pre-war dreams. On a visit to Toronto in 1966 she met an air force veteran, and they were married in 1969. Apart from liking each other, his was an ear that understood. As Emmy says: "Anybody who was not involved can only touch the rim of our experience."

Each year she tries to return to Holland for Remembrance Day, on May 4, and for Liberation Day, on May 5.

I'll be there to pay tribute to those who fought for freedom and lost their lives. At 7:30 in the evening, with flags at half mast, people will start their silent walks to monuments and graves all over the country, where, at 8.00 o'clock, everybody will remember in silence.

Appendix — List of Members of The Royal Air Forces Escaping Society, Canadian Branch, 1992.

Active Members

ADAMS, ROBERT W.   Toronto, Ont.
BATES, ROBERT W.   Bracebridge, Ont.
BAUSET, PIERRE   Lorraine, Que.
BEATON, JOSEPH J.   Ottawa, Ont.
BIDDLE, GORDON   Oshawa, Ont.
BILLING, JERRY   South Woodslee, Ont.
BJARNASON, STEFAN A.   Don Mills, Ont.
BLANCHET, PIERRE G.   Montreal, Que.
BOCKUS, DAVID   Scarborough, Ont.
BODIE, A. R.   Vancouver, B.C.
BRENNAN, HAROLD J.   Peterborough, Ont.
BROAD, STEVEN P.   Knowlton, Que.
BROOK, STANLEY   Markham, Ont.
BRUNELLE, PAUL   St. Lambert, Que.
BULMAN, E. L.   Riverview, N.B.
CARTER, G.   Ploubazlanec, France
CHARTERS, ROBERT B.   Mississauga, Ont.
CHASTER, J. BARRY   New Westminster, B.C.
CHENEY, DONALD H.   Gloucester, Ont.
CHRISTIE, V. B.   Lethbridge, Alta.
CLEE, HUGH A. M.   Ocean Park, B.C.
COMPTON, HARRY M.   Ottawa, Ont.
COOK, WILLIAM F.   Goderich, Ont.
COTE, J. ANATOLE   Fossambault, Que.
COWAN, STEWART F.   Bobcaygeon, Ont.
COX, DOUGLAS M.   Bridgewater, N.S.
DE PAPE, RAYMOND A.   Willowdale, Ont.
DEETH, GEORGE F.   Mississauga, Ont.
DENNSTEDT, W. G.   Moosomin, Sask.
DICKS, J. B.   Halifax, N.S.
DILWORTH, A. A.   Towson, Md. U.S.A.
DIX, JOHN H. J.   Toronto, Ont.
DONNELL, A. C.   Kingston, Ont.
DONOVAN, GERALD H.   Woodstock, N.B.
DUNGEY, ELMER B.   Toronto, Ont.
EVANS, DONALD A.   Vancouver, B.C.
FALKOWSKI, J.   Peterborough, Ont.
FEDORUK, MICHAEL   Edmonton, Alta.
FIRESTONE, HARVEY   Bolton, Ont.
FLINTOFT, JOHN   Kingston, Ont.

FORMAN, J. M. Ottawa, Ont.
FORSYTH, DONALD A. Ottawa, Ont.
FRAME, JAMES South Surrey, B.C.
FRAME, L. W. Victoria, B.C.
FRITH, ROBERT A. Peterborough, Ont.
FRY, C. W. Nepean, Ont.
FURNEAUX, ROBERT V. London, Ont.
GARRITY, R. C. B. Pointe Claire, Que.
GAY, S. Kingston, Ont.
GEOFFRION, LOUIS St. Bruno, Que.
GOLDBERG, DAVID Hamilton, Ont.
GOLDSMITH, JOHN E. Sydney, B.C.
GOUINLOCK, JACK Don Mills, Ont.
GREENBURGH, LOU Winnipeg, Man.
HAGEN, FRED Winterburn, Alta.
HALL, JOHN D. Vancouver, B.C.
HARLTON, J. E. Riverhurst, Sask.
HARMSWORTH, FRANK Midland, Ont.
HEALEY, JOSEPH P. Ennismore, Ont.
HIGH, DAVID Edmonton, Alberta
HODDER, WALTER Montreal, Que.
HOLLOWAY, MAURICE E. Ottawa, Ont.
HUGHES, R. C. Willowdale, Ont.
HULEATT, RICHARD R. Kingston, Ont.
HUTCHINSON, J. A. Winnipeg, Man.
JENNINGS, D. R. Truro, N. S.
JOHNSON, R. G. Charlottetown, P.E.I.
JONES, A. R. White Rock, B.C.
KELLY, W. J. Willowdale, Ont.
KEMP, A. F. Winnipeg, Man.
KIDD, R. M. Deaconsfield, Que.
KNOWLTON, W. R. Willowdale, Ont.
KORPELA, OLIVER Sudbury, Ont.
KOWALSKI, MICHAL R. Montreal, Que.
LAIDLAW, ALAN F. Winnipeg, Man.
LAWRENCE, STANLEY Toronto, Ont.
LEIGH, CLAYTON Hillsburgh, Ont.
LENNIE, DONALD A. Edmonton, Alta.
LEREW, JOHN Vancouver, B.C.
LESLIE, STUART M. Vancouver, B.C.
LINDSAY, R. P. Don Mills, Ont.
LLEWELLYN, D. E. Georgetown, Ont.
LYNCH, THOMAS Markham, Ont.
MACGILLIVRAY, D. KEITH London, Ont.

MacINTYRE, D. P.   Islington, Ont.
MacLEAN, ANGUS   Belle River, P.E.I.
MACPHERSON, W.B.   Truro, N.S.
MARKLE, ALEX G.   Victoria, B.C.
MARTIN, A.   Belfast, Ireland
MASON, E. B.   Ottawa, Ont.
McCLURE, G. C.   Toronto, Ont.
McCOY, D. A.   Edmonton, Alta.
McCREIGHT, V.   Kanata, Ont.
McGREGOR, N. R.   Port Coquitlam, B.C.
McLARTY, D.   Ottawa, Ont.
McLERNON, ROY A.   Knowlton, Que.
McMILLAN, DAVID   Vineland, Ont.
MIDDLEMASS, G.   Edmonton, Alta.
MILLAR, G.   Houston, Tex. U.S.A.
MILLAR, JOHN B.   Victoria, B.C.
MOFFAT, JAMES   Lachine, Que.
MONAGHAN, A.   Rossana, Victoria, Australia
MORAN, A.   Windsor, Ont.
MORGAN, G. R.   West Bank, B.C.
MORROW, J.   Scarborough, Ont.
MUSGROVE, GERALD A.   Wyevale, Ont.
NEAL, J. A.   Calgary, Alta.
NOAKES, E. E.G.   Don Mills, Ont.
NORDIN, G. M.   Scottsdale, Arizona
OGILVIE, A. M.   Ottawa, Ont.
OTTEN, J. F.   Lakefield, Ont.
PATRICK, E. R.   Toronto, Ont.
PATRICK, KEITH   Stevensville, Ont.
PETRACHENKO, WILLIAM   Welland, Ont.
PETSCHE, JOSEPH   Burlington, Ont.
PHILLIPS, S.   Cote St-Luc, Que.
POOHKAY, ALAN   Black Creek, B.C.
POOHKAY, WILLIAM   Edmonton, Alta.
POTTAGE, A.   Black Creek, B.C.
POWELL, E. A.   Saskatoon, Sask.
RATTNER, CYRIL   Willowdale, Ont.
REAIN, FRED   Cambridge, Ont.
RENEAU, GORDON   Islington, Ont.
RICHARDS, F. H.   Oakville, Ont.
ROBILLARD, L.   Montreal, Que.
ROPER, P.   Montreal, Que.
SCOTT, R. A.   Etobicoke, Ont.
SHANNON, BOB   Montreal, Que.
SHAUGHNESSY, G. JOSEPH   Ohaton, Alta.

SHERK, R. J. F.   Willowdale, Ont.
SMITH, DONALD V.   St. Catharines, Ont.
SMITH, M. B.   London, Ont.
SPENCER, A. E.   Nepean, Ont.
STACEY, A. G.   Guelph, Ont.
STEVENS, HERBERT L.   Coldwater, Ont.
STIRLING, J. W.   Ottawa, Ont.
TAYLOR, FLETCHER V.   Mississauga, Ont.
THOMAS, J. C.   Islington, Ont.
TROTTIER, ERNEST   Etobicoke, Ont.
TRULL, JOHN C.   Mississauga, Ont.
WALTER, BRUCE H.   Westlake Village Cal, U.S.A.
WATKINS, J.C.   South Surrey, B.C.
WATLINGTON, H.   Somerset, Bermuda
WATSON, W. C.   London, Ont.
WIENS, R. C.   Montreal, Que.
WILBY, T. R.   Fredericton, N.B.
WILSON, E. LYALL   Dartmouth, N.S.
WOODHOUSE, K. B.   Saskatoon, Sask.
WRIGHT, ALBERT   Belleville, Ont.

Deceased Members

BANVILLE, REDMOND T.   Montreal, Que.
BARTLEY, LEONARD   Ottawa, Ont.
BASTOW, G. H.   St. Johns, Nfld.
BEAUCHESNE, NOEL, Ottawa, Ont.
BENNETZ, MALCOLM   Argentina
BOWLBY, ARTHUR T.   Ottawa, Ont.
BROOKS, B. II.   Ottawa, Ont.
BUDD, A. C. DENIS   Victoria, B.C.
CAMPBELL, J. L.   Don Mills, Ont.
CHAPPELL, C. D. R.   London, Ont.
CLEMENTS, R. S.   Kelowna, B.C.
DALPHOND, MEL   Summerland, B.C.
DAVIDSON, RUSSELL   Peterborough, Ont.
DeBREYNE, ARTHUR   St. Lambert, Que.
DeMONE, HAROLD   Lehave, N.S.
DESAUTELS, R. V.   Willowdale, Ont.
FOY, J. H.   Toronto, Ont.
FREW, G. SUMNER   Westmount, Que.
GIBB, G.W.   St. Paul d'Abbotsford, Que.
GILCHRIST, PETER   Toronto, Ont.
HARE, CHRIS   Toronto, Ont.
HARRISON, D.   Thornhill, Ont.
HOLMES, P.   Don Mills, Ont.

JONES, W.   Agincourt, Ont.
JONES, W. F.   Picton, Ont.
KELLOW, R. G.   Winnipeg, Man.
LAMBERT, A.   Westfield, N.B.
LOGAN, L. E.   Manotick, Ont.
McCAULEY, D.   Oakville, Ont.
McELROY, L. R.   Chalk River, Ont.
McPHERSON, D. A. B.   Lindell Beach, B.C.
MOLNAR, E. J.   Goderich, Ont.
NEIL, M.   Pointe-Claire, Que.
NOLAN, D. K.   Ottawa, Ont.
PRICE, E.   Pembroke, Ont.
RAFTER, R.   Mississauga, Ont.
RUTHERFORD, D.   Corbyville, Ont.
SEMPLE, ERROL Q.   London, Ont.
SHERIDAN, R.   Burford, Ont.
SHERWOOD, L.D.   Sydney, N.S.
SIMPSON, T.   Wawa, Ont.
SWIDA, S.   Toronto, Ont.
TARRAS, M.   Montreal, Que.
TURENNE, E.   Winnipeg, Man.
WATSON, J. H.   Waterdown, Ont.
WHITNALL, PHILLIP   Peterborough, Ont.

Name index

Printed in Canada